EMS Notes

EMT & Paramedic Field Guide

Ehren Myers, RN
Consultants
Dave Paul, EMT-P
Jason Cunningham, FF/EMT-Basic

Purchase additional copies of this book at your health science bookstore or directly from F.A. Davis by shopping online at www.fadavis.com or by calling 800-323-3555 (US) or 800-665-1148 (CAN)

A Davis's Notes Book

F.A. Davis Company • Philadelphia

F. A. Davis Company
1915 Arch Street
Philadelphia, PA 19103
www.fadavis.com

Copyright © 2009 by F. A. Davis Company

All rights reserved. This book is protected by copyright. No part of it may be reproduced, stored in a retrieval system, or transmitted in any form or by any means, electronic, mechanical, photocopying, recording, or otherwise, without written permission from the publisher.

Printed in China by Imago

Last digit indicates print number: 10 9 8 7 6 5 4 3 2 1

Publisher, Nursing: Robert G. Martone
Developmental Editor: William Welsh
Director of Content Development: Darlene D. Pedersen
Project Editor: Christina C. Burns
Manager of Art and Design: Carolyn O'Brien
Cover Design: Elizabeth DiFebo
Consultant: Dave Paul, EMT-P

Reviewers: Amanda Brame, BSN, CEN, EMT-B, ENPC, RN; Deneen Little Colsin, BA, LP, RN; Kathleen Curtis, MSN, RN; Theresa Delahoyde, MSN, RN; Grant Fraser, MD; Kenneth D. Hoffman, CRNA, Anne Larson, BA, BC, MN, PhD, RN; Phillip D. Levy, MD, MPH; Dawn McKay, CCRN, MSN, RN; Stephen J. Nardozzi, EMT-Basic, EMT-Paramedic; Karen Reilly, ANP-BC, Melissa Robinson, EMT, LPN; Polly Gerber Zimmerman, CEN, FAEN, MBA, MS, RN

As new scientific information becomes available through basic and clinical research, recommended treatments and drug therapies undergo changes. The author(s) and publisher have done everything possible to make this book accurate, up to date, and in accord with accepted standards at the time of publication. The author(s), editors, and publisher are not responsible for errors or omissions or for consequences from application of the book, and make no warranty, expressed or implied, in regard to the contents of the book. Any practice described in this book should be applied by the reader in accordance with professional standards of care used in regard to the unique circumstances that may apply in each situation. The reader is advised always to check product information (package inserts) for changes and new information regarding dose and contraindications before administering any drug. Caution is especially urged when using new or infrequently ordered drugs.

Authorization to photocopy items for internal or personal use, or the internal or personal use of specific clients, is granted by F. A. Davis Company for users registered with the Copyright Clearance Center (CCC) Transactional Reporting Service, provided that the fee of $.25 per copy is paid directly to CCC, 222 Rosewood Drive, Danvers, MA 01923. For those organizations that have been granted a photocopy license by CCC, a separate system of payment has been arranged. The fee code for users of the Transactional Reporting Service is: 8036-2038-1/09 0 + $.25.

Pulse Oximetry

Finding	Intervention
SpO_2 >95%	• Considered normal and generally requires no invasive intervention* • Continue routine monitoring of Pt
SpO_2 91%–94%	• Considered borderline* • Assess probe placement, and adjust if necessary • Begin oxygen at 2 L/min titrated to SpO_2 >95%
SpO_2 85%–90%	• Elevate head, and encourage Pt to breathe deeply • Assess airway and suction as needed • Administer oxygen, and titrate to SpO_2 >95% • If condition worsens or fails to improve, assist ventilations manually, and prepare to intubate
SpO_2 <85%	• Administer 100% oxygen, set Pt upright, encourage deep breathing and suction as needed • Assist ventilations manually, and prepare to intubate if condition worsens or fails to improve • Consider reversal agents for possible drug-induced respiratory depression

*__Caution:__ Consider readings within the overall context of the Pt's medical history and physical exam. **NEVER** withhold treatment based solely on a "normal" SpO_2 reading (e.g., a Pt who is hypovolemic may have a normal SpO_2, which may mislead you to overlook a potentially fatal condition).

AIRWAY

AIRWAY

Conditions That May Produce False SpO₂ Readings

False Highs	False Lows
• Anemia	• Cool extremities
• Alkalosis	• Drugs (vasoconstrictors)
• CO (carbon monoxide) Poisoning	• Nail polish/nail infection
• Hypovolemia	• Pt movement
• Pt movement	• Poor peripheral circulation
	• Reynaud's disease

Capnography Waveform Monitors

Normal waveform: normal range 35–45 mm Hg

AB = baseline
BC = expiratory upslope
CD = expiratory plateau
D = peak CO₂ concentration
DA = inspiratory slope

Interpreting Waveforms: Intubated Pts

Flat waveform (near 0)

- Esophageal intubation
- ET tube dislodgement
- ET tube obstruction
- Loss of circulatory function

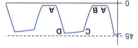

↓ $Etco_2$ with loss of plateau

- ET cuff leak or deflation
- ET tube dislodgement
- ET tube obstruction

Sudden ↑ in $Etco_2$

- Return of spontaneous circulation during CPR

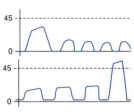

Interpreting Waveforms: Non-Intubated Pts in Distress

- Helpful in determining source of respiratory distress when Pt presentation and/or signs and symptoms are vague.

"Shark fin" appearance

- Suggests asthma or COPD
- Look at PMH and medications (e.g., inhalers, steroids)

Normal and upright

- Consider heart failure
- Look at PMH and medications (e.g., diuretics, beta blockers, digoxin, antihypertensives)

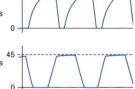

Oxygen Delivery Equipment

	Flow Rate	O_2 Delivered
Nasal cannula	1–6 L/min	22%–44%
Simple face mask	6–10 L/min	35%–60%
Non-rebreather mask	10–15 L/min	up to 100%
Venturi mask	4–8 L/min	24%–40%
Bag-valve-mask (BVM)	15 L/min	up to 100%

Basic Airway Devices

Oropharyngeal airway (OPA)

- Measure from corner of mouth to earlobe
- Open mouth using chin lift
- Insert upside down, and rotate 180° as it passes crest of tongue (not for small children)
- **Alternate method** (all ages): Use tongue depressor, **insert right side up;** follow normal curve of oral cavity

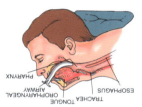

OROPHARYNGEAL AIRWAY
TRACHEA
TONGUE
OROPHARYNGEAL AIRWAY
ESOPHAGUS
PHARYNX

Nasopharyngeal airway (NPA)

- Measure from tip of nose to earlobe
- Diameter should match Pt's smallest finger
- Lubricate tip using water-soluble lubricant, and insert with bevel side facing in.

Contraindicated in presence of facial trauma

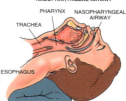

Basic Airway Management

Head-Tilt, Chin-Lift

Jaw-Thrust Maneuver

AIRWAY

BMV

One-Person Technique

Two-Person Technique

Cricoid Pressure

- Reduces gastric inflation
- Reduces risk of aspiration
- Displaces vocal cords posteriorly and helps to bring them into view

Contraindications

- Active vomiting
- Cervical spine injuries
- Cricotracheal trauma

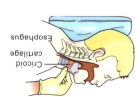

Continuous Positive Airway Pressure (CPAP)

Indications (inclusion criteria): Respiratory distress consistent with **CHF, pulmonary edema, COPD (asthma, emphysema, bronchitis)** or **pneumonia** and:

- RR >20/minute
- SpO_2 <95%
- Use of accessory muscles during respiration

Contraindications (exclusion criteria)

- Respiratory or cardiac arrest
- Unable to maintain patent airway (includes tracheotomy)
- Decreased level of consciousness
- Respiratory distress related to trauma (pneumothorax)
- SBP <90 mm Hg (monitor BP closely during treatment)
- Pneumothorax or chest trauma
- Inadequate respiratory effort/agonal respirations
- Pt younger than 12 years old
- Pt with increased risk for aspiration (e.g., stroke Pt)
- Nausea, vomiting, or active GI bleed or nose bleed
- Inadequate face-to-mask seal

Procedure

- Determine whether Pt meets inclusion criteria for CPAP
- Rule out pneumothorax
- Give 100% oxygen, and begin continuous SpO_2 monitoring
- Place CPAP mask (ensure tight seal over mouth and nose)
- Begin CPAP at 5–10 cm of PEEP
- Adjust/tighten mask as needed for air leaks
- Coach Pt to improve tolerance/efficacy of therapy
- Decrease or discontinue CPAP for SBP <90 mm Hg
- If respiratory status deteriorates, discontinue CPAP, and manually ventilate Pt or intubate as indicated

AIRWAY

Approximate Oxygen Tank Life (at 10 cm PEEP)

D cylinder	Approximately 25–30 minutes
E cylinder	Approximately 40–50 minutes
M cylinder	Approximately 4 hours

Rapid Sequence Intubation (RSI)

Preoxygenate with 100% oxygen
- Non-rebreather mask for at least 30–60 seconds
- If breathing inadequate, use BVM with cricoid pressure

Cricoid pressure (for unresponsive or paralyzed Pts)
- Maintain until intubation complete, cuff inflated, correct tube placement confirmed, and ET tube secured
- **BURP technique:** Backward, Upward, Rightward Pressure

Head trauma, stroke, or increased ICP
- Lidocaine 1 mg/kg IV over 30–60 seconds

Sedation and induction drugs
- **Midazolam** 0.1–0.2 mg/kg IV (if SBP >100 mm Hg)
- **Etomidate** 0.2–0.4 mg/kg IV (etomidate preferred over midazolam if SBP <100 mm Hg)
- **Fentanyl** 2–4 mcg/kg IV, IM
- **Propofol** 2–3 mg/kg IV
- **Thiopental** 2–5 mg/kg IV
- **Ketamine** 1–2 mg/kg IV

Paralytics (neuromuscular blocking agent [NMBA])*
*Paralytics have *no* sedative properties; Pt *must* be sedated
Nondepolarizing NMBA
- **Succinylcholine:** 1.5 mg/kg IV. Wait for paralysis to occur. Avoid use in conditions which may cause hyperkalemia (e.g., burns >24 hours after injury, trauma, renal failure, prolonged bed rest, closed head injuries, etc.).

Depolarizing NMBA

- **Vecuronium:** 0.1–0.2 mg/kg IV (for long-duration paralysis)
- **Rocuronium:** 0.6–1.2 mg/kg IV

If unable to intubate within 30 seconds, resume BVM ventilations with cricoid pressure for several minutes.

Intubate Pt

- **Atropine:** 0.5 mg IV (for bradycardia during intubation)
- Inflate ET tube cuff and secure ET tube with holder
- Confirm correct ET tube placement
- Reassess tube placement after repositioning or transferring Pt or any unexpected change or deterioration in Pt status

Troubleshooting Intubation Complications (DOPE)

Dislodgement

- Confirmed by absent breath sounds and no $EtCO_2$ detected
- Remove ET tube, and manually ventilate Pt with BVM*
- Suction as needed, and re-intubate as soon as possible

If right main-stem intubation suspected (absent breath sounds on the left), withdraw ET tube in 1-cm increments until equal breath sounds achieved with ventilations.

Obstruction

- Suction ET tube to clear secretions
- If unable to clear obstruction or pass suction catheter, extubate and manually ventilate Pt with a BVM
- Suction as needed and reintubate as soon as possible

Pneumothorax

- Auscultate chest for equal and adequate air movement
- If there is unequal chest wall movement and/or decreased air movement on one side, consider pneumothorax
- Needle chest decompression for tension pneumothorax

AIRWAY

AIRWAY

Equipment

- Assess and replace airway equipment as necessary
- If ineffective ventilation continues and no physical or mechanical cause can be found, consider sedating Pt

Colorimetric End-Title CO_2 Detectors

- **Yellow** indicates tracheal intubation* (**y**ellow = **y**es)
- **Tan** indicates low CO_2 (**t**an = **t**roubleshoot possible causes)
- **Purple** indicates esophageal intubation (**p**urple = **p**roblem).

  Emesis and carbonated beverages can cause false-positives.

Indications for Advanced Airways

- **Inability to protect or maintain airway** (e.g., coma, GCS <8, severe AMS, stroke, intoxication, etc.)
- **Inadequate ventilation or oxygenation** (e.g., cardiac arrest, apnea, pulmonary edema, decreased lung compliance [asthma, COPD, emphysema, etc.])
- **Anticipated deterioration** (e.g., expanding neck hematoma)

ET Tube

Ideal for Pts requiring PPV (e.g., pulmonary edema, asthma).

- **Contraindications:** Intact gag reflex, epiglottitis (pediatric cases), basilar skull fractures (avoid nasal intubation), caustic ingestion, known esophageal disease or trauma
- **Immobilize c-spine if indicated**
- **Pre-oxygenate with 100% oxygen**
- **Position Pt's head in sniffing position** (except for trauma)
- **Test patency of balloon:** use-10 mL syringe; deflate balloon, but leave syringe attached to inflation port

- **Open and assess airway:** lift Pt's jaw up, and open
- Remove dentures or foreign bodies, and suction if needed
- **Insert laryngoscope blade:** insert in right side of mouth
- Sweep tongue left while advancing blade
  - **Straight blade:** insert blade under epiglottis
  - **Curved blade:** insert blade into vallecula
- **Bring cords into alignment:** without changing angle of blade, lift upward and forward (do not touch Pt's teeth)
- **Pass tube under direct visualization:** from right corner of mouth, pass tube through vocal cords into trachea
- **Withdraw stylet:** connect bag-valve device
- **Inflate balloon:** Use 10 mL of air
- **Confirm proper tube placement:**
  - Auscultate epigastria and bilateral lung fields
  - Esophageal/CO_2 detector, capnography, oximetry
- **Secure tube:** use commercial ETT holder per protocol
- Insertion depth noted at level of Pt's teeth

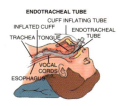

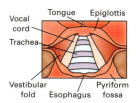

AIRWAY

Laryngeal Mask Airway (LMA)

Note: LMA cannot deliver PPV

- **Contraindications**: conscious (non-sedated) Pt, gag reflex, severe oropharyngeal trauma
- **Immobilize c-spine if indicated**
- **Preoxygenate with 100% oxygen**
- Completely deflate cuff so it forms a smooth "spoons shape"
- Lubricate posterior surface of mask with water-soluble lubricant
- Hold LMA like a pen (index finger placed at junction of cuff and tube)
- With Pt head extended and neck flexed, flatten LMA tip against hard palate.
- Maintain pressure on tube while pushing cranially with index finger
- Advance mask until resistance is felt at base of hypopharynx
- Maintain cranial pressure, and remove index finger
- Inflate cuff (without holding tube) with enough air to obtain seal

(Images courtesy of LMA North America Inc.)

Sizing Chart: Never Overinflate Cuff

LMA	Pt Size	Max Cuff Vol
1	Neonate up to 5 kg	Up to 4 mL
1.5	Infant 5–10 kg	Up to 7 mL
2	Infant 10–20 kg	Up to 10 mL
2.5	Child 20–30 kg	Up to 14 mL
3	Child 30–50 kg	Up to 20 mL
4	Adult 50–70 kg	Up to 30 mL
5	Adult 70–100 kg	Up to 40 mL
6	Adult >100 kg	Up to 50 mL

King LT-D/LTS-D Airways

Can be used to deliver PPV

- **Contraindications:** Pts <34 inches tall or <12 kg, intact gag, caustic ingestion, esophageal disease or trauma
- **Immobilize c-spine if indicated**
- **Preoxygenate with 100% oxygen**
- Test cuff patency with maximum air volume (see sizing chart above), and remove all air from both cuffs
- Lubricate (water-soluble) distal tip and posterior aspect of tube

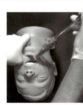

AIRWAY

AIRWAY

- Position Pt in sniffing position (for trauma, place in neutral position)
- Open Pt's mouth using chin-left method with nondominant hand
- Insert tip of tube into corner of Pt's mouth at 45°–90° angle, and rotate tube back to midline as you advance tube under Pt's tongue (orientation line toward Pt's chin)
- Advance tube until base of connector aligns with teeth
- Inflate cuff (see following chart)
- It may be necessary to withdraw tube slightly until ventilation becomes easy

Combitube Airway

Pt Size	Tube Size	Color	Cuff Vol
Child 34-45" (12-25 kg)	2.0 (LT only)	Green	25-35 mL
Child 41-51" (25-35 kg)	2.5 (LT only)	Orange	30-40 mL
Adult 4-5 ft	3 (LT/LTS)	Yellow	40-60 mL
Adult 5-6 ft	4 (LT/LTS)	Red	60-80 mL
Adult >6 ft	5 (LT/LTS)	Purple	70-90 mL

Combitube cannot deliver PPV

- **Contraindications:** Pts <4 feet tall, Pts <16 years old, intact gag, caustic ingestion, known esophageal disease, esophageal trauma
- Immobilize c-spine if indicated

14

- **Pre-oxygenate with 100% oxygen**
- **Insertion:** Insert blindly into mouth, and gently advance tube until Pt's teeth or gums are aligned between the two black rings
- **Inflate blue port:** using larger syringe and blue inflation port, inflate pharyngeal cuff
- **Inflate white port:** using smaller syringe and white inflation port, inflate distal cuff
- **Ventilation:** Ventilate through longer, blue tube marked #1
  - **If lung sounds present and no gastric sound heard,** continue ventilation through blue tube (#1)
  - **If lung sounds absent and gastric sounds heard,** remove BVM device from blue (#1) tube, and ventilate through shorter, clear tube (#2)
- Secure tube and reassess placement periodically and with any Pt change

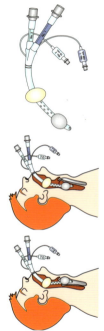

Reprinted by permission of Nellcor Puritan Bennett Inc., Pleasanton, California

AIRWAY

Pt Height	>5 ft	4-5 ft
Tube size	41 fr	37 fr
Blue port	100 mL	85 mL
White port	15 mL	12 mL

Needle Cricothyrotomy

Indications: airway obstruction where oral (including LMA, King, Combitube, etc.) or nasal intubation unsuccessful

- Locate landmarks: cricothyroid membrane, just below thyroid cartilage (Adam's apple)
- Prepare insertion site with antiseptic
- Attach over-the-needle catheter to 3 mL syringe
- **Adults: 10 g–14 g, 3½" over-the-needle catheter**
- **Children <12 years: 14 g, 1¾" over-the-needle catheter**
- Stabilize larynx, and insert needle at 45° angle in a downward direction along midline (toward carina)
- Maintain negative pressure on syringe during insertion
- Advance catheter, and discard needle after successfully entering trachea (confirmed by aspiration of air)
- Reconnect 3 mL syringe (discard plunger) to inserted 14 gauge catheter, then connect syringe to BVM using a 7.5 mm ET tube adapter (see following illustrations for setup)
- Ventilate Pt for 1 second
- Allow Pt to exhale for 4 seconds

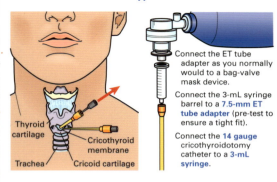

- Connect the ET tube adapter as you normally would to a bag-valve mask device.
- Connect the 3-mL syringe barrel to a **7.5-mm ET tube adapter** (pre-test to ensure a tight fit).
- Connect the **14 gauge** cricothyroidotomy catheter to a **3-mL syringe.**

Resuscitation Maneuvers

Head-Tilt, Chin-Lift

Jaw-Thrust Maneuver (Known or suspected trauma)

Pulse Check: Adult/Child (carotid)

Hand Placement: Adult/Child (lower half of sternum; use heel of one hand for child)

Relief of Foreign Body: Conscious Adult/Child (use chest thrusts for pregnant or obese Pts)

Relief of Foreign Body: Unresponsive Adult/Child (same as for CPR)

Resuscitation Maneuvers

Head-Tilt, Chin-Lift: Infants (do not hyperextend neck)

Pulse Check: Infants (brachial)

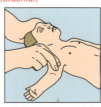

Back Blows and Chest Thrusts: Infants (always support infant's head and neck)

One Rescuer (one finger width below nipples)

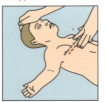

Two Rescuers (both thumbs, hands encircling chest)

CPR Quick Reference (All Ages*)

Determine unresponsiveness

- **Adult**: first call 911; get help and/or AED if available
- **Child or infant**: call 911 after 2 minutes (five cycles) of CPR

Airway: open airway

- **All ages**: head-tilt, chin-lift; if trauma suspected, use jaw-thrust method

Breathing: assess for breathing

- If not breathing, give two slow breaths at 1 sec/breath
- If unsuccessful, reposition airway, and reattempt to ventilate; if still unsuccessful, see Choking Quick Reference next section)

Circulation: check for pulse for up to 10 seconds

- Pulse present, but Pt not breathing: begin rescue breathing
- No definite pulse after 10 seconds: start chest compressions

Defibrillation/AED (AED may not reflect updated AHA standards; follow AED voice prompts)

- Give 2 minutes of CPR between shocks
- **Adults**: do not use pediatric pads (must be >8 yr or >80 lb)
- **Child**: use adult pads if pediatric pads unavailable
- Recheck pulse every 2 minutes and after each shock

	Adult	Child and Infant	Newborn
Ventilations	10–12/min; ET: 8-10/min	15–20/min; ET: 8–10/min	40–60/min
Pulse Check	Carotid	**Child:** carotid **Infant:** brachial	Brachial or umbilicus
Events/Min	100/min	100/min	120/min
Ratio	30:2 (1 or 2 rescuers)	30:2 (15:2 if 2 rescuers)	3:1 (1 or 2 rescuers)
Depth	1½–2 in.	½–⅓ depth of chest	⅓ depth of chest
Hand Positioning	Lower half of sternum	**Child:** same as adult; **Infant NB:** one finger width below nipple line	

***Adult:** adolescent and older; **child:** 1 yr to adolescent; **infant:** <1 yr; **newborn:** birth to 1 mo

Choking Quick Reference (All Ages)

Assess for airway obstruction

- Grasping at throat with hands
- Inability to speak, breathe, cough, or cry (infants)

Conscious victim

- **Able to cough effectively (all ages)**
  - Keep victim calm, and encourage coughing
- **Unable to breathe or cough effectively**
  - **Adult/child:** abdominal thrusts until obstruction relieved or victim becomes unresponsive
  - **Infant:** alternate five back blows and five chest thrusts until obstruction relieved or unresponsiveness occurs
  - **Pregnant/obese victims:** use chest thrusts until obstruction relieved or victim becomes unresponsive

ACLS/12 LEAD

ACLS/12 LEAD

Unresponsive victim

- **Adults:** call 911 **first**, and then begin CPR
- **Child:** call 911 **after** five cycles of CPR
- Lay victim flat on back, and look inside mouth while opening airway
- Use finger sweep and attempt to remove obstruction (only if obstruction visible)
- Attempt to give two rescue breaths
- Begin CPR if breaths do not go in
- **Repeat steps:** inspect mouth, remove obstruction if seen, give 2 rescue breaths, give 30 chest compressions, and repeat until obstruction relieved

Recovery Position

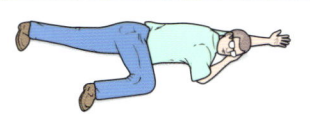

Pulseless Arrest

Asystole/PEA

- Confirm asystole in two leads
- **CPR:** perform five cycles of CPR (about 2 min)
- **Epinephrine** 1 mg IV or IO (2-2.5 mg ET) every 3-5 min or **vasopressin** 40 units IV or IO one time only (may be used to replace first or second dose of epinephrine)
- **Atropine:** 1 mg IV or IO (2-3 ET) every 3-5 min (max 3 mg) for asystole or bradycardic PEA.

V-fib or pulseless VT

- Perform five cycles of CPR (shock first, if witnessed)
- **Shock:** biphasic 120-200 J; monophasic 360 J
- Resume CPR for 2 min

22

Goal: *To give all medications without interrupting CPR*

- **Epinephrine** 1 mg IV or IO (2-2.5 mg ET) every 3-5 min or **vasopressin** 40 units IV or IO one time only; may use to replace first or second dose of epinephrine
- **Shock:** biphasic 120-200 J; monophasic: 360 J
- **Consider antiarrhythmics** (after 2 min CPR)
- **Amiodarone:** 300 mg IV or IO; repeat 150 mg in 3-5 min
- **Lidocaine:** 1-1.5 mg/kg IV or IO; repeat 0.5-0.75 mg/kg every 5-10 min; max 3 mg/kg
- **Magnesium:** 1-2 g IV or IO for torsade de pointes

Search for and manage reversible causes

Hypovolemia	Toxins
Hypoxia	Tamponade (cardiac)
Hydrogen ion (acidosis)	Tension pneumothorax
Hypo/Hyperkalemia	Thrombosis (coronary)
Hypoglycemia	Thrombosis (pulmonary)
Hypothermia	Trauma

Unstable Arrhythmias

- Unstable: any arrhythmia associated with serious signs and symptoms: CP, decreased BP, SOB, or AMS
- Any unstable arrhythmia requires immediate intervention

Unstable bradycardia (HR <60 bpm)

- **Pace:** prepare for transcutaneous pacing (TCP); **do not delay** for second-degree type 2 or third-degree AV block
- **Atropine:** 0.5 mg IV every 3-5 min to maximum 3 mg
- Consider **epinephrine** 2-10 mcg/min or **dopamine** 2-20 mcg/kg/min infusion if TCP ineffective or unavailable
- Definitive care may require transvenous pacing (ED only)
- Search for and manage reversible causes

Unstable tachycardia: all types

- **Perform immediate synchronized cardioversion**
- Monomorphic* VT and A-fib: 100 J, 200 J, 300 J, 360 J
- SVT and A-flutter: may start with 50 J
- Polymorphic* VT: **treat as pulseless VT;** defibrillate (unsynchronized cardioversion) at 360 J
- Consider *torsade de pointes* with **all** polymorphic VT
- Premedicate whenever possible: sedative and analgesics
- If synchronization delayed and clinical situation critical, go immediately to unsynchronized cardioversion at 360 J
- If cardioversion successful, begin antiarrhythmic infusion of **lidocaine** at 1-4 mg/min
- **Ventricular ectopy (including nonsustained VT)**
- Refer to specific arrhythmia below. Never give antiarrhythmics for ventricular escape rhythms/beats
- **Lidocaine** 1-1.5 mg/kg IV; repeat 0.5-0.75 mg/kg every 5-10 min (maximum 3 mg/kg); **infusion:** 1-4 mg/min

*Monomorphic = all QRS are same shape and size
*Polymorphic = QRS differ in shape and size

Stable Arrhythmias

Note: treatment should not be based on HR alone; if Pt is otherwise asymptomatic (**no** CP or SOB, stable BP, etc.), Pt should be transported for definitive in-hospital treatment

- Begin supportive care, and search for reversible causes
- If Pt becomes unstable, see **Unstable Arrhythmias**
- Contact OLMC for ongoing treatment options

Bradycardia (HR <60 bpm)

- Monitor and supportive care as needed
- Common causes of symptomatic bradycardia include excellent physical conditioning (e.g., runners, athletes), medication (e.g., beta blockers, digoxin)

24

Narrow-complex tachycardia
Regular rhythm (SVT: HR >150 bpm)

- **Valsalva's maneuver:** instruct Pt to cough or bear down
- **Adenosine:** 6-mg rapid (over 1-3 sec) IV push followed with 20-mL NS flush; may repeat adenosine for recurrence SVT at 12 mg every 1-2 min (max 30 mg)

Irregular rhythms

- Most likely **a-fib/a-flutter** or **multifocal atrial tachycardia**
- Definitive care may require rate control with **diltiazem** or **beta blockers** once Pt has arrived at hospital

Wide-complex tachycardia
Regular rhythm (VT or uncertain rhythm)

- **Amiodarone:** 150 mg IV given over 10 min; repeated as needed to a maximum of 2.2 g/24 hr
- Prepare for **synchronized cardioversion** (100 J initially)

Irregular and polymorphic rhythms

- **Torsade de pointes: magnesium** 1-2 g over 5-60 min followed by magnesium infusion
- **A-fib with WPW:** antiarrhythmics (e.g., **amiodarone** 150 mg IV over 10 min); **WPW:** HR usually >250 bpm, presence of delta wave, wide QRS; avoid adenosine, beta blockers, Ca-channel blockers, and diltiazem

Automatic External Defibrillators (AEDs)

- **Assessment:** determine unresponsiveness and assess ABCs
  - Children 1–8 yr: get help/AED after 2 min of CPR
  - Adults ≥8 yr: get help/AED immediately
- **CPR:** perform CPR until AED arrives
- **Power:** turn on AED and follow voice prompts
- **Attach pads:** stop CPR, attach appropriate-size pads to Pt, and plug pad cable into AED unit if needed
  - Position pads according to manufacturer's guidelines

ACLS/12 LEAD

Manual Defibrillation

- **Power:** turn on, and verify all cables connected
- **Lead select:** turn "Lead Select" to "Paddles" or "Defibrillator"
- **Select energy level: biphasic:** 200 J; **monophasic:** 360 J
- **Paddle placement*:** sternum (upper right sternal border) and cardiac apex (lower left-lateral chest); if using **hands-free defibrillation pads** follow manufacturer's guidelines

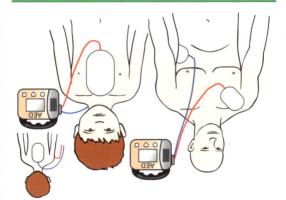

- **Analyze:** press "Analyze" button, and wait for instructions (do not make contact with Pt while AED analyzes rhythm)
- **Shock:** say "Shock indicated, stand clear," and ensure no one in contact with Pt
- Fully automatic units analyze rhythm and shock if indicated
- Semiautomatic units analyze rhythm and instruct operator to press "Shock" button if indicated

- **Verify rhythm:** confirm V-fib or pulseless VT
- **Charge defibrillator:** say "Charging, stand clear"
- **Clear:** say "I'm going to shock on three. One, I'm clear; two, you're clear; three, everybody's clear"
- **Defibrillate: biphasic:** 200 J; **monophasic:** 360 J
- **Reassess rhythm:** refer to appropriate algorithm

Hand-held paddles: apply 25 lb of pressure to both paddles, and simultaneously depress both paddle discharge buttons

Hands-free defibrillation pads: do not contact pads; depending on type of defibrillator, either press "Shock" button on defibrillator or simultaneously depress both paddle discharge buttons (while docked in defibrillator)

Synchronized Electrical Cardioversion

Indication

- Symptomatic stable or unstable tachycardia (with pulses)

Contraindication (when to use unsynchronized mode)

- No pulse, severe (prearrest) shock, or polymorphic VT

Technique

- Sedate when clinical situation permits
- Turn on defibrillator, attach ECG electrodes, press "Synch" button, and verify that R waves are sensed by machine
- It may be necessary to adjust gain until each R wave has synch marker
- **Energy level:** select energy level based on arrhythmia
    - Monomorphic* VT and a-fib: 100 J, 200 J, 300 J, 360 J
    - A-flutter and SVT: may start with 50 J
    - Polymorphic* VT: **treat as pulseless VT;** defibrillate (unsynchronized cardioversion) at 360 J
- Apply conductive medium to paddles, and position at sternum and apex (position hands-free defibrillation pads per package instructions)
- **Charge:** say "Charging, stand clear"

- **Clear:** say "I'm going to shock on three. One, I'm clear; two, you're clear; three, everybody's clear"
- **Cardioversion:** apply 25 lb pressure (N/A for hands-free pads) to both paddles, and press and hold both defibrillator buttons simultaneously until shock delivered
  Note: delays in cardioversion normal; do not release discharge buttons until shock delivered
- **Assess rhythm:** see appropriate algorithm for treatment
- **Caution:** Most defibrillators default back to nonsynchronized mode after each synchronized cardioversion; if subsequent synchronized cardioversion is needed, confirm that the defibrillator is in the synchronized mode
  Note: if QRS too wide for machine to identify R waves, switch to unsynchronized cardioversion (same steps as above, but turn lead select to "Paddles" or "Defibrillator" mode)

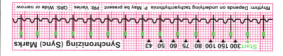

Transcutaneous Pacing (TCP)

Indications

- Symptomatic second-degree type II or third-degree AV block
- Symptomatic bradycardia unresponsive to atropine
- Bradycardia with ventricular escape rhythms
- May be useful in witnessed rhythm degradation to asystole
- Overdrive pacing of tachycardia refractory to drug therapy or electrical cardioversion (performed by physician only)
- When standby or demand pacing is indicated

Contraindications

- Severe hypothermia (not recommended for asystole)

Pacing modes

- **Demand** (synchronous) mode senses Pt's heart rate and paces only when heart rate falls below predetermined rate
- **Fixed** (asynchronous) mode paces at predetermined rate regardless of Pt's heart rate

Procedure

- **Pads:** apply pacing electrodes to Pt per package instructions
- **Power:** turn pacemaker on, and ensure cables connected
- **Rate:** set demand rate to approximately 60 bpm, and adjust up or down, based on Pt's response once pacing initiated
- **Current:** output ranges 0–200 milliamperes (mA)
- **Technique:** increase mA from minimum setting until consistent capture* is achieved, then increase by 2 mA

Capture characterized by pacer spikes, a widened QRS, and broad T waves. Pulses may not be palpable. Avoid using carotid artery to confirm mechanical capture because muscular jerking (from pacing) can mimic a carotid pulse.

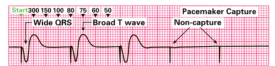

ACLS/12 LEAD

Standard 12-Lead Placement

V1: 4th ICS, right sternal border
V2: 4th ICS, left sternal border
V3: midway, between V2 and V4
V4: 5th ICS, midclavicular line
V5: 5th ICS, midway between V4 and V6
V6: 5th ICS, midaxillary line

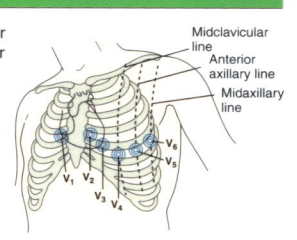

Modified Chest Leads (MCL₁, MCL₆, MC₄R)

Monitor lead III (Note: white and black leads do not change)

■ **MCL₁: red** lead on V_1 (4th ICS, right sternum)
■ **MCL₆: red** lead on V_6 (5th ICS, midaxillary line)
■ **MC₄R: red** lead on **right** 5th ICS at midclavicular line

Standard Three Lead

Lead-I
White (RA) — (LA) Black
Lead-III
(LL) Red
Lead-II

MCL Leads

Midclavicular
White | Black
Midaxillary
MCL₁(V₁)
MCL₆(V₆)
MC₄R

ECG Basics

Normal ECG parameters
Normal sinus rhythm (NSR): 60–100 bpm
Sinus bradycardia: <60 bpm
Sinus tachycardia: >100 bpm
Paroxysmal supraventricular tachycardia (PSVT) >150 bpm

Systematic approach to ECG assessment
Rate: normal (60–100), fast (>100), or slow (<60)?
Rhythm: regular or irregular?
P waves: present? are they 1:1 with QRS?
PRI: normal (0.12–0.20 sec)? consistent?
QRS: normal (0.06–0.10 sec) or wide (>0.10 sec)?
Extra: extra or abnormal complexes?

ACLS/12 LEAD

Components of the ECG

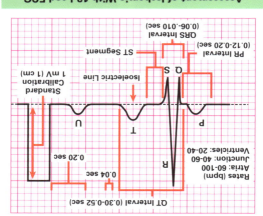

Assessment of Ischemia With 12-Lead ECG

Assess quality of 12-lead tracing

- Lead aVR should have predominantly negative deflection
- Confirm 1 mV (two large boxes) of standard calibration

Look for lead changes suggestive of an MI*

- **LBBB (new)**: *diagnosis of AMI confounded by LBBB
- **QRS**: >0.10 sec
- **V1, V2**: predominantly negative (QS in V1)
- **T-wave inversion (ischemia)**: should appear symmetrical; T-wave inversion in I, V5, V6 suggestive of LBBB

- **ST elevation (injury):** 1 mm or more of ST elevation in two or more contiguous leads confirms MI; *elevation usually associated with reciprocal ST depression in other leads*
- **Significant Q waves (infarct):** *suggestive of MI; large Q wave normal in aVR (not used in diagnosing AMI); small Q wave (<0.4 sec) can be normal in leads I, aVL, V5, V6*
- **ST depression (consistent with NSTEMI):** *may be present in V1–V4 without reciprocal ST elevation (posterior MI)*

Assessment of Acute MI Patterns

ST Elevation Pattern	Area of MI and Related Findings
II, III, and aVF	Inferior (↓BP, use NTG/MS cautiously)
I, aVL, V5, V6	Lateral (LV dysfunction, AV blocks)
V1, V2	Septal (BBBs common)
V3, V4	Anterior (CHF, CHB, BBBs common)
V4R–V6R	RV (↓BP, a-fib/-flutter, PACs, AV blocks)
V1–V4 (ST depression)	Posterior (LV dysfunction)

Reciprocal Lead Changes

Leads With ST Elevation	Reciprocal ST Depression
II, III, aVF	I, aVL, V3, V4
I, aVL, V5, V6	II, III, aVF
V3, V4	II, III, aVF
No ST elevation (NSTEMI?)	V1–V4 (suspect posterior MI)

ACLS/12 LEAD

ACLS/12 LEAD

Differentiating Wide-Complex Tachycardias

SVT With Aberrancy	Ventricular Tachycardia
• **I, aVL**: positive • **V1**: triphasic • Associated P waves	• **I, aVL**: negative • **V1**: biphasic or positive • **aVR**: positive • **Concordance** in V1–V6 (all negative or all positive) • **Fusion** or **capture** beats

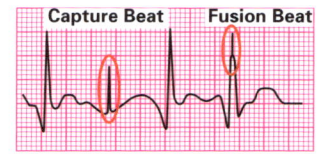

Capture Beat   Fusion Beat

Differentiating RBBB From LBBB

LBBB	RBBB
• **QRS**: >0.10 sec • **V1, V2**: predominantly negative (QS in V1) • **I, V5, V6**: blunted, upright QRS with T-wave inversion	• **QRS**: >0.10 sec • **V1, V2**: predominantly positive, rSR' or rR' (rabbit ears) • **I, V5, V6**: slurred S wave

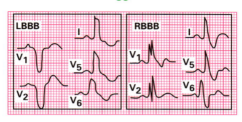

Sample ECG Rhythms

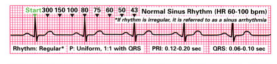

Normal Sinus Rhythm (HR 60-100 bpm)
*If rhythm is irregular, it is referred to as a sinus arrhythmia

Rhythm: Regular* | P: Uniform, 1:1 with QRS | PRI: 0.12-0.20 sec | QRS: 0.06-0.10 sec

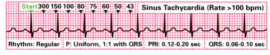

Sinus Tachycardia (Rate >100 bpm)

Rhythm: Regular | P: Uniform, 1:1 with QRS | PRI: 0.12-0.20 sec | QRS: 0.06-0.10 sec

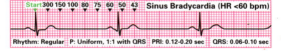

Sinus Bradycardia (HR <60 bpm)

Rhythm: Regular | P: Uniform, 1:1 with QRS | PRI: 0.12-0.20 sec | QRS: 0.06-0.10 sec

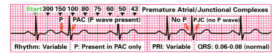

Premature Atrial/Junctional Complexes

Rhythm: Variable | P: Present in PAC only | PRI: Variable | QRS: 0.06-0.08 (normal)

ACLS/12 LEAD

ACLS/12 LEAD

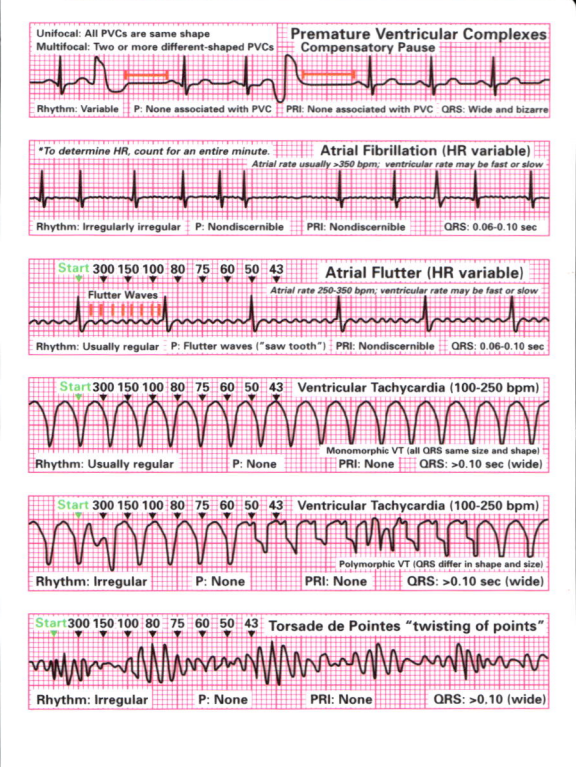

Unifocal: All PVCs are same shape			**Premature Ventricular Complexes**	
Multifocal: Two or more different-shaped PVCs			**Compensatory Pause**	
Rhythm: Variable	P: None associated with PVC	PRI: None associated with PVC	QRS: Wide and bizarre

			Atrial Fibrillation (HR variable)	
*To determine HR, count for an entire minute.			Atrial rate usually >350 bpm; ventricular rate may be fast or slow	
Rhythm: Irregularly irregular	P: Nondiscernible	PRI: Nondiscernible	QRS: 0.06-0.10 sec

Start 300 150 100 80 75 60 50 43			**Atrial Flutter (HR variable)**	
Flutter Waves			Atrial rate 250-350 bpm; ventricular rate may be fast or slow	
Rhythm: Usually regular	P: Flutter waves ("saw tooth")	PRI: Nondiscernible	QRS: 0.06-0.10 sec

Start 300 150 100 80 75 60 50 43			**Ventricular Tachycardia (100-250 bpm)**	
			Monomorphic VT (all QRS same size and shape)	
Rhythm: Usually regular	P: None	PRI: None	QRS: >0.10 sec (wide)

Start 300 150 100 80 75 60 50 43			**Ventricular Tachycardia (100-250 bpm)**	
			Polymorphic VT (QRS differ in shape and size)	
Rhythm: Irregular	P: None	PRI: None	QRS: >0.10 sec (wide)

| Start 300 150 100 80 75 60 50 43 | | | **Torsade de Pointes "twisting of points"** | |
| Rhythm: Irregular | P: None | PRI: None | QRS: >0.10 (wide) |

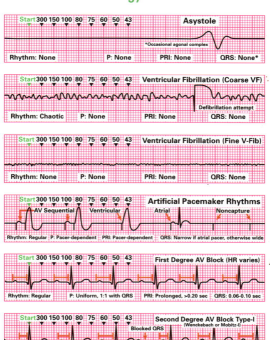

Second Degree AV Block Type-II (Mobitz-II)

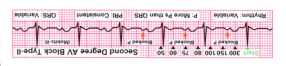

Start 300 150 100 75 60 50
Blocked P Blocked P Blocked P

Rhythm: Variable | P: More Ps than QRS | PRI: Consistent | QRS: Variable

Third Degree AV Block (Complete Heart Block)

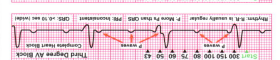

Start 300 150 100 75 60 50 43
P waves   P waves

Rhythm: R-R is usually regular | P: More Ps than QRS | PRI: Inconsistent | QRS: >0.10 sec (wide)

Junctional Rhythms (HR 40-60 bpm*)

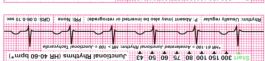

Start 300 150 100 75 60 50 43

*HR 61-100 = Accelerated Junctional Rhythm; HR > 100 = Junctional Tachycardia

Rhythm: Usually regular | P: Absent (may also be inverted or retrograde) | PRI: None | QRS: 0.06-0.10 sec

Wolfe-Parkinson White (WPW)

Start 300 150 100 75 60 50 43
Delta waves

Rhythm: Irregularly irregular | P: None | PRI: None | QRS: >0.10 (wide) due to presence of delta wave

WPW is abnormal accessory pathway that bypasses the normal route through AV node; this prematurely depolarizes a portion of the ventricles and causes delta wave (slurring of the initial portion of QRS); PRI shortened (nondiscernible in a-fib) and QRS widened >0.10 sec

Effect of Medication on ECG

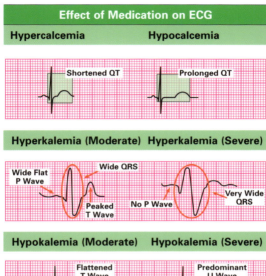

Effect of Hypothermia on ECG

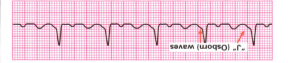

"J" (Osborn) waves

- Seen in severe hypothermia (temp <87°; 3°F).
- Often associated with prolonged PRI, QRS, QT interval
- Check leads II, III, V4, V5, V6

Abdominal Pain

Clinical findings
Neuro: anxiety, restlessness
Resp: may have dyspnea secondary to breathing itself
CV: tachycardia, hypotension
Skin: Pt may have a fever, or skin may be cool, pale, diaphoretic
GI/GU: anorexia, N/V, constipation, diarrhea, GI bleeding, GU bleeding/discharge, missed period, pregnancy
MS: abdominal tenderness, rigidity, guarding, pulsatile mass, bruising, trauma, weakness, fatigue, malaise

EMT—basic/intermediate

- Establish and manage ABCs as indicated
- Place Pt in position of comfort and keep NPO
- Administer supplemental O_2 titrated to VS
- Obtain and document baseline VS and monitor frequently
- Obtain finger-stick blood glucose level
- Obtain SAMPLE history
- Obtain a focused symptom analysis (OPQRST); focus on location (epigastric may be ACS), radiation, guarding, rigidity, femoral pulses, pulsatile abdominal masses (AAA), sexually active female (ectopic pregnancy), diabetes (DKA), bowel tones, last PO intake

Paramedic

- Attach ECG monitor, and manage dysrhythmias per ACLS
- Follow AMI protocol as indicated: initiate AMI checklist
- Obtain IV access, and titrate to SBP >90 mm Hg
- **Ondansetron:** 4 mg slow IV or IM for vomiting
- Consult with OLMC regarding pain management

MEDICAL EMERG

Abdominal Organs

Work from area of least pain toward area of most pain

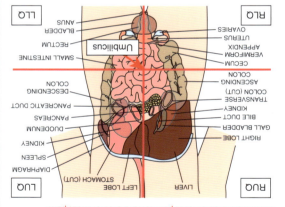

RUQ: Liver, Left Lobe (cut), Stomach (cut), Diaphragm, Spleen, Kidney, Duodenum, Pancreas, Pancreatic Duct, Descending Colon

LUQ: Right Lobe, Gall Bladder, Bile Duct, Kidney, Transverse Colon (cut), Ascending Colon

RLQ: Cecum, Vermiform Appendix, Uterus, Ovaries

LLQ: Small Intestine, Rectum, Bladder, Anus

Umbilicus

Allergic Reaction: Anaphylaxis

Clinical findings
Neuro: anxiety, restlessness
Resp: dyspnea, bronchospasm, wheezing, stridor, swelling of tongue or throat, respiratory arrest
CV: hypotension, localized or systemic edema, CV collapse
Skin: rash, itching, hives, cool, pale, cyanosis, diaphoresis
EMT—basic/intermediate

■ Remove source of allergy; immediately remove stinger(s); scraping preferred (tweezers may inject more venom), but **do not delay removal** if only tweezers available

- Establish ABCs, and insert nasal or oral airway if indicated
- Administer high-flow O_2, or manually ventilate as indicated
- Elevate legs, and keep Pt warm if exhibiting signs of shock
- Administer medications as permitted by protocol (see below)

Paramedic

- Assess need for advanced airway, and intubate as indicated
- Obtain IV access, and titrate to SBP >90 mm Hg
- Attach ECG monitor, and manage dysrhythmias per ACLS

Management by Severity of Signs and Symptoms*

Mild: itching, rash or hives only	**Diphenhydramine:** 25–50 mg IV, IM **Cimetidine:** 300 mg IV, IM, PO
Moderate: above s/s + swelling of lips or tongue	**Dexamethasone:** 10 mg IV, IM *or* **Methylprednisolone:** 40–125 mg IV, IM **Albuterol:** 2.5 mg nebulized in 3-mL NS
Severe: above s/s + dyspnea	**Epinephrine (1:1,000):** 0.3–0.5 mg SC *(may be administered by EMT-I or EMT-P)*
Critical: above s/s + airway closure, hypotension **(anaphylaxis)**	**IV fluids:** goal SBP >90 mm Hg **Epinephrine (1:10,000):** 0.1 mg (1 mL) IV **Dopamine:** start at 10 mcg/kg/min **Glucagon:** 1 mg IV, IM *(if unresponsive to epinephrine or Pt taking beta blockers)*

*Give all drugs up to and including the Pt level of severity

Altered Mental Status (AMS)

Clinical (suggestive) Findings
Neuro: (*see GCS/AVPU scales*); pupils constricted bilaterally (narcotic OD/CNS depressant), unequal pupils (CVA, brain injury), pupils dilated bilaterally (CNS stimulant, cocaine, amphetamine)
Resp: Depressed (opioid OD), Cheyne-Stokes (CVA), Kussmaul or

MEDICAL EMERG

MEDICAL EMERG

fruity odor on breath (DKA), apneustic (brainstem injury), odor of alcohol (intoxication), sweet almond odor (cyanide exposure)
CV: HTN and decreased HR (↑ ICP), hypotension (sepsis, MI, OD, internal bleeding), dysrhythmias (*see ACLS algorithms*)
Skin: Cool and diaphoretic (hypoglycemia, vasovagal response), warm and flushed (spinal injury, hyperglycemia)
GI/GU: N/V, incontinence
MS: Weakness, fatigue, abnormal flexion or extension, trauma

EMT—basic/intermediate
- Establish ABCs, and insert nasal or oral airway if indicated
- Take full c-spine precautions if traumatic injury suspected
- Elevate legs and keep Pt warm if exhibiting signs of shock
- Transport Pt on left side, and suction airway as needed
- Administer high-flow O₂, or manually ventilate as indicated
- Obtain VS, assess pupils, and establish a baseline GCS
- Assess for stroke (see *stroke screening tool at end of this tab*)
- Obtain finger-stick blood glucose level

Paramedic
- Assess need for advanced airway, and intubate as indicated
- Obtain IV access, and titrate to SBP >90 mm Hg
- Attach ECG monitor, and manage dysrhythmias per ACLS
- **Naloxone:** 0.4–2 mg IV, IM, SC, ETT for opioid overdose
- **Flumazenil:** 0.2–0.5 mg IV for benzodiazepine overdose

AVPU Scale

A	**Alert**	Pt alert and requires no stimulation
V	**Verbal**	Pt responds to verbal stimulation only
P	**Pain**	Pt responds to painful stimulation only
U	**Unresponsive**	Pt unresponsive to any stimulation

44

Differential Diagnosis of AMS

	Opiate	Stimulant	Neuro Event	Hypoglycemia	DKA	Alcohol
Onset	Nondiagnostic	Nondiagnostic	Sudden	Sudden	Slow	Nondiagnostic
CNS	Depressed, unresponsive	Stimulated	Depressed, unresponsive	Depressed, seizure, coma	Awake, weak, tired, fatigue	Depressed, may be aggressive
Pupils	Constricted	Dilated	Unequal	Normal, PERRL	Normal, PERRL	Constricted
Resp	Slow	Rapid	Neurological; Cheyne-stokes	Normal	Deep, rapid; Kussmaul	Low or normal
Breath	Normal	Normal	Normal	Normal	Fruity odor	Alcohol odor
HR	Low or normal	Rapid	Normal to rapid	Normal or fast	Rapid, weak, thready	Normal or rapid
BP	Low or normal	Elevated	HTN	Normal or high	Normal or low	Normal or low
Skin	Normal	Normal	Cool, pale, diaphoretic	Cool, pale, diaphoretic	Warm and dry	Normal
Temp	Normal	Moderate to high	Normal to increased	Normal	Increased	Normal or low

MEDICAL EMERG

MEDICAL EMERG

Chest Pain

Clinical findings

Neuro: anxiety, restlessness, dizziness, lightheadedness, syncope, sense of "impending doom"

Resp: SOB, tachypnea

CV: tachycardia or bradycardia, signs of CHF

Skin: coolness, pallor, cyanosis, diaphoresis

MS (ACS): weakness, fatigue; substernal or epigastric sensation of a dull, achy pain or chest pressure, heaviness, squeezing, or tightness, which may radiate to the left jaw, ear, neck, shoulder and/or left arm (onset is usually rapid, lasting >30 min)

GI/GU: N/V

EMT—basic/intermediate

- Establish and manage ABCs per protocol
- Transport in position of comfort, reassure, and keep calm
- Administer high-flow O_2 titrated to SpO_2 >95%
- Obtain baseline VS, and focused symptom analysis (OPQRST)

Paramedic

- **Aspirin:** 325 mg PO chewable
- **Nitroglycerin:** 0.4 mg SL q3–5 min $\times$ 3 (only if SBP >100)
- Attach ECG monitor, and manage dysrhythmias per ACLS
- Obtain IV access, and titrate to SBP >90 mm Hg
- **Morphine:** 2–4 mg IV *or* fentanyl: 25–50 mcg IV
- Initiate or review fibrinolytic check list

Noncardiac Types of Chest Pain

- **Aortic aneurysm:** tearing pain, radiation to back, may be discrepancy between right and left pulse and/or BP
- **Cholecystitis:** RUQ, referred to right shoulder/scapula, fever, N/V, anorexia, or recent high-fat meal consumption
- **Musculoskeletal:** increases with inspiration/palpation
- **Pleurisy:** sharp/stabbing, increases with inspiration
- **Pneumonia:** fever, productive cough, crackles/rhonchi

- **Pulmonary embolism:** sharp/pleuritic, sudden onset, anxiety, SOB, cough, ↑HR, ↑RR, diaphoresis, ↓SpO$_2$, hemoptysis
- **Ulcer/gastric reflux:** burning epigastric pain, positional (pain worsens when lying down), pain increases after eating

Ischemic CP Fibrinolytic Checklist

Ischemic CP Fibrinolytic Checklist

CP >15 min and <12 hr → No → **Stop**

Yes ↓

ST elevation or new LBBB → No

Yes ↓

Contraindications (all must be checked "NO")

	Yes	No
SBP >180 mm Hg	☐	☐
DBP >110 mm Hg	☐	☐
SBP difference >15 mm Hg R-L	☐	☐
Structural CNS disease	☐	☐
Head trauma w/in 3 mo	☐	☐
GI bleed w/in 6 wk	☐	☐
Surgery w/in 6 wk	☐	☐
Major trauma w/in 6 wk	☐	☐
Pregnant	☐	☐
CPR lasting >10 min	☐	☐
Serious systemic disease	☐	☐

Criteria for high risk Pts. (if any are checked "YES", Pts. should be transferred to PCI facility)

	Yes	No
HR >/= 100 and SBP <100 mm Hg	☐	☐
Pulmonary edema	☐	☐
Signs of shock	☐	☐
Contraindications (see above)	☐	☐

Source: American Heart Association

MEDICAL EMERG

Diabetic Emergencies

Hyperglycemia (DKA, HHNS)

Clinical findings
Classic Pt presentation: gradual onset; deep, rapid respirations (Kussmaul); fruity odor on breath; warm, dry; flushed skin; excessive thirst, excessive urination, abdominal cramping, N/V, mental status may range from normal to comatose

EMT—basic/intermediate
- Establish and manage ABCs per protocol
- Administer supplemental O_2 titrated to SpO_2 >95%
- Obtain a thorough SAMPLE history, and assess GCS
- Obtain finger-stick blood glucose level

Paramedic
- Attach ECG monitor, and manage dysrhythmias per ACLS
- Obtain large-bore IV access, and titrate to SBP >90 mm Hg
- Consider fluid challenge with isotonic solution (NS or LR)

Hypoglycemia (Diabetic Coma, Insulin Shock)

Clinical findings
Classic Pt presentation: rapid onset; cool, pale, diaphoretic skin; HA, dizziness, blurred vision, tremors, tachycardia, restlessness, decreased LOC, behavioral changes (Pt may become combative), seizures and/or coma in severe cases

EMT—basic/intermediate

- Establish and manage ABCs per protocol
- Administer 100% O₂ via NRB mask or BVM if indicated
- Obtain a thorough SAMPLE history, and assess GCS
- Obtain finger-stick blood glucose level

Oral glucose: 20 g PO (Pt *must* be alert and oriented)
Paramedic

- Attach ECG monitor, and manage dysrhythmias per ACLS
- Obtain IV access, and titrate to SBP >90 mm Hg
- **Dextrose (D₅₀):** 25 g IV only *or* **glucagon:** 1 mg IM if IV access unavailable
- Reassess blood glucose level and GCS *(EMT-B, I and P)*

Hypoglycemia Compared With Hyperglycemia

	Hypoglycemia	Hyperglycemic Conditions	
	Insulin Shock	**DKA**	**HHNS**
Hx	Recent insulin shot, missed meal, excessive exercise	Infection, stress, trauma, insufficient insulin intake	Pneumonia, UTI, dehydration, AMS, immobility
Onset	Rapid (minutes)	Gradual (days)	Gradual (weeks)
Neuro	Confusion, delirium, coma, seizures	Irritability, HA, double or blurred vision	Fatigue, impaired vision, HA, coma, seizure, delirium
CV	Weak, rapid HR, SBP variable	HR normal to fast, SBP variable	**Early:** tachycardia **late:** hypotension
Resp	Normal	Deep and rapid (Kussmaul)	Tachypnea, may be depressed

Continued

MEDICAL EMERG

Hypoglycemia Compared With Hyperglycemia—cont'd

	Hypoglycemia	Hyperglycemic Conditions	
	Insulin Shock	**DKA**	**HHNS**
Breath	Normal	Fruity odor	No fruity odor
Skin	Cool, pale, moist	Warm, dry, flushed	Itchy, poor turgor
MS	Weakness, tremor, twitch	Muscle wasting	Weakness
GI/GU	N/V	Polydipsia, N/V, abdominal cramps, polyuria, dehydrated	Polyuria, decreased fluid intake
FSBG	<80 mg/dL	>180 mg/dL	>800 mg/dL
Rx	Glucose IV or PO, glucagon	IV, insulin, potassium	IV, insulin, potassium

DKA: diabetic ketoacidosis
HHNS: hyperglycemic, hyperosmolar, nonketotic syndrome
FSBG: finger-stick blood glucose (chem-strip)

Hypertensive Emergency

Clinical findings
Neuro: HA, visual disturbances, restlessness, anxiety, confusion, AMS, disorientation, seizures, slurred speech
Resp: SOB, dyspnea
CV: SBP >220 mm Hg or DBP >140 mm Hg, CP, tachycardia, dysrhythmias, pulmonary edema, CHF (pedal or dependent edema and JVD if HTN secondary to CHF)
Skin: flushed or cool, pale, diaphoretic
GI/GU: N/V
MS: weakness, fatigue, hemiparesis (CVA)

EMT—basic/intermediate

- Establish and manage ABCs per protocol
- Assess pupils, and establish baseline GCS score
- Assess for stroke (see *stroke screening tool* at end of this tab)
- Administer high-flow O_2, or manually ventilate as indicated
- Rapid transport with head elevated to position of comfort
- Minimize stimulation, and keep Pt calm
- Obtain baseline VS, and record BP in both arms

Paramedic

- Attach ECG monitor, and manage dysrhythmias per ACLS
- Obtain IV access, and run TKO (30 mL/hr)
- Initiate ischemic CP pre-hospital checklist if ACS suspected
- Initiate ischemic stroke checklist if stroke suspected
- Reduction of BP in the field: Must consult with OLMC

Pharmacologic Management*

- **Nitroglycerin:** 04 mg SL tablet or spray; may repeat every 5 min to three doses (hold for SBP <90 mm Hg)
- **Labetalol:** 10 mg slow IV over 1–2 min; may double or repeat dose every 10 min to 150 mg
- **Nitroprusside:** 0.1–10 mcg/kg IV infusion

*Caution: treatment should be directed by symptoms and not blood pressure alone; use extreme caution, as too rapid lowering of BP can precipitate cerebral and myocardial ischemia and diminished renal blood flow

Increasing Intracranial Pressure (ICP)

Clinical findings
Cushing reflex: HTN, bradycardia, unequal pupils, irregular respirations, hyperthermia
Neuro: AMS, HA, sensitivity to light, irritability, double or blurred vision, seizures, hemiparesis, GCS <8, unequal pupils
Resp: abnormal respirations, tachypnea (late)

MEDICAL EMERG

CV: HTN, bradycardia (late), widening pulse pressure (late)
GI/GU: N/V
MS: weakness, decreased motor function, posturing

EMT—basic/intermediate

- Establish and manage ABCs per protocol
- Assess pupils, and establish baseline GCS score
- Controlled hyperventilation: decrease $Paco_2$, causing cerebral vasoconstriction and decreased ICP; **Note:** If capnography monitoring available, goal should be $ETCO_2$ of 30 mm Hg
- Rapid transport with head elevated to 30 degrees, maintain head in neutral alignment, and avoid flexion or rotation of neck
- Closely monitor VS and neurological status (AVPU/GCS)

Paramedic

- Assess need for advanced airway, and intubate as indicated
- Attach ECG monitor, and manage dysrhythmias per ACLS
- Obtain IV access, and run at TKO; if Pt becomes hypotensive, titrate IV to SBP >90 mm Hg (avoid D_5W)
- **Mannitol 20%:** 0.5–1 g/kg IV over 5–10 min

Abnormal Extension (decerebrate posturing)

Abnormal Flexion (decorticate posturing)

Overdose and Poisoning

Poison Control (United States: 1-800-222-1222)

Clinical (suggestive) findings
CNS depressants: (opioids, sedatives): constricted pupils, drowsiness, weakness, coma, respiratory depression, pulmonary edema, apnea, bradycardia, hypotension, hypothermia
CNS stimulants: (cocaine, amphetamines): dilated pupils, anxiety, agitation, HA, psychotic, tachypnea, tachycardia, dysrhythmias, HTN, CP, diaphoresis, hyperthermia
Carbon monoxide (CO): cherry-red lips and/or skin, weakness, fatigue, HA, dizziness, visual disturbances, ataxia, coma, dysrhythmias, respiratory distress, N/V
Caustics (acids, alkalis): chemical burns to the area of exposure or mouth and GI tract if ingested, pain, N/V, respiratory distress
Hydrocarbons (gasoline, oil): respiratory distress, odor on breath if ingested, bronchospasm, pulmonary edema, seizure
Organophosphates (OPP): *s*alivation, *l*acrimation, *u*rination, *d*efecation, *g*astric upset, *e*mesis, *m*uscle twitching (SLUDGEM)
EMT—basic/intermediate

- Protect yourself and crew from HAZMAT or violent Pts
- Remove from source, and remove clothing and jewelry
- Establish and manage ABCs per protocol
- Transport Pt on left side, and suction airway as needed
- Administer supplemental O_2 titrated to SpO_2 >95%
- Activated charcoal: 1 g/kg PO or NG (*Caution: ineffective for treatment of heavy metals, alcohols, caustics, hydrocarbons, or potassium or potassium cyanide*)

Paramedic

- Assess need for advanced airway, and intubate as indicated
- Attach ECG monitor, and manage dysrhythmias per ACLS
- Obtain IV access, and titrate to SBP >90 mm Hg

Caution: avoid Ipecac as vomiting may complicate or worsen clinical management of OD or poisoning

MEDICAL EMERG

Antidotes and Reversals

This is a reference and is not intended to replace EMS protocol.

All Pts: crew/scene safety, ABCs, supportive care, transport

Acetaminophen (APAP, Tylenol)
- **Activated charcoal**: 1 g/kg (**peds**: same) PO, NG
- **N-acetylcysteine**: 150 mg/kg in 250-mL D_5W IV, IO over 60 min (**peds <40 kg**: same dose except use less D_5W); **PO route** (if awake and not vomiting): 140 mg/kg (**peds**: same)

Aspirin (ASA, Bayer, Excedrin)
- **Activated charcoal**: 1 g/kg (**peds**: same) PO, NG
- **Sodium bicarbonate 8.4%**: 1 mEq/kg (**peds**: same) IV, IO

Beta blockers (metoprolol, Lopressor, atenolol, Tenormin)
- **Activated charcoal**: 1 g/kg (**peds**: same) PO or NG
- **Glucagon**: 3 mg (150 mcg/kg) IV, IO followed by 3 mg/hr (**peds**: 3 mg/hr) infusion

Calcium channel blockers (Adalat, Cardizem, Isoptin)
- **Activated charcoal**: 1 g/kg (**peds**: same) PO, NG
- **Calcium chloride 10%**: 1-4 g (**peds**: 20-25 mg/kg) slow IV, IO

Carbon monoxide (CO)
- See General HAZMAT Decontamination

Caustics (acids and alkalis)
- See General HAZMAT Decontamination

Cholinergics (organophosphate, carbamates, nerve gas)
- Remove from source and remove Pt clothing and jewelry
- Decontaminate with copious NS or water
- **Atropine**: 2-5 mg (**peds**: 0.05 mg/kg) IV, IO, IM every 3-5 min
- **Pralidoxime*** (**2-PAM**): 600 mg IM or may infuse 1-2 g over 15-30 min (**peds**: 20-50 mg/kg IM or infuse over 15-30 min)
- *Not recommended for carbamates
- **Do not induce vomiting if substance ingested**; if Pt alert with gag reflex, give water 5 mL/kg (max 200 mL) PO

Antidotes and Reversals—cont'd

All Pts: Crew/scene safety, ABCs, supportive care, transport

CNS stimulants (cocaine, methamphetamine, speed, crank)
- Protect self and crew, wait for law enforcement
- Minimize sensory stimulation, treat symptoms of ACS
- **Activated charcoal:** 1 g/kg (**peds:** same) PO if ingested
- **Midazolam:** 1–2 mg (**peds:** 0.05–0.2 mg/kg) IV, IO

Cyanide poisoning
- Protect self and crew, extricate Pt, remove Pt clothing
- **Amyl nitrite:** 1 ampule crushed and inhaled every 30 sec
- **Na nitrite:** 300 mg (**peds:** 10 mg/kg) IV, IO over 2–5 min
- **Na thiosulfate:** 125 g (**peds:** 412.5 mg/kg) IV, IO over 5 min
- **Hydroxocobalamin:** 5 g (**peds:** 70 mg/kg) IV over 15 min

EPS (extrapyramidal symptoms)
- Symptoms associated with phenothiazines and tranquilizers
- **Diphenhydramine:** 25–50 mg (**peds:** 1 mg/kg) IV, IO, IM

Hallucinogens (LSD, PCP, some mushrooms, mescaline, THC)
- Protect self and crew, wait for law enforcement
- Minimize sensory stimulation
- **Diazepam:** 2–5 mg (**peds:** 0.1–0.2 mg/kg) IV, IO

Narcotics/opioids (heroin, methadone, Demerol, oxycodone)
- **Naloxone:** 0.4–2 mg (**peds:** 0.1 mg/kg, max 2 mg) IV, IO, IM
- **Nalmefene:** 0.5 mg/70 kg (**peds:** 0.25 mcg/kg) IV, IO, IM

Sedative-hypnotics (benzodiazepines, Rohypnol)
- **Flumazenil:** 0.2–0.5 mg (**peds:** 0.01 mg/kg) IV, IO, IM

Tricyclic antidepressants (TCA, nortriptyline, amitriptyline)
- Watch for tachycardia with widened QRS
- Do not induce vomiting; rapid transport, O$_2$, monitor, IV
- **Sodium bicarbonate 8.4%:** 1 mEq/kg (**peds:** same) IV, IO

MEDICAL EMERG

Respiratory Distress

Clinical findings
Neuro: anxiety, restlessness, confusion, AMS
Resp: dyspnea, tachypnea, use of accessory muscles, sternal retractions, pursed-lip breathing (emphysema), wheezing, stridor, cough, rales, crackles, orthopnea, pink frothy sputum (pulmonary edema/CHF), thick white sputum (asthma)
CV: tachycardia, HTN, pulmonary edema (CHF), pedal or dependent edema, jugular vein distention (JVD)
Skin: cyanosis, coolness, pallor, diaphoresis
GI/GU: decreased or no urinary output
MS: weakness, lethargy, fatigue, exhaustion

EMT—basic/intermediate
- Establish and manage ABCs per protocol
- Place Pt in position of comfort if Pt status allows
- Administer high-flow O_2 or manually ventilate as indicated
- Begin CPAP at 5–10 cm PEEP **if indicated**
- Assess breathing (rate, depth, effort, lung sounds, cyanosis)
- Obtain baseline VS, noting BP and HR
- Do not encourage paper bag rebreathing as a treatment for hyperventilation syndrome (HVS); all HVS should receive O_2 until causes other than anxiety can be ruled out

Paramedic
- Assess need for advanced airway and intubate as indicated
- Attach ECG monitor, and manage dysrhythmias per ACLS
- Obtain IV access, and run at TKO (30 mL/hr)

Etiology-Specific Treatment

Asthma/status asthmaticus/bronchospasm

- Initiate CPAP therapy at 5–10 cm PEEP
- **Albuterol**: 25 mg nebulized in 3-mL NS
- Consider **ipratropium**: 0.5 mg (given with albuterol)
- Consider **methylprednisone**: 125 mg IV
- Consider **epinephrine**: 0.3–0.5 mg of 1:1000 SC

COPD (chronic bronchitis and emphysema)

- Initiate CPAP therapy at 5–10 cm PEEP
- **Albuterol**: 25 mg nebulized in 3-mL NS
- Consider **ipratropium**: 0.5 mg (given with albuterol)
- Consider **methylprednisone**: 125 mg IV

CHF/pulmonary edema

- Initiate CPAP therapy at 5–10 cm PEEP
- **Nitroglycerin**: 0.4 mg SL every 3–5 min × 3, hold if SBP <100 mm Hg
- **Furosemide**: 0.5–1 mg/kg IVP (some EMS systems administer a dose equaling Pt oral dose)

Hyperventilation syndrome (HVS)

- Offer reassurance, and attempt to calm Pt
- Benzodiazepines may help reduce anxiety
- $Etco_2$ <30 suggestive of HVS

MEDICAL EMERG

Differentiating Lung Sounds

Rales/Crackles	Simulated by rolling hair near the ear between two fingers, best heard on inspiration in the lower bases, unrelieved by coughing, (CHF, pneumonia)
Wheezes	High-pitched squeaking sounds, best heard on expiration over all lung fields, unrelieved by coughing (asthma, COPD, bronchitis, emphysema)
Rhonchi	Coarse, harsh, loud gurgling or rattling; best heard on expiration over bronchi and trachea, often relieved by coughing (bronchitis, pneumonia)
Stridor	**Life-threatening**; harsh, high-pitched, easily audible on inspiration, progressive narrowing of the upper airway requiring immediate attention (**partial airway obstruction, croup, epiglottitis**)

Differentiating Respiratory Diseases

	Asthma	Bronchitis	Heart failure	Emphysema	Pneumonia
Lung Sounds	Wheezes, mostly expiratory	Coarse rhonchi, wheezing	Crackles, rales	Wheezes	Crackles, rales, rhonchi
Onset	Usually sudden	**Acute:** rapid **Chronic:** varies	Nighttime, early morning	Exacerbations sudden	Gradual
Home Meds	Beta-adrenergic inhalers, steroids, home O_2	**Acute:** may be on antibiotics **Chronic:** inhalers, steroids, home O_2	Diuretics, beta blocker, ACE inhibitors, steroids, home O_2	Beta-adrenergic inhalers, steroids, home O_2	Antibiotics
Comorbidity	Smoking, allergies	Smoking, URI	HTN, MI	Smoking	URI, fatigue, infection
Cough	Dry, sometimes thick, white mucus	Productive, yellow, green, light brown	Productive, pink frothy	Dry, may produce mucous plugs	Productive, yellow, green, light brown
Fever	None	**Acute:** elevated **Chronic:** none	None	None	Elevated
Exacerbation	Exercise, allergens	Exercise, allergens	Lying supine	Exercise, allergens	Exercise, lying supine if severe

MEDICAL EMERG

MEDICAL EMERG

Seizure/Status Epilepticus

Clinical findings
Neuro: loss of consciousness (blank stare if absence seizure)
Resp: cyanosis, inability to breathe adequately, apnea
MS: repetitive jerking movements of all extremities
GI/GU: urinary or fecal incontinence
Progression of seizure

- **Aura** (before seizure starts): Warning or recognition by Pt that seizure imminent (not present in all seizures)
- **Ictal phase:** active seizing
- **Postictal phase** (after seizure subsides): AMS, extremely confused, frightened, lethargic and disoriented

Types of seizures

- **Simple partial** (focal): unusual sensations, Pt remembers event
- **Complex partial:** abnormal behavioral-motor movements
- **Generalized absence** (petit mal): no movement, blank stare
- **Tonic-clonic** (grand mal): localized or full-body convulsions
- **Status epilepticus:** life-threatening; recurring seizures between which Pt does not regain consciousness

EMT—basic/intermediate

- Protect Pt from injury by clearing immediate area
- Do not attempt to restrain Pt during seizure
- Establish and manage ABCs per protocol
- Take full C-spine precautions if traumatic injury suspected
- Transport Pt on left side, and suction airway as needed
- Administer high-flow O_2, or manually ventilate as indicated
- Obtain VS, assess pupils, and establish baseline GCS
- Obtain finger-stick blood glucose level
- Document seizure description: aura, onset, type, duration

Paramedic

- Assess need for advanced airway, and intubate as indicated
- Attach ECG monitor, and manage dysrhythmias per ACLS
- Obtain IV access, and titrate to SBP >90 mm Hg
- **Lorazepam**: 1–4 mg slow IV *or* **diazepam**: 5–10 mg slow IV *(may give both PR or IN if no IV; **Note**: dose may vary)*
- **Dextrose 50%**: 25 gram slow IV for confirmed hypoglycemia

Shock/Hypotension

Clinical findings
Neuro: AMS, anxiety, restlessness (early), confusion, coma
Resp: Tachypnea, dyspnea
CV: Hypotension, decreased capillary refill, reflex tachycardia, jugular vein distention (tamponade/tension pneumothorax)
Skin: Coolness, pallor, diaphoresis, cyanosis
GI/GU: N/V
MS: Weakness, fatigue

EMT—basic/intermediate

- Establish and manage ABCs as indicated
- Full c-spine precautions for trauma
- Administer high-flow O_2, or manually ventilate as indicated
- Control bleeding with direct pressure or pressure dressing
- Rapid transport (supine position, elevate legs, and keep warm)
- Assess baseline VS, LOC (AVPU/GCS), and lung sounds
- If critical trauma, perform secondary survey and other nonessential interventions while moving to trauma center

Paramedic

- Assess need for advanced airway, and intubate as indicated
- Attach ECG monitor, and manage dysrhythmias per ACLS
- **Rate problem**: see respective ACLS algorithm
- Start two large-bore IVs, and titrate to SBP >90 mm Hg
- Identify and correct cause (hemorrhage, dehydration)

MEDICAL EMERG

Shock-specific pre-hospital management

- **Anaphylactic shock:** see beginning of this tab
- **Cardiogenic shock:** if lungs clear, give 250–500-mL fluid challenge to normalize SBP and HR; if pulmonary congestion (rales or crackles) present, adjust IV to TKO, and initiate CPAP therapy; consider vasopressors
- **Hypovolemic shock:** establish two large-bore IVs (NS/LR), and titrate to SBP >90 mm Hg; immobilize c-spine for trauma
- **Neurogenic shock:** ABCs, O_2, immobilize c-spine for trauma IV fluids, lie flat, consider vasopressors
- **Rate problem:** refer to bradycardia or tachycardia algorithm
- **Septic shock:** ABCs, O_2, IV fluids, consider vasopressors

Shock: Differential Diagnosis

	Anaphylactic (Allergic Reaction)	Cardiogenic (Pump Failure)	Hypovolemic (Low Volume)	Neurogenic (Spinal Shock)	Septic (Septicemia)
Pathophysiology	Vasodilatation, fluid shifts, laryngeal and peripheral edema, bronchospasms	↓CO d/t lack of contractile force, ↓BP, ↓tissue perfusion	Intravascular volume causing ↓tissue perfusion	Profound vasodilation causing ↓BP and ↓tissue perfusion	Circulatory failure d/t systemic inflammatory response, capillary leak syndrome, and ↓tissue perfusion
Common Etiology	Acute, life-threatening allergic reaction to specific antigen	AMI, acute pulmonary edema, tamponade, right or left heart failure	Low circulating volume d/t burns, hemorrhage, third spacing, trauma, dehydration	Traumatic spinal cord injury, anesthesia	Endotoxin release usually from gram-negative organism

Continued

MEDICAL EMERG

Shock: Differential Diagnosis—cont'd

	Anaphylactic (Allergic Reaction)	Cardiogenic (Pump Failure)	Hypovolemic (Low Volume)	Neurogenic (Spinal Shock)	Septic (Septicemia)
Clinical Findings	Respiratory distress, hypotension, edema, rash; cool, pale skin; possible seizure activity	↑HR, weak pulses, ↑capillary refill, cyanosis, dysrhythmias, AMS; cool, clammy skin	↓BP, ↑HR, weak pulses, ↑capillary refill, cyanosis, dysrhythmias, AMS; cool, clammy skin	↓BP, ↓HR, bounding pulse; pale, warm, and dry skin	Flushed, warm skin vasodilation (early) ↑temp, ↓UO (late) vasoconstriction (late)

Stroke

Clinical findings
Neuro: AMS, unequal pupils, agitation, confusion, HA, visual disturbances, aphasia, dysphasia, dysarthria, dizziness, vertigo
Resp: Cheyne-Stokes pattern
CV: hypertension, dysrhythmias
Skin: coolness, pallor, diaphoresis, cyanosis
GI/GU: N/V
MS: weakness, ataxia, clumsiness, facial droop
EMT—basic/intermediate

- Establish and manage ABCs per protocol; use c-spine precautions if Pt comatose or trauma suspected
- If Pt cannot tolerate sitting upright, position **on affected side**
- Suction airway, and clear secretions as needed
- Administer high-flow O_2, or manually ventilate as indicated
- Assess pupils, and establish baseline GCS score
- Obtain baseline VS, and record BP in both arms
- Obtain finger-stick blood glucose level

Paramedic

- Assess need for advanced airway, and intubate as indicated
- Attach ECG monitor, and manage dysrhythmias per ACLS
- Obtain IV access, and titrate to SBP >90 mm Hg (avoid D_5W)

MEDICAL EMERG

Pre-hospital Stroke Screening Tool

Facial droop Ask Pt to smile	**Normal:** both sides of face move equally **Abnormal:** droop or unequal movement
Arm drift Have Pt hold arms out for 10 sec	**Normal:** arms move equally or not at all **Abnormal:** one arm drifts compared to other
Abnormal speech Have Pt say, "Let sleeping dogs lie."	**Normal:** repeats phrase without slurring **Abnormal:** slurred or inappropriate words or inability to speak
Interpretation: with any abnormal result, Pt should be considered for transport to designated stroke center	

Ischemic Stroke Checklist for tPA

All boxes *must* be checked before tPA can be given; a physician with expertise in ischemic stroke may modify list

YES! Inclusion Criteria (all YES boxes must be checked)
- ☐ Age 18 or older
- ☐ Clinical diagnosis of ischemic stroke with neurological deficit
- ☐ Time of symptom onset (when Pt was last seen normal) well established as <3 hr before treatment would begin

NO! Exclusion Criteria (all NO boxes must be checked)
- ☐ Intracranial hemorrhage on non-contrast CT
- ☐ Clinical presentation suggestive of subarachnoid hemorrhage despite normal CT
- ☐ History of intracranial hemorrhage

Ischemic Stroke Checklist for tPA—cont'd

- ☐ Uncontrolled HTN: at time treatment should begin, SBP >180 mm Hg or DBP >110 mm Hg despite repeated treatments
- ☐ Known AVM, neoplasm, or aneurysm
- ☐ Witnessed seizure at stroke onset
- ☐ Active internal bleeding or acute trauma
- ☐ Platelet count <100,000/mm³
- ☐ Heparin received within 48 hr resulting in aPTT that is higher than the upper limit of normal for laboratory
- ☐ Current anticoagulant use with an INR >17 or a PT >15 sec
- ☐ Within 3 months of intracranial or intraspinal surgery, serious head trauma, or previous stroke
- ☐ Arterial puncture within past 7 days

Relative Contraindications

- Minor or rapidly improving stroke symptoms
- Lumbar puncture (LP) within 21 days
- Major surgery or serious trauma within 14 days
- GI or urinary tract hemorrhage within 21 days
- AMI within 3 months or post-MI pericarditis
- Blood glucose of <50 or >400 mg/dL

MEDICAL EMERG

Suicidal/Combative Pts

- Ensure safety of yourself and crew, and wait for scene to be cleared by law enforcement prior to entering
- Be aware of items at scene or medical equipment that may be used as a weapon
- Observe closely for signs of potential violence (e.g., threatening posture, agitation, threatening language, etc.)
- Observe pupils (dilated = CNS ↓; constricted = CNS ↑)
- Demonstrate confidence, but avoid arguing or confrontation
- Maintain safe distance between yourself and Pt
- Never allow Pt to block your exit from scene
- Restrain Pts who are danger to themselves or others

Restraint Guidelines

Indication

- Restrain Pts who display behavior or threats that create or imply a danger to themselves or others

Procedure

- Attempt first to control the Pt with verbal counseling
- Restraints should never interfere with management of ABCs
- Only restraints approved for EMS should be used
- Ensure that enough help is available (ideally, one person for each limb and one for applying restraints)
- Pregnant women should be restrained in a left-lateral recumbent position to help prevent supine hypotension

Chemical restraints: *Consult OLMC for orders*
- **Droperidol: adults:** 1.25–2.5 mg (**peds:** 0.1 mg/kg) IV or IM
- Use physical restraints as well, because duration of chemical restraints unpredictable and Pts can emerge unexpectedly

Document

- Medical necessity
- Explanation to Pt
- Pt refusal to comply with EMS and/or law enforcement
- Evidence of Pt incompetence (e.g., intoxication, AMS)
- Type of restraint used (e.g., wrist, ankle, chemical)
- **Distal CSM:** before and after applying and every 5 min

MEDICAL EMERG

Triage Criteria for Critical Trauma

Vital Signs and LOC
- SBP <90 mm Hg
- RR <10 or >29
- AMS, unconsciousness
- GCS <14
- RTS <11
- Pt has no memory of event

Anatomical Injuries
- Penetrating injuries to head, neck, torso, and extremities proximal to elbows or knees
- Trauma and burns
- Two or more long-bone fractures
- Flail chest
- Open/depressed skull fracture
- Amputation proximal to wrist or ankle
- Paralysis
- Major burn injury
- Pelvic fractures

Mechanism of Injury
- Ejection from same vehicle
- Death in same vehicle
- MVA impact >40 mph
- Intrusion of passenger compartment >12 in
- Vehicle deformity >20 in
- MVA involving a rollover
- Falls >20 ft
- Pedestrian run over or thrown
- Extrication time >20 min
- Auto vs pedestrian or bike >5 mph
- MCA >20 mph with rider thrown from motorcycle

Comorbidity
- Pregnancy
- Pre-existing disease
- Intoxication
- Bleeding disorder
- Age <5 y or >55 y
- Environmental extremes

TRAUMA/ HAZMAT

Note: All Pts with a high suspicion of critical trauma, despite absence of clinical findings, may be transported to a trauma center for evaluation at the paramedic's discretion

Primary Trauma Survey

Airway management and c-spine immobilization

- Open airway: use jaw-thrust method, assign C-spine control
- Assess for compromise/obstruction
- Suction airway to clear blood, secretions, debris
- Have C-collar applied

Breathing and ventilation

- Respirations: presence, rate, depth, quality, and effort
- Inspect and palpate chest, and auscultate lung fields for diminished or absent breath sounds
- Manually ventilate with a BVM if breathing inadequate

Circulation and hemorrhage control

- Pulse: presence, quality, regularity
- Begin chest compressions if no palpable pulse
- Skin: color, temperature, moisture, capillary refill
- Control hemorrhage with direct pressure

Disability

- Determine and establish baseline GCS score
- Pupils: PERL (pupils equal and reactive to light)

Expose/environment

- Remove Pt clothing, and assess Pt for injury and hemorrhage
- Maintain body temperature by keeping Pt covered
- Log roll to inspect and palpate posterior surfaces
- Immobilize entire body using c-spine collar/long board

TRAUMA/HAZMAT

Secondary Trauma Survey

Vital signs
- BP, HR, RR, lung sounds, skin color, and temperature
- Assess every 3–5 min or with any change in Pt status

SAMPLE history
- **S:** signs and symptoms (S/S)
- **A:** allergies or sensitivities to medications
- **M:** medication (prescription or OTC) taken on a regular basis
- **P:** past medical or surgical history
- **L:** last meal eaten or last beverage
- **E:** events leading up to the injury

Head-to-Toe Assessment

Head and face
- Pupils: reassess equality and reactivity to light (PERL)
- Contusions, abrasions, lacerations, asymmetry
- Abnormalities of the eyes, eyelids, ears, mouth, mandible
- Soft-tissue injuries, skull depressions, abnormal mobility

Neck and c-spine
- Contusions, abrasions, lacerations, deformity
- Tracheal deviation/jugular vein distention (JVD)
- Tenderness, crepitus, subcutaneous emphysema

Chest and lungs
- Contusions, abrasions, lacerations, deformity, paradoxical movement, penetrating or sucking chest wounds, splinting, guarding, sternal retractions, steering wheel bruises
- Anterior lung fields: diminished/absent breath sounds
- Tenderness, crepitus, subcutaneous emphysema

Abdomen

- Distention, contusions, abrasions, lacerations, penetrations, ecchymosis, transverse umbilical contusion (seat-belt sign)
- All quadrants: tenderness, guarding, softness, rigidity

Pelvis and perineum

- Contusions, abrasions, lacerations, hematoma, ecchymosis
- Perineal injury/bleeding
- Pelvic tenderness/instability/limb foreshortening
- Pelvic fracture: shortened, externally rotated leg

Back (performed during log roll onto long board)

- Contusions, abrasions, lacerations, penetrations, deformity
- Spinal tenderness/deformity
- Posterior lung fields: diminished/absent breath sounds

Extremities

- Deformity, open fractures, lacerations, hematoma, ecchymosis, tenderness, crepitus, abnormal movement
- Distal CSM: assess before and after splinting

Neurological status

- Reassess GCS score, pupils, and sensory and motor function every 3–5 min or with any change in Pt status

Special Considerations

Pregnancy

- Immobilize pregnant women (>24 wk) in the left lateral position if possible to avoid compression of vena cava

Mechanism of injury

- **Motor vehicle accidents (MVA):** direction of impact, speed at impact, condition of vehicle, use of seat belts or airbags, ejection from vehicle, any other passenger from the same vehicle killed, delayed transport due to extrication

TRAUMA/HAZMAT

TRAUMA/HAZMAT

- **Falls**: from what height and onto what type of surface?
- **Penetrating trauma**: weapon, site and depth of injury, underlying organs, caliber/velocity of bullet

Indications for Spinal Immobilization

Neurological findings
- AMS, GCS <15, unequal or unresponsive pupil(s)
- Loss of consciousness or loss of memory of incident
- Neurological deficits/symptoms

Associated findings
- Spinal tenderness and/or spinal deformity
- Distracting injury
- Communication barrier
- Alcohol or drug involvement

Mechanism of injury
- Fall >10 ft
- Auto versus pedestrian
- Penetrating injuries of head, chest, back, abdomen, pelvis
- Significant blunt force trauma to head, neck, or back

Pupil Gauge (mm)

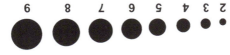

2   3   4   5   6   7   8   9

74

Glasgow Coma Score (GCS)

Eyes Open	Spontaneously 4	
	To command (infant: to noise/voice) ...3	
	To pain 2	
	Unresponsive 1	
Best Verbal	Oriented (infant: coos/babbles) 5	
	Confused (infant: irritable) 4	
	Inappropriate (infant: cries to pain) 3	
	Incomprehensible (infant: grunts/moans) .2	
	Unresponsive 1	
Best Motor	Obeys commands (infant: spontaneous) .6	
	Localizes pain 5	
	Withdraws from pain 4	
	Abnormal flexion 3	
	Abnormal extension 2	
	Unresponsive 1	
	Total	

TRAUMA/HAZMAT

TRAUMA/HAZMAT

Revised Trauma Score (RTS)

Resp Rate	10–29/min 4	
	>29/min 3	
	6–9/min 2	
	1–5/min 1	
	Apnea 0	
SBP	>89 .4	
	76–89 3	
	50–75 2	
	1–49 1	
	Pulseless 0	
GCS Score	13–15 4	
	9–12 3	
	6–8 .2	
	4–5 .1	
	3 0	
	Total	

Basic Trauma Management

Goal: rapid assessment, airway control, c-spine immobilization, hemorrhage control, and rapid transport with IVs done en route

EMT—basic/intermediate

- Establish and manage ABCs with full C-spine precautions
- Administer high-flow O$_2$, or assist ventilations manually
- Control external bleeding with direct pressure
- Maintain normal body temperature
- Rapid transport to appropriate trauma center

Paramedic

- Assess need for advanced airway, and intubate as indicated
- Use of pneumatic anti-shock garment (PASG) controversial and varies by region (follow local protocol)
- Start two large-bore IVs en route titrated to SBP >90 mm Hg
- Attach monitor en route, and manage dysrhythmias

Head Trauma

Watch for abnormal respiratory patterns; changes in LOC and pupils; S/S of increasing ICP, seizures, and posturing

- Assess pupils, and establish a baseline AVPU/GCS
- Inspect ears for blood/CSF leak; allow nosebleed to drain if CSF leak present: protect airway and suction as needed
- Check blood glucose level with all AMS

Chest Trauma

Watch for respiratory distress, shock, JVD, sub-Q emphysema

- **Flail chest:** unstable segment of ribs, paradoxical movement with respiration: stabilize flail segment with bulky dressing
- **Impaled object:** stabilize in place with 4×4 and tape; do not remove object unless it interferes with resuscitation
- **Open/sucking chest wound:** three-sided, occlusive dressing; if tension pneumothorax develops, remove dressing
- **Tension pneumothorax:** respiratory distress, absent breath sounds on affected side, tracheal deviation; perform needle decompression on affected side

TRAUMA/HAZMAT

Comparing Types of Chest Trauma

Impression	Pneumothorax	Hemothorax	Tamponade
	Respiratory distress		Shock
Heart	Normal sound	Can be muffled	Muffled
Lungs	Diminished on affected side		Normal
Trachea	Shifted away	May be shifted	Midline
Neck Veins	Distended	Distended	Distended
Percussion	Hyperresonant	Dull	Normal

Needle Chest Decompression

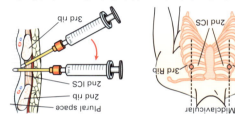

- **Locate landmark:** begin at midclavicular line on clavicle of affected side, and palpate down one rib to first space below that rib; this is the second intercostal space (space immediately after clavicle is first intercostal space)
- **Prepare site:** prepare insertion site with antiseptic
- **Insert catheter:** 10 g–12 g, 3" (peds: <12 yr: 14 g, 1⅜"), over-the-needle catheter at a 45° angle (parallel to sternum) over the top of the third rib to avoid nerves and vessels
- Rush of air indicates entrance into pleural space
- Advance catheter, remove needle, stabilize catheter
- Attach a one-way valve, and monitor Pt for improvement

Abdominal Trauma

Watch for guarding, bruising, rigidity, distention, or hypotension: suspect internal hemorrhage

- Establish ABCs, c-spine precautions, hemorrhage control
- Start two large-bore IVs titrated to SBP >90 mm Hg
- Pt meets criteria for critical trauma with any penetration

Impaled objects

- Secure in place with 4×4 and tape
- Do not remove object unless it interferes with resuscitation

Eviscerations

- Cover with saline-soaked, sterile gauze
- Do not inflate abdominal compartment if using PASG
- Do not replace organs back into abdominal cavity

Extremity Trauma

- Immobilize extremity in place, and assess distal CSM before and after immobilization; leave fingertips and toes exposed
- Do not attempt to reduce fractures
- Cover any exposed bone with NS-soaked gauze dressing
- Apply traction splint to mid-shaft femur fractures
- Consider using PASG to splint lower extremity fractures (use varies by region)
- Consider **morphine** (2–4 mg IV) or **fentanyl** (25–50 mcg IV) for moderate to severe pain (for isolated extremity injury only)
- Pt meets criteria for critical trauma with two or more long-bone fractures or any amputation proximal to wrist or ankle

TRAUMA/HAZMAT

TRAUMA/HAZMAT

Amputations

- **Manage life-threatening injuries first;** irrigate debris from amputated part with saline; wrap part in gauze moistened with saline; avoid soaking the gauze, which causes tissue to become macerated and diminishes viability (especially digits)
- Place wrapped part into a zip-lock bag (note time on bag), and place sealed bag into a container of ice water
- Immobilize partial amputations in anatomical position

Abuse

Child abuse

- Unlikely mechanism of injury (story does not match injury)
- Details of injury change from person to person
- Burns (scalding or cigarettes) or wire marks
- Fractures or dislocation in a child younger than 2 years
- Multiple injuries in various stages of healing
- Unexcused delay in seeking medical attention
- History inconsistent with child's developmental stages
- Overly protective parent (interferes with assessment)
- Unusual fear of parent or desire to please parent
- Withdrawn or aggressive behavior
- Malnutrition, insect infestation, or disheveled appearance

Sexual abuse (molestation/)

- Bruised or bleeding genitalia or blood-stained underwear
- Painful urination or itching of genital area
- Sexually transmitted disease (STD) or pregnancy
- Inappropriate display of sexual behavior

Elder abuse

- Malnourishment and unexplained dehydration
- Poor hygiene (body/clothing soiled with urine and feces)
- Clothing inappropriate for weather/season
- Signs of inappropriate use of restraints (bruising/abrasions of wrists and ankles)

Pre-hospital management

- Assess and ensure scene safety and wait for police
- Remove victim from abusive environment
- Avoid any confrontation with alleged abuser
- Assess and manage ABCs and treat injuries per protocol
- Take full c-spine precautions if indicated
- Discourage sexual assault victims from bathing, douching, urinating, or changing clothes prior to going to ED
- Minimize disturbance of crime scene or potential evidence
- File report with appropriate authorities or protective services when abuse is either witnessed or suspected

Bites and Stings

- Goal is **early notification and transport** to hospital
- Follow standard protocol for supporting ABCs
- Always ensure scene safety before entering
- Carefully remove any remaining, visible venom apparatus*
- Keep Pt warm and calm, and avoid excessive movement
- Apply cold compress**/sterile dressing to affected area
- Remove rings and constricting jewelry from affected area
- Immobilize extremity with loose splint to restrict movement
- Keep affected area **below** level of heart
- Attempt to identify insect or animal for correct antidote
- Manage allergic reaction/anaphylaxis

Arachnid (spiders) and scorpions

- **Black widow**: abdominal rigidity, HA, dizziness, shoulder and backache, N/V, sweating, salivation

*Remove stingers by scraping only
**Do not use cold compresses or ice on affected area

TRAUMA/HAZMAT

- **Brown recluse:** reddish blister/ulcer surrounded by whitish blue "bull's eye"
- **Scorpion:** bark scorpion (SW United States) only lethal species in United States; anticipate shock-support ABCs, immediate transport

Hymenoptera (bees, wasps, ants)

- Avoid tweezers as squeezing venom sac will inject more venom
- If Pt has Epi-Pen, assist with administration

Snake envenomation

- Anticipate shock-support ABCs, immediate transport
- Avoid practices such as tourniquets or excision and suction
- Do not attempt to capture or kill snake; if safely possible, bring **dead** snake to hospital in a sealed, rigid container

Marine animal

- **Jellyfish/sea anemones:** carefully remove visible tentacles or spines; irrigate skin with 5% acetic acid (household vinegar), isopropanol, or seawater **Do not use fresh water**
- **Sea urchin/sea cucumber/stingray:** carefully remove spines if possible, and immerse affected area in water as warm as Pt can tolerate without scalding (<110°F/42°C)

Burns

Burn assessment

- **First degree:** epidermis (sunburn-like, no blistering)
- **Second degree:** epidermis and partial dermis (blistering)
- **Third degree:** penetrating the dermis and underlying tissues (full-thickness, eschar, and/or whitish-gray appearance)
- Percentage of total body surface area (TBSA) involved (count only second- and third-degree burns); For small, irregularly shaped burns, palm of hand is equal to 1%
- Age of Pt (age + TBSA = % probability of mortality)

- Pulmonary injury (smoke inhalation, toxic fumes)
- Associated injuries (airway burns and other trauma)
- Chemical/electrical burns, carbon monoxide poisoning
- Pre-existing diseases (potential for exacerbation)

EMT—basic/intermediate

- Establish and manage ABCs per protocol
- Use c-spine precautions for obvious or suspected trauma
- Administer high-flow O_2, or manually ventilate as indicated
- Rapid transport to burn center if Pt meets inclusion criteria

Paramedic

- Assess need for advanced airway, and intubate as indicated
- Anticipate laryngospasm/airway complications
- Start two large-bore IVs (LR), and titrate to SBP >90 mm Hg
- Attach ECG monitor, and manage dysrhythmias per ACLS

Fluid Resuscitation: First 24 Hours*

Indications

- Adults with second- or third-degree burns >20% of TBSA
- Children >1 y with second- or third-degree burns 15% or greater TBSA
- All infants with second- or third-degree burns of 10% or greater TBSA

Management (Parkland Formula)

- 4 mL × kg × %TBSA burned (second- plus third-degree burn injury)
- Infuse half over the first 8 hr (from time of burn)
- Infuse remaining half over the next 16 hr

---

*Start from time of injury

TRAUMA/HAZMAT

Inclusion Criteria for Transfer to Burn Center

- Second- or third-degree burns >10% TBSA in Pts <10 yr or >50 yr
- Second- or third-degree burns >20% TBSA in Pts of other age groups
- Second- or third-degree burns that involve the face, hands, feet, genitalia, perineum, or major joints
- Third-degree burns >5% TBSA in Pts of any age group
- Electrical burns, including lightning injury
- Chemical burns or inhalation injury
- Pts with pre-existing disease or simultaneous trauma

Rule of Nines

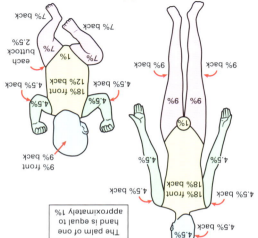

The palm of one hand is equal to approximately 1%

Cold Injury: Frostbite

Clinical findings
General: white, waxy, mottled appearance; loss of sensation
First degree: erythema; edema; waxy, hard, white plaques
Second degree: Formation of clear blisters within 24 hr
Third degree: formation of blood-filled blisters
Fourth degree: full-thickness (muscle, tendons, bones)
Thawing: red, warm, edema; burning, stinging, painful

EMT—basic/intermediate

- Remove Pt from cold environment
- Establish and maintain ABCs per protocol
- Anticipate and manage hypothermia per protocol
- Replace wet, restrictive clothing with warm, dry blankets to protect Pt from further heat loss or hypothermia
- Avoid excessive or rough handling of Pt or affected area
- Do not massage frostbitten area
- Leave blisters intact
- Remove jewelry, and keep affected area slightly elevated
- First degree: position Pt with affected area against warm body surface (e.g., placing frostbitten fingers into axilla)
- Encourage warm, nonalcoholic beverage unless contraindicated by AMS or trauma

Paramedic

- ECG: manage dysrhythmias per hypothermia protocol
- Obtain IV access in a non-frostbitten extremity
- **Morphine** 1–4 mg IV or **fentanyl** 25–50 mcg IV for pain

Rapid Thawing Procedure

Caution: avoid thawing procedures if refreezing likely

- Submerse affected area in warm water (38°–42°C/102°–108°F) for 10–30 min (may use warm wet packs)
- Carefully separate digits with cotton or gauze

TRAUMA/HAZMAT

- Elevate extremity slightly to minimize swelling
- Extremely painful: manage pain as needed

Drowning—Near Drowning—Submersion

EMT—basic/intermediate
- Bathtub and bucket drowning; consider child abuse
- Note length of time Pt was in or under water, water temperature, and whether fresh or salt water
- Obtain quick history from on-scene personnel or bystanders (diving or boating accident, alcohol, etc.)
- Remove victim from water using c-spine precautions; **Note:** this should be attempted only by trained personnel
- Establish and manage ABCs per protocol
- Administer high-flow O₂ via NRB mask, or provide positive-pressure ventilations (PPV) or CPAP if indicated
- Remove wet garments, and protect Pt against heat loss by using warm blankets and insulating equipment
- Anticipate and manage hypothermia per protocol
- Manage associated traumatic injuries per trauma protocol

Paramedic
- Assess need for advanced airway, and intubate as indicated
- Attach ECG monitor, and manage dysrhythmias per ACLS*
- Obtain IV access, and titrate to SBP >90 mm Hg

Special considerations
*Cold water submersion: Pt chance of survival may increase significantly if submersion occurs in cold water; therefore, resuscitation should continue while aggressive attempts are implemented to restore normal core temperature; withhold drugs until core temperature >30°C

Scuba Diving: Decompression Sickness (DCS)

S/S: joint pain, AMS, fatigue, visual disturbances, increased RR and HR, hypotension, N/V, cyanosis, seizure activity

- Remove Pt from water: manage ABCs normally
- **Do not** place Pt in Trendelenburg's position (increases ICP)
- Transport to facility with hyperbaric O_2 capabilities
- Consider aspirin for potential blood coagulation disorder
- Needle chest decompression for tension pneumothorax

High-Altitude Illness

EMT—basic/intermediate

- Extricate victim to a lower altitude; **Note:** this should only be attempted by personnel trained in mountain rescue
- Establish and manage ABCs per protocol
- Administer high-flow O_2 via NRB mask or provide positive-pressure ventilations (PPV) or CPAP if indicated
- Remove wet garments and protect Pt against heat loss by using warm blankets and insulating equipment
- Anticipate and manage hypothermia per protocol
- Manage associated traumatic injuries per trauma protocol

Paramedic

- Assess need for advanced airway, and intubate as indicated
- Attach ECG monitor, and manage dysrhythmias per ACLS
- Obtain IV access, and titrate to SBP >90 mm Hg

Specific high-altitude illnesses
Acute mountain sickness (AMS)

- Most common at or above 2500 m (8200 ft)
- **S/S:** fatigue, lethargy, anorexia, N/V, insomnia, dizziness, increased HR or RR (progresses to HACE; see following)
- **Management:** ABCs, O_2, descent, supportive care

TRAUMA/HAZMAT

TRAUMA/HAZMAT

High altitude cerebral edema (HACE)

- Most common at or above 4800 m (15,750 ft)
- **S/S:** (severe AMS) ataxia and/or altered mental status in addition to any one of the signs of acute mountain sickness
- **Management:** ABCs, immediate descent, O₂, hyperbaric therapy (Gamow bag/tent); consider Decadron 8 mg IM, IV

High altitude pulmonary edema (HAPE)

- Most common at or above 4500 m (14,760 ft)
- **S/S:** dyspnea, SOB, crackles, cyanosis, dry cough (progresses to pink, frothy sputum), tachycardia, tachypnea, mild fever
- **Management:** ABCs, descent, O₂, CPAP, rewarming, hyperbaric therapy; consider nifedipine 10 mg PO
- Can also occur in residents of high altitude who travel to low altitude and then return to altitude (re-ascent HAPE)

Hyperthermia

Differentiating Heatstroke and Heat Exhaustion

	Heatstroke	Heat Exhaustion
Core Temp	>104°F (40°C)	<104°F (40°C)
Skin	Dry, hot, flushed (late) Can be moist (early)	Profuse sweating
Neuro	Significant AMS	Fatigue, HA, agitation
S/S Common to Both	Tachypnea, N/V, tachycardia, weakness, fatigue, dehydration, hypotension	

EMT—basic/intermediate

- Remove Pt from heat source, and loosen or remove clothing
- Establish and manage ABCs per protocol

- Administer high-flow O₂, or manually ventilate as indicated
- Obtain baseline VS including core temperature
- Begin rapid cooling measures if indicated
- Obtain finger-stick blood glucose level
- Transport Pt supine with feet elevated if exhibiting S/S of shock

Paramedic

- Assess need for advanced airway, and intubate as indicated
- Attach ECG monitor, and manage dysrhythmias per ACLS
- Obtain IV access, and bolus with 500–1000 mL of NS

Rapid Cooling Measures

- Indicated for a core temperature >104°F (40°C)
- Remove clothing from Pt if not already done
- Use a fan to increase airflow over disrobed Pt while misting with warm water (warm water helps to prevent shivering)
- Place ice packs to axilla and groin
- Diazepam or lorazepam helps suppress shivering
- **Caution:** To avoid risk of hypothermia, stop cooling measure once core temperature reaches 102°F (39°C)

Hypothermia

Initial therapy for all Pts

- Establish and maintain ABCs per protocol
- Remove wet garments, and protect Pt against heat loss and wind chill by using blankets and insulating equipment
- Transport in supine position, and avoid rough movement
- Monitor core temperature and cardiac rhythm
- **ECG:** manage dysrhythmias as outlined in the following chart; **Note:** watch for tachycardia (early), bradycardia (late), and J waves

TRAUMA/HAZMAT

Pulse and Breathing Present   No Pulse or Respiration

34°C-36°C (mild)
- Passive rewarming
- Active external rewarming

30°C-34°C (moderate)
- Passive rewarming
- Active external rewarming of truncal areas only

<30°C (severe hypothermia)
- Active internal rewarming sequence (see Active Internal Rewarming)

Active Internal Rewarming
- Warm IV fluids (43°C)
- Warm humid O₂ (42°C-46°C)
- Peritoneal lavage (use only potassium-free fluid)
- Extracorporeal rewarming

Continue rewarming until:
- A core temperature of >35°C is achieved *or*
- Return of spontaneous circulation *or*
- Resuscitative efforts cease

- Initiate CPR
- Defibrillate VF/VT: biphasic 200 J; monophasic 360 J
- Intubate and confirm placement
- Ventilate with warm humidified O₂ (42°C-46°C)
- Establish IV, and infuse warm normal saline (43°C)

Core temperature <30°C
- Continue CPR, withhold drugs, limit to one shock for VF/VT
- Rapid transport
- Active internal rewarming sequence (see Active Internal Rewarming)

Core temperature <30°C
- Continue CPR
- Drugs as indicated but spaced longer apart
- Repeat shocks for VF/VT as core temperature rises
- Rapid transport
- Active internal rewarming (see Active Internal Rewarming)

Rape: Sexual Assault

Emergency management

- Do not enter scene until cleared by law enforcement
- Manage ABCs, and treat injuries as indicated; use C-spine precautions if head or spinal trauma suspected
- Do not disturb crime scene or potential evidence
- Avoid examining genitalia except to control hemorrhage
- Discourage Pt from bathing, douching, urinating, or changing clothes prior to arriving in ED
- Transport to a facility, if possible, specifically equipped for examining and collecting sexual assault evidence

HAZMAT/Weapons of Mass Destruction (WMD)

Type of Incident	Agency	Phone Number
Biological agents	CDC 24-hr USAMRIID	770-488-7100 888-872-7443
Chemical/HAZMAT	CHEMTREC	800-424-9300
Radiation release	REAC/TS	423-576-3131

Responding to a HAZMAT/WMD incident

Protect yourself and crew first; do not rush in

- **Scene survey:** assess risk to crew; consider potential for secondary devices (terrorist attack), weather conditions, proximity of exposure, access/egress routes, staging area
- **Identify hazard:** vehicle placards, container labels, shipping papers, and if accidental (HAZMAT) or intentional (WMD)
- **Available resources:** fire department, HAZMAT unit, police
- Enter only after scene has been determined safe
- Approach cautiously from upwind and uphill
- Position vehicle well away from liquids, smoke, vapors, etc.

TRAUMA/HAZMAT

TRAUMA/HAZMAT

- Instruct bystanders to retreat to a safe distance
- **DTS Rule**: keep maximum safe *Distance* from source, minimize exposure *Time*, use appropriate *Shielding* (PPE)

Hazardous Material Classification

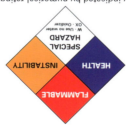

- Hazard severity indicated by numerical rating that ranges from 0 (minimal hazard) to 4 (severe hazard)
- The white (bottom) quadrant represents **special hazards**: **W** indicates unusual reactivity with water; **OX** indicates material is an oxidizer

Hazard Classes and Placard Colors

Class	Type	Color Code
1	Explosives	Orange
2	Gases	Red or green
3	Liquids	Red
4	Solids	Red and white
5	Oxidizers and organic peroxides	Yellow
6	Poisonous and etiological agents	White
7	Radioactive materials	Yellow and white
8	Corrosives	Black and white
9	Miscellaneous	Black and white

Rapid Assessment of Unknown Biological Agent

	Response	Skin	Flu-Like/GI	Neuro	PPE Level
Anthrax (Cutaneous)		Boil-like lesion forms ulcers			Standard[1]
Anthrax (Inhalation)	Cough, dyspnea		High fever		Standard[1]
Botulism				Slurred speech	Standard[1]
Plague	Bloody sputum		Rapid onset		Droplet[2]
Smallpox		Rash: head/extremities	Rapid onset		Airborne[4] and contact[3]
Tularemia	Cough, dyspnea		High fever, chills, N/V, diarrhea		Standard[1]
Hemorrhagic Fevers		Late-onset rash	High fever, diarrhea	HA, fatigue	Airborne[4]

[1]Standard precautions: gloves, frequent hand washing, routine equipment disinfection
[2]Droplet: standard precautions plus mask (use mask on Pt as well)
[3]Contact: standard precautions plus mask and gown
[4]Airborne: standard precautions plus mask and gown and strict Pt isolation

TRAUMA/HAZMAT

Rapid Assessment of Unknown Chemical Agent

	Odor	Neuro	Resp	Other S/S	PPE Level*
Nerve Agents sarin, soman, tabun, VX	**Soman/tabun**: fruity odor **Sarin/VX**: odorless	Twitching, spasms, paralysis, seizures	Dyspnea, wheezing	Symptoms of SLUDGEM	Maximum including respirator
Vesicants mustard, lewisite, phosgene	**Mustard** Garlic **Lewisite** Geraniums **Phosgene** Fresh hay	Sensitivity to light	Productive cough, oral-nasal irritation and bleeding, sore throat, laryngitis	Erythema, blisters, burning, stinging	Maximum including respirator
Chlorine Phosgene Tear gas	Sharp, irritating odor		Tearing; eye, nasal, oral irritation; dyspnea		Standard[†]
Cyanide	Mild; bitter almonds	Confusion, HA, seizure, coma	Gasping, respiratory arrest	Flushing, sweating (cyanosis rare)	Standard[†]

*Level of PPE after Pt has been extricated from source of chemical exposure
[†]Standard precautions: gloves, frequent hand washing, routine equipment disinfection

General HAZMAT Decontamination Guidelines

Protect yourself and crew first; hold back until scene safe
Organophosphate (OPP)/carbamate exposure

- Remove Pt from source, and remove Pt clothing and jewelry
- Decontaminate with copious NS or water
- **Atropine:** 2–5 mg (**peds:** 0.05 mg/kg) IV, IM repeated every 3–5 min until signs of SLUDGEM resolve
- **Pralidoxime* (2-PAM):** 600 mg IM or may infuse 1–2 g over 15–30 min (**peds:** 20–50 mg/kg IM or infuse over 15–30 min)
- *Not recommended for carbamates
- **Do not induce vomiting if substance ingested!** If Pt alert with gag reflex, give water 5 mL/kg (max 200 mL) PO

Carbon monoxide (CO) exposure

- Remove Pt from source and remove Pt clothing
- **High-flow O₂**
- Rapid transport for hyperbaric therapy

Cyanide exposure

- See Chemical and Nerve Agents, last section this tab
- Extricate Pt, remove Pt clothing and jewelry, support ABCs
- **Hydroxocobalamin:** 5 g (**peds:** 70 mg/kg) IV infused over 15 min *or* cyanide antidote kit

Hydrocarbon (methylene chloride, xylene) exposure

- *Common in inhalation (huffing/sniffing) of aerosol fumes*
- Remove Pt from source, and remove Pt clothing
- **Do not induce vomiting if substance ingested**
- Decontaminate with copious NS or water

Ammonia or chlorine exposure

- Remove Pt from source, and remove Pt clothing
- Decontaminate with copious NS or water
- Manage pulmonary edema per standard protocol

TRAUMA/HAZMAT

Caustic (acids and alkalis) exposure

- Remove Pt from source, and remove Pt clothing
- **Solid (powder) corrosive:** brush off dry particles
- **Liquid corrosive:** decontaminate with copious NS or water
- **Do not induce vomiting if substance ingested;** if Pt alert with gag reflex, give water or milk: 200–300 mL (peds: 15 mL/kg)

Biological Agents

Anthrax (inhalation, cutaneous)

- **S/S: inhalation:** initial flu-like symptoms progress to severe respiratory difficulty and shock; **cutaneous:** marked by boil-like lesion that forms an ulcer with a black center
- **EMS risk: low:** inhalation anthrax cannot be transmitted from person to person (cutaneous anthrax can, but is rare)
- **Pre-hospital care:** use standard precautions, support ABCs

Botulism

- **S/S:** progressive, descending muscle weakness that leads to full-body paralysis, respiratory failure, drooping eyelids, slurred speech, difficulty swallowing, dry mouth
- **EMS risk: none:** not spread from person to person
- **Pre-hospital care:** use standard precautions, support ABCs; botulinum antitoxin; pre-hospital use not recommended

Hemorrhagic fevers (Ebola virus, Hantavirus, Marburg, etc.)

- **S/S: early:** high fever, HA, fatigue, diarrhea, rash; **late:** hematemesis, diarrhea, rash, bleeding mucous membranes
- **EMS risk: high:** transmitted from person to person or from contaminated surface to person
- **Pre-hospital care:** use contact precautions, support ABCs; antibiotics: doxycycline or ciprofloxacin given in hospital

Plague
- **S/S:** fever, cough, chest pain, hemoptysis
- **EMS risk: high:** Pts are contagious until they have completed 72 hr of antibiotic treatment
- **Pre-hospital care:** Use droplet precautions, support ABCs; antibiotics: doxycycline or ciprofloxacin given in hospital

Smallpox
- **S/S:** skin lesions (pox): more prominent on head and extremities; lesions all appear to be of the same age (chickenpox concentrated around trunk, and lesions appear to be in different stages of healing)
- **EMS risk: high:** From onset of rash until lesions have scabbed over and fallen off (approximately 3 weeks)
- **Pre-hospital care:** airborne/contact precautions, ABCs

Chemical and Nerve Agents

Vesicants (mustard gas, lewisite, phosgene)
- **S/S:** erythema, blistering, burning, itching and stinging of skin, tearing and burning of eyes, sore throat, productive cough, laryngitis, irritated, bloody nose, light sensitivity
- **EMS risk: high:** avoid contact with agent or fumes
- **Pre-hospital care:** use maximum PPE, decontamination with copious water, support ABCs; **for lewisite** (severe cases): British anti-lewisite (**BAL**) administered 3 mg/kg deep IM

Nerve agents (sarin, VX, soman, tabun)
- **S/S:** SLUDGEM as well as coma and seizures
- **EMS risk: high:** avoid contact with agent or fumes
- **Pre-hospital care:** use maximum PPE, remove Pt from source; remove Pt clothing, decontaminate with copious water; support ABCs aggressively, and administer antidote

TRAUMA/HAZMAT

- **Mark-I kit: atropine:** 2–5 mg (**peds:** 0.05 mg/kg) IM every 3–5 min until signs of SLUDGEM resolve; **pralidoxime (2-PAM):** 600 mg IM or may infuse 1–2 g over 15–30 min (**peds:** 20–50 mg/kg IM or infuse over 15–30 min)
- **Diazepam:** 5–10 mg (**peds:** 0.2 mg/kg) IV for seizures

Pulmonary agents (chlorine, diphosgene, PFIB)

- **S/S:** eye and nasal irritation, tearing, chest pressure, cough, choking, hemoptysis, rales, pulmonary edema
- **EMS risk: low:** avoid contact with agent or fumes
- **Pre-hospital care:** use standard precautions, remove Pt from source, decontaminate with copious water, support ABCs

Cyanide

- **S/S:** gasping, flushing, faintness, sweating, confusion, HA, seizure, coma, respiratory/cardiac arrest (cyanosis rare)
- **EMS risk: low:** avoid contact with agent or fumes
- **Pre-hospital care:** Remove Pt from source, remove clothing, support ABCs aggressively, administer antidote
- **Hydroxocobalamin:** 5 g (**peds:** 70 mg/kg) IV infused over 15 min *or* cyanide antidote kit

Pediatric Quick Reference (Vital Signs, Equipment, Electricity, Drugs)

Age	Term	2 mo	4 mo	6 mo	1 yr	3 yr	6 yr	8 yr	10 yr	11 yr	12 yr
Length (in.)	18-20	20-22	22-24	24-27							
Weight (lb)	7	9	11	13-15	18-20	22-24	26-31	33-40	42-48	53-62	66-79
Weight (kg)	3	4	5	6-7	8-9	10-11	12-14	15-18	19-22	24-28	30-36
SBP (lower limit)	>60	>60	>60	>60	>70	>76	>82	>86	>90	>90	>90
SBP (critical)	<50	<50	<50	<50	<50	<50	<60	<60	<70	<70	<70
HR	85-205	85-205	99-190	99-190	99-190	60-140	60-140	60-140	60-100	60-100	60-100
RR	30-60	30-60	30-60	30-60	30-60	22-34	18-30	18-30	18-30	18-30	12-16

Continued

Age	Term	2 mo	4 mo	6 mo	1 yr	3 yr	6 yr	8 yr	10 yr	11 yr	12 yr
Laryngo-scope blade*				*Straight blade					*Straight/curved		
ET tube (mm, cuffed)	3.0	3.0	3.0	3.0	3.0	4.0	4.5	5.0	5.5	6.0	6.0
ET tube (uncuffed)	3.5	3.5	3.5	3.5	4.0	5.0	5.5	6.0	6.5	7.0	7.0
ETT insertion depth (cm at gums/teeth)	9–10.5	9–10.5	9–10.5	9–10.5	9–12	12–15	14–17	15–18	17–20	18–21	18–21
Defibrillate: 2 j/kg	6	8	10	13	17	20	26	33	40	53	66
Defibrillate: 4 j/kg	12	16	20	26	34	40	52	66	80	106	132
Cardiovert: 0.5–1 j/kg	3	4	5	7	9	10	13	17	20	27	33

Continued

Age	Term	2 mo	4 mo	6 mo	1 yr	3 yr	6 yr	8 yr	10 yr	11 yr	12 yr
Cardiovert: 2 j/kg	6	8	10	13	17	20	26	33	40	53	66
Adenosine (mg) 1st 0.1/0.2 mg/kg 2nd	0.3 0.6	0.4 0.8	0.5 1	0.65 1.3	0.85 1.7	1 2.1	1.3 2.6	1.7 3.3	2.1 4.2	2.7 5.4	3.3 6.6
Aniodarone (mg) 5 mg/kg	15	20	25	32	42	52	65	80	105	130	165
Atropine IV (mg) 0.02 mg/kg	0.1	0.1	0.1	0.13	0.17	0.21	0.26	0.33	0.42	0.5	0.5
Atropine ET (mg) 0.03 mg/kg	0.1	0.1	0.1	0.2	0.26	0.32	0.4	0.5	0.6	0.8	1
Calcium chloride 10% (mg) 20 mg/kg	60	80	100	130	170	210	260	330	420	530	660
Charcoal (g) 1 g/kg	3	4	5	6.5	8.5	10	13	16.5	21	27	33

Continued

Age	Term	2 mo	4 mo	6 mo	1 yr	3 yr	6 yr	8 yr	10 yr	11 yr	12 yr
Colloid or blood (mL) 10 mL/kg	30	40	50	65	85	105	130	165	210	270	330
Dextrose 25% (g) 0.5 g/kg	1.5	2	2.5	3.25	4.25	5.25	6.5	8.25	10.5	13.3	16.5
Diazepam IV (mg) 0.2 mg/kg	0.6	0.8	1	1.3	1.7	2	2.6	3.3	4.2	5.3	6.6
Diazepam rectal (mg) 0.3 mg/kg	1.5	2	2.5	3.3	4.2	5	6.5	8	10	8	10
Diphenhydramine (mg) 1.25 mg/kg	4	5	6	8	11	13	16	21	26	33	41
Epinephrine IV (mg) (1:10,000) 0.01 mg/kg	0.03	0.04	0.05	0.07	0.09	0.1	0.13	0.17	0.21	0.27	0.33

Continued

Age	Term	2 mo	4 mo	6 mo	1 yr	3 yr	6 yr	8 yr	10 yr	11 yr	12 yr
Epinephrine ET (mg) (1:1,000) 0.1 mg/kg	0.3	0.4	0.5	0.65	0.85	1	1.3	1.7	2.1	2.7	3.3
Etomidate (mg) 0.3 mg/kg	0.9	1.2	1.5	2	2.5	3.2	4	5	6.3	8	10
Fentanyl (mcg) 3 mcg/kg	9	12	15	20	25	32	40	50	63	80	100
Flumazenil (mg) 0.01 mg/kg	0.03	0.04	0.05	0.07	0.09	0.1	0.13	0.16	0.2	0.2	0.2
Fosphenytoin (mg-PE) Load 15 mg-PE/kg	45	60	75	100	130	160	200	250	315	400	500
Furosemide (mg) 1 mg/kg	3	4	5	6.5	8.5	10	13	17	21	27	33

Continued

Age	Term	2 mo	4 mo	6 mo	1 yr	3 yr	6 yr	8 yr	10 yr	11 yr	12 yr
Glucagon (mg) 0.5–1 mg/kg	0.5	0.5	0.5	0.5	0.5	0.5	0.5	0.5	1	1	1
Ketamine (mg) 2 mg/kg (>5 kg)	–	–	–	13	17	20	26	3	42	50	66
Lidocaine IV (mg) 1 mg/kg	3	4	5	6.5	8.5	10	13	17	20	27	33
Lidocaine ET (mg) 2–3 mg/kg	6–9	8–12	10–15	13–20	17–26	20–30	26–40	34–50	40–60	54–80	66–100
Lorazepam (mg) 0.05 mg/kg	0.15	0.2	0.25	0.3	0.4	0.5	0.7	0.8	1	1.3	1.7
Magnesium sulfate (mg) 50 mg/kg	150	200	250	325	425	525	650	820	1050	1325	1650
Mannitol (g) 1 g/kg	3	4	5	6.5	8.5	10	13	17	21	27	33

Continued

Age	Term	2 mo	4 mo	6 mo	1 yr	3 yr	6 yr	8 yr	10 yr	11 yr	12 yr
Midazolam (mg) 0.3 mg/kg	0.9	1.2	1.5	2	2.5	3.2	4	5	6.3	8	10
Naloxone (mg) 0.1 mg/kg	0.3	0.4	0.5	0.65	0.85	1	1.3	1.6	2	2	2
NS or LR (mL) 10 mL/kg	30	40	50	65	85	105	130	165	210	270	330
NS or LR (mL) 20 mL/kg	60	80	100	130	170	210	260	325	420	530	660
Pancuronium (mg) 0.2 mg/kg	0.6	0.8	1	1.3	1.7	2.1	2.6	3.3	4.2	5.3	6.6
Phenobarbital (mg) Load 20 mg/kg	60	80	100	130	170	210	260	330	420	530	660
Phenytoin (mg) Load 15 mg/kg	45	60	75	98	128	158	195	248	308	390	488

Continued

Age	Term	2 mo	4 mo	6 mo	1 yr	3 yr	6 yr	8 yr	10 yr	11 yr	12 yr
Procaina-mide (mg) 15 mg/kg	45	60	75	98	128	158	195	248	308	390	488
Propofol (mg) 3 mg/kg	9	12	15	20	25	32	40	50	63	80	100
Rocuronium (mg) 1 mg/kg	3	4	5	7	9	10	13	16	21	27	33
Sodium bicarbonate 4.2% (mEq) 1 mEq/kg	3	4	5	6.5	8.5	10	13	16.5	21	27	33
Succinyl-choline (mg) 2 mg/kg (atropine 1st)	6	8	10	13	17	20	26	30	40	53	66
Vecuronium (mg) 0.2 mg/kg	0.6	0.8	1	1.3	1.7	2.1	2.6	3.3	4.2	5.3	6.6

Pediatric Intraosseous (IO) Access

Caution: contraindicated if long bone to be used is fractured.

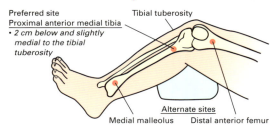

Preferred site
Proximal anterior medial tibia
- 2 cm below and slightly medial to the tibial tuberosity

Tibial tuberosity

Alternate sites
Medial malleolus   Distal anterior femur

IO Insertion Techniques

Manual insertion technique

- Observe standard precautions
- Cleanse area with antiseptic
- Flex and support knee with a sandbag or towel roll
- Palpate tibial tuberosity (bony prominence just below knee)
- Locate insertion site (flat area ~ 2 cm distal and slightly medial to tibial tuberosity; preferred insertion site)
- Hold limb firmly above site of insertion, usually at level of knee; avoid placing hand behind site of insertion to avoid accidental injury of own hand
- Insert IO needle at 90 degrees to the skin (slightly angled towards foot to avoid growth plate)
- While maintaining constant pressure, advance IO needle using a twisting motion
- Entrance into marrow cavity is confirmed by a "pop" and cessation of resistance

PEDS/OB

- Remove trocar, and attach 10-mL syringe
- Aspirate marrow (may or may not be successful)
- Attach connector, and flush catheter with 10-mL NS
- Secure catheter and tubing, and begin infusion
- Assess for signs of infiltration, including pain, swelling, inflammation, and leakage of fluid from IO site
- D/C IO, and apply pressure bandage if infiltration suspected

Intraosseous driver (EZ IO) technique

- Insertion site: **proximal anterior medial tibia only**
- Stabilize leg using opposite hand (avoid path of needle)
- Insert EZ IO needle using 90-degree angle, and gently power needle until you feel a "pop"
- Remove driver from needle set, remove stylet from catheter, and confirm catheter stability and placement

Pediatric Trauma Score

	+2	+1	—1	Score
Weight	>20 kg	10–20 kg	<10 kg	
Airway	Normal	Maintained	Unmaintained	
SBP	>90	50–90	<50	
LOC	Awake	Obtunded	Unresponsive	
Open Wounds	None	Minor	Major	
Fractures	None	Closed	Open, multiple	
Transport to trauma center if score is ≤8				**Total**

APGAR Score

		1 min	5 min
Appearance	Pink torso and extremities ..2 Pink torso, blue extremities .1 Blue all over 0		
Pulse	>100 ....2 <100 ....1 Absent 0		
Grimace (Irritability)	Vigorous cry ....2 Limited cry ....1 No response to stimulus ...0		
Activity	Actively moving ....2 Limited movement ....1 Flaccid 0		
Respiratory Effort	Strong loud cry ....2 Hypoventilation, irregular ..1 Absent 0		
	Total		

8–10: normal; 4–6: moderate depression; 0–3: aggressive resuscitation (see following section).

PEDS/OB

Initial Steps to Neonatal Resuscitation[1]

Assess respirations, HR, and color

30 sec
- **Temperature**: provide warmth (dry; use radiant warmer)
- **Airway**: position on back or side, neck slightly extended in a "sniffing" position, and suction (mouth first, then nose)
- Dry, stimulate,* reposition

   *Note: if meconium present and baby **NOT** vigorous, suction mouth and trachea first
   If baby fails to improve (apnea, cyanosis, HR <100)

30 sec
- **Breathing**: positive pressure ventilation (PPV) at 40–60 breaths/min with 100% O_2 using infant BVM

   If HR remains <60 bpm despite adequate ventilation/O_2

30 sec
- **Circulation**: chest compressions at 120 events/min (3 compressions with 1 ventilation every 2 sec)
- **Drugs**: reassess efforts, intubate, and administer drugs
  - **Epinephrine (1:10,000)**: 0.1–0.3 mL/kg IV (0.3–1 mL/kg ET)
  - **NS**: 10 mL/kg IV, IO, or umbilicus over 5–10 min
  - **Naloxone**: 0.1 mg/kg IV, IM (for respiratory depression despite PPV *and* maternal narcotic within last 4 hr)

   Note: consider intubation at any step during resuscitation

---

[1]American Academy of Pediatrics (AAP), Neonatal Resuscitation Textbook, 5th edition, 2006 AAP, with permission.

Neonatal Equipment Size and Depth[2]

Gestational age (wk)	<28	28–34	34–38	>38
Weight	<1 kg	1–2 kg	2–3 kg	>3 kg
Tracheal tube (mm)	2.5	3.0	3.5	3.5–4.0
ET insertion depth (cm from upper lip)	6–7 cm	7–8 cm	8–9 cm	9–10 cm
Laryngoscope (straight)	0	0	0–1	1
Suction catheter (ET)	5–6 fr	6–8 fr	8 fr	8–10 fr

Rapid Newborn Drug Reference

Note: follow all drugs with 0.5–1.0 mL NS flush

- **Adenosine:** [SVT] 0.1 mg/kg IV, IO; second dose 0.2 mg/kg
- **Atropine:** [RSI, second-line bradycardia] **IV, IO:** 0.02 mg/kg (minimum 0.1 mg; maximum 0.5 mg) **ET:** 0.03 mg/kg
- **Dextrose 10% (D10):** [hypoglycemia] 0.2 g/kg IV only
- **Diazepam:** [seizures] **IV, IO:** 0.2 mg/kg; **rectal:** 0.5 mg/kg
- **Dopamine:** [hypotension] 2–20 mcg/kg/min IV infusion
- **Epinephrine (1:10,000):** [bradycardia, asystole] 0.1–0.3 mL/kg IV, IO, umbilicus (consider 0.3–1 mL/kg for ET route)
- **Flumazenil:** [benzodiazepine OD] 0.01 mg/kg IV, IO
- **Lidocaine:** [VF/pulseless VT] **IV, IO:** 1 mg/kg; **ET:** 2–3 mg/kg
- **Lorazepam:** [seizures—second line] 0.05–0.1 mg/kg IV, IO
- **Naloxone:** [narcotic OD] 0.1 mg/kg rapid IV, IO, IM
- **NS or LR:** 10 mL/kg IV, IO, or umbilicus over 5–10 min
- **Phenobarbital:** [seizures] 20 mg/kg slow IV, IO (1 mg/kg/min)

---

[2]American Academy of Pediatrics (AAP), Neonatal Resuscitation Textbook, 5th edition, 2006 AAP, with permission.

- **Phenytoin:** [seizure] 15 mg/kg IV, IO (loading dose)
- **Sodium bicarbonate 4.2%:** [confirmed acidosis] 1 mEq/kg slow IV, IO (dilute 8.4% with equal amount NS for 4.2%)

Pediatric Advanced Life Support (PALS)

Bradycardia (HR <60 bpm)

Asymptomatic
- Observe and support ABCs as needed

Symptomatic: severe cardiopulmonary compromise
- **Chest compressions:** 100/min; ratio 30:2 (15:2 if two rescuers)
- **Epinephrine: IV or IO** [1:10,000] 0.01 mg/kg (0.1 mL/kg) every 3–5 min; **ET** [1:1,000] 0.1 mg/kg (0.1 mL/kg) every 3–5 min
- **Atropine:** 0.02 mg/kg IV, IO, may repeat one time; minimum single dose 0.1 mg; max total dose 1 mg
- **Consider cardiac pacing:** same as adults but use pediatric pads, placed anterior-to-posterior, set rate to 100 bpm

Note: if bradycardia due to suspected increased vagal tone or primary AV block, give atropine as first-line drug

Tachycardia: Poor Perfusion*

Narrow-Complex (0.08 sec or less)
- 12-lead to evaluate tachycardia if clinically practical
- Consider vagal maneuvers
- **Immediate cardioversion:** 0.5–1 J/kg (repeat at 2 J/kg) *or*
- **Adenosine:** 0.1 mg/kg (max first dose 6 mg) rapid IV push; may give second dose at 0.2 mg/kg (max second dose 12 mg)

*If tachycardia associated with adequate perfusion, consider pharmacological cardioversion before electrical cardioversion

Wide-Complex (>0.08 sec)

- **Immediate cardioversion:** 0.5–1 J/kg (repeat at 2 J/kg)
- **Antiarrhythmic:** consider *one* of the following:
  - Amiodarone: 5 mg/kg IV, IO bolus over 20–60 min *or*
- **Procainamide:** 15 mg/kg IV, IO over 30–60 min

Pediatric Pulseless Arrest

V-Fib/Pulseless VT

- **Defibrillate:** initially 2 J/kg; all subsequent shocks at 4 J/kg
- **CPR** (five cycles): rate: 100/min; ratio: 30:2 (15:2 if two rescuers)
- **Defibrillate:** 4 J/kg, then resume CPR immediately
- **Epinephrine: IV, IO** [1:10,000] 0.01 mg/kg (0.1 mL/kg) every 3–5 min; **ET** [1:1,000] 0.1 mg/kg (0.1 mL/kg) every 3–5 min
- **Defibrillate:** 4 J/kg, then resume CPR immediately
- **Antiarrhythmic:** consider *one* of the following:
  - **Amiodarone:** 5 mg/kg IV, IO bolus *or*
  - **Lidocaine:** 1 mg/kg (max 100 mg) IV, IO, ET (2 mg/kg) *or*
  - **Magnesium:** *(if torsade de pointes)* 25–50 mg/kg IV, IO (max 2 g)

Asystole: Pulseless Electrical Activity (PEA)

- **CPR** (5 cycles): rate: 100/min; ratio: 30:2 (15:2 if 2 rescuers)
- **Epinephrine: IV, IO** [1:10,000] 0.01 mg/kg (0.1 mL/kg) every 3–5 min; **ET** [1:1,000] 0.1 mg/kg (0.1 mL/kg) every 3–5 min
- **Continue CPR:** perform five cycles, then reassess rhythm

Pediatric Developmental Milestone

Age	Developmental Milestones
1 mo	Cries to communicate, reflex activity, eye contact
2 mo	Coos, smiles, frowns, tracks objects, lifts head
3 mo	Turns from back to side, sits with support
4 mo	Turns from back to abdomen, lifts head, bears weight on forearms, holds head erect, places everything in mouth, grasps with hands, laughs
5-6 mo	Turns onto back, uses hands independently, plays with toes, puts feet into mouth, sits alone leaning forward on hands, holds baby bottle, extends arms to be picked up, stranger anxiety
7-8 mo	Begins to crawl, bears weight on feet when supported, pulls to standing position, sits alone without support, increased fear of strangers, walks along side furniture, well-developed crawl
9-10 mo	May begin to walk and climb, vocabulary of one or two words, understands "No!", shakes head to indicate "No!", follows simple directions
12 mo	Walks alone or with assistance, falls frequently while walking, points with finger
15-18 mo	Walks independently, throws overhand, pulls/pushes toys, uses blocks, runs vigorously, jumps in place, vocabulary of 8-10 words
2 yr	Runs well, climbs stairs, names objects, phrases of two to three words, becoming potty trained
3-4 yr	Rides tricycle, turns doorknobs, dresses self, uses short sentences, hops on one foot, catches ball
6-12 yr	Physically coordinated, uses complete and complex sentences, extensive vocabulary, swims, skates, rides bicycle, reads, forms social groups

Common Childhood Illnesses

Croup
- **S/S**: Gradual onset, usually at night (fall and winter) **Low-grade fever,** harsh, **"barking seal"** cough, hoarse voice. May have sore throat or chest discomfort from coughing.
- **Avoid examining airway.** Administer cool, nebulized mist, racemic epinephrine, IV fluids, and steroids.

Epiglottitis
- **S/S**: Rapid onset, **high-grade fever, inspiratory stridor,** muffled voice, difficulty breathing, upright, leaning forward, difficult and painful swallowing, excessive drooling.
- **Do not examine airway!** Rapid transport, oxygen, minimize agitation, ventilate with BVM or intubate if airway obstructs.

Measles (Rubella)
- **S/S**: Koplik's spots (small red spots with bluish-white centers). Progresses to red, blotchy rash along hairline and behind ears, rapidly spreads to chest and back and then thighs and feet.

Chickenpox (Varicella)
- **S/S**: Red pimple-like spots. Starts on trunk and then spreads to rest of body. Pimples progress to red teardrop blisters, eventually break open and scab over.

Respiratory Syncytial Virus (RSV)
- **S/S Child <3 yo**: High fever, severe cough, tachypnea, expiratory wheezes, and orthopnea.
- **S/S Child >3 yo**: Congestion, runny nose, cough, sore throat, low-grade fever, HA, and general malaise.

Meningitis
- **S/S**: Stiff neck, headache, high fever, vomiting, confusion, drowsiness, lethargy, seizures; rash near axilla, hands, and feet; small hemorrhages under skin (petechiae).

Gastroenteritis
- S/S: Abdominal cramping, bloating, diarrhea (may be bloody and contain mucus), n/v, fever and dehydration.

Respiratory Syncytial Virus (RSV)

S/S Child <3 yr	RSV usually progresses to a lower respiratory tract infection; symptoms include: • High fever, severe cough, tachypnea, expiratory wheezes, orthopnea
S/S Child <3 yr	Symptoms usually mimic mild cold or URI • Congestion, runny nose, cough, sore throat, low-grade fever, HA, general malaise
EMS treatment	• Supportive care • Bronchodilators for relieving bronchospasm

Meningitis

Definition	• Infection/inflammation of meninges and CSF
Incidence	• Most common in children <5 years
Onset	• Rapid but may be 1–2 days after exposure
Etiology	• Bacterial (more serious) or viral (less serious)
S/S	• Stiff neck, headache, high fever, vomiting • Confusion, drowsiness, lethargy, seizures • Rash near axilla, hands, feet • Small hemorrhages under skin (petechiae)
EMS treatment	• Supportive care, strict standard precautions • Severe cases: management of cerebral edema, dehydration, shock, seizures

Gastroenteritis (Stomach Flu)

S/S	• Abdominal cramping and bloating • Diarrhea (may be bloody and contain mucus) • Nausea, vomiting, fever • **Dehydration:** lethargy, decreased tears and saliva, sunken fontanelle, fewer than four wet diapers/day
EMS treatment	• Supportive care • IV fluids, antiemetic per protocol

Obstetrical Complications

Hyperemesis Gravidarum

Clinical findings

- **Onset:** anytime during pregnancy
- **Neuro:** fatigue, malaise
- **CV:** hypotension, tachycardia
- **F and E:** dehydration, electrolyte imbalances
- **GI/GU:** Nausea, vomiting

EMT—basic/intermediate

- ABCs, supportive care
- **Position mother on left side:** relieves compression of IVC, enhances venous return and uteroplacental perfusion
- Obtain finger-stick blood glucose level

Paramedic

- Start large-bore IV (D_5NS or D_5LR preferred), titrate to SBP >90 mm Hg (dehydration may result in hypotension)
- **Ondansetron:** 4 mg IV, IO, IM

PEDS/OB

Supine Hypotensive Syndrome

When a pregnant woman lies on her back, heavy gravid uterus compresses IVC and results in pooling of blood in legs, decreased venous return, a fall in CO, and hypotension (relieved by maintaining mother in left-lateral position)

Clinical findings

- **Onset:** becomes more pronounced as pregnancy progresses
- **Neuro:** dizziness, syncope, fatigue
- **CV:** hypotension, tachycardia
- **Skin:** pallor, diaphoresis
- **GI/GU:** Nausea

EMT—basic/intermediate

- ABCs, supportive care
- **Position mother on left side:** relieves compression of IVC, enhances venous return and uteroplacental perfusion

Paramedic

- Start large-bore IV, titrate to SBP >90 mm Hg

Normal Changes With Pregnancy

- Resp rate: increases
- HR: increases
- BP: lower first half, no change last half
- Temperature: slight increase
- Blood glucose: increase may indicate gestational diabetes

Preeclampsia/Eclampsia

Preeclampsia: HTN, proteinuria, and edema during pregnancy
Eclampsia: seizures during pregnancy
Note: PIH is HTN during pregnancy but without proteinuria

Clinical findings (preeclampsia)

- **Onset:** 20 weeks gestation (can continue 6 weeks postpartum)
- **Neuro:** hyperreflexia, clonus, HA, visual disturbances
- **CV:** SBP >140, DBP >90, edema, vasospasm
- **GI/GU:** RUQ/epigastric pain, nausea, vomiting; oliguria
- **Severe preeclampsia:** SBP >160 or DBP >110

EMT—basic/intermediate

- **All hypertensive pregnant Pts should be considered high risk for eclampsia (seizures) until clinically proved otherwise**
- Establish and manage ABCs per protocol
- **Position mother on left side:** relieves compression of IVC, enhances venous return and uteroplacental perfusion
- Minimize sensory stimulation (dim lights, gentle transport)
- Administer high-flow O_2, or manually ventilate as indicated
- Obtain finger-stick blood glucose level
- Transport to an appropriate facility for high-risk deliveries

Paramedic

- Start large-bore IV, titrate to SBP >90 mm Hg
- Assess edema, deep tendon reflexes, presence of clonus
- **If condition deteriorates to *eclampsia* (maternal seizures):**
  - **Magnesium sulfate:** 1–4 g slow IV; *or*
  - **Lorazepam:** 1–4 mg slow IV; *or*
  - **Diazepam:** 5–10 mg slow IV

Placenta Abruptio Versus Placenta Previa

	Placenta Abruptio	Placenta Previa
Onset	May occur during prenatal or intrapartum period	Often as early as 28 weeks but may not occur until onset of labor
Neuro	Anxiety, fear, restlessness	Anxiety, fear, restlessness
Resp	Tachypnea if in shock	Usually unremarkable

Continued

	Placenta Abruptio	Placenta Previa
CV	Signs of shock	May exhibit shock
Skin	Cool, pale, diaphoretic	Usually unremarkable
GI/GU	Dark red vaginal bleeding; bleeding may be concealed, depending on grade of abruptio	Painless, bright red bleeding
MS (pain)	Severe tearing sensation, abdominal and low back	Usually unremarkable

EMT—basic/intermediate

- Follow standard precautions
- Establish and manage ABCs per protocol
- **Position mother on left side:** relieves compression of IVC, enhances venous return and uteroplacental perfusion
- Administer high-flow O_2, or manually ventilate as indicated
- Transport to appropriate facility for high-risk deliveries
- Apply clean perineal pad, note time to assess amount of bleeding; (do not perform vaginal examination at any point)
- Monitor VS and for signs of shock every 3–5 min
- Monitor bleeding: amount and character of blood or clots
- Assess for signs of occult bleeding (including rigid, board-like abdomen) and constant abdominal pain

Paramedic

- Start large-bore IV, titrate to SBP >90 mm Hg

Emergency Delivery: Uncomplicated

Clinical findings (imminent delivery)

- Contractions usually regular, <2 min apart and progressively increasing in frequency and duration
- Low back and abdominal pain and/or cramping
- Urge to have bowel movement or strong urge to push
- Bulging vaginal opening or crowning of baby's head

Emergency management

- Assess contractions (regularity, duration, frequency)
- Assess status of membranes: rupture manually if intact
- Instruct Pt to take slow, deep breaths during contractions
- If birth imminent, instruct Pt to push during contractions
- Discourage pushing between contractions
- With gloved hand, apply gentle pressure against baby's head to prevent explosive delivery and tearing of perineum
- **Head:** as head delivers, examine neck for looped cord and gently slip it over baby's head if present
- Suction mouth first and then nose before next contraction (tear away amniotic sac if covering face)
- **Shoulders:** position hands on either side of baby's head, gently guide baby downward until upper shoulder emerges, guide baby upward as body emerges
- Keep baby at same level as perineum until cord is cut
- Hypothermia can occur rapidly in newborns; dry and wrap baby's body and head (not face) in dry, warm blankets
- Reassess airway, suction mouth and nose as needed
- Stimulate respirations with vigorous rubbing and drying
- **Cord:** clamp at 8 and 10 inches from baby (cut in between)
- Position baby (skin-to-skin) on mother's abdomen or chest
- Do not pull on umbilical cord if placenta has not delivered
- Encourage breastfeeding, or massage mother's abdomen to stimulate uterine contractions
- Assess cord vessels: normally three vessels (one vein, two arteries)

PEDS/OB

PEDS/OB

- Save placenta for analysis by receiving hospital physician
- Document APGAR at 1 and 5 minutes postpartum
- Assess for postpartum complications (e.g., hemorrhage)

Complicated Delivery

EMT-basic/intermediate (all scenarios)

- Follow standard precautions
- Establish and manage ABCs per protocol
- Administer high-flow O_2, or manually ventilate as indicated
- Rapid transport to appropriate facility
- Anticipate likelihood of managing two critical Pts, request second EMT to assist during transport

Paramedic (all scenarios)

- Start large-bore IV, titrate to SBP >90 mm Hg

Meconium-Stained Amniotic Fluid

EMT—basic/intermediate
During delivery

- Suction mouth first, then nose, with bulb syringe prior to delivery of shoulders to prevent aspiration of meconium

After delivery

- If baby not vigorous, minimize stimulation, and delay ventilation until meconium can be suctioned from airway

Paramedic
If baby depressed (HR <100, depressed RR/muscle tone)

- Intubate newborn's trachea, but **do not** ventilate
- Apply suction, withdraw ET tube to clear meconium
- Repeat process until no further meconium can be suctioned
- During process administer 100% O_2 via blow-by
- Ventilate newborn using bag-valve device after suctioning

Cord Presentation (Prolapsed Cord)

EMT—basic/intermediate

- Trendelenburg's position (left-lateral if birth not imminent)
- Relieve cord pressure with gentle pressure to baby's head
- Monitor cord pulses, and cover with saline-soaked gauze
- Discourage mother from pushing during contractions to minimize cord pressure (panting helps avoid pushing)

Breech Presentation

EMT—basic/intermediate

Buttocks first: if baby has delivered to umbilicus level, gently extract baby's legs; gently extract enough cord in order to relieve tension on cord during delivery

Both feet first: support baby's legs and buttocks, gently pull during contractions until shoulders delivered

- Avoid pulling on baby once shoulders have delivered
- Place gloved fingers between baby's face and vaginal wall to create airway for baby until head delivers

Limb Presentation

EMT—basic/intermediate

- Place mother in Trendelenburg's position to slow delivery
- Support presenting limb, assess pulse if possible
- Discourage mother from pushing during contractions (panting instead helps avoid pushing)

Vaginal Bleeding

EMT—basic/intermediate

- Do not perform vaginal examination or attempt vaginal packing

Antepartum (before delivery)

- Apply perineal pad; note time to assess amount of bleeding
- **Position mother on left side**: relieves compression of IVC, enhances venous return and uteroplacental perfusion

Postpartum hemorrhage

- Massage mother's abdomen, or encourage breastfeeding
- Control external bleeding with direct (external) pressure

Paramedic

- Establish second large-bore IV, titrate to SBP >90 mm Hg
- **Oxytocin:** (postpartum hemorrhage only) 10 U mixed in 1000 mL LR titrated to effect (give 3–10 U IM if no IV)

Emergency Medications

This is a reference only and is not meant to be exhaustive in clinical content. Doses are guidelines only. Actual dosing may vary depending on Pt's clinical status. Always follow protocol.

IV Fluid Drip Rate Table (gtt/min)

	Rate: mL/hr								
	30	50	75	100	125	150	175	200	250
10 gtt/mL Set	5	8	13	17	21	25	29	33	42
12 gtt/mL Set	6	10	15	20	25	30	35	40	50
15 gtt/mL Set	8	13	19	25	31	37	44	50	62
20 gtt/mL Set	10	17	25	33	42	50	58	67	83
60 gtt/mL Set	30	50	75	100	125	150	175	200	250

Note: TKO = 30 mL/hr

Abciximab (ReoPro) (GP IIb/IIIa Platelet Inhibitor)

UA/NSTEMI (PCI planned within 24 hr): 0.25 mg/kg IV 10–60 min before procedure, then infuse 0.125 mcg/kg/min
PCI only: 0.25 mg/kg IV, then 10 mcg/min infusion
Contraindicated: active internal bleeding, neurovascular event, major surgery or trauma within 1 mo, platelet count <150,000/mm³, concomitant use of another GB IIb/IIIa inhibitor
Side effects: increased bleeding and bruising, GI irritation
Precautions: must be given with heparin

EMS DRUGS

Activated Charcoal (Absorbent, Antidote)

OD/poisoning: 1 g/kg PO, NG

Peds: same as adults

Contraindicated: concurrent use with syrup of ipecac
Side effects: constipation, N/V, diarrhea
Precautions: ineffective for treatment of heavy metals, alcohols, caustics, hydrocarbons, potassium, potassium cyanide
U.S. poison control: 1-800-222-1222

Adenosine (Adenocard) (Antiarrhythmic)

Narrow-complex PSVT: 6-mg rapid IV push; repeat with 12 mg in 1–2 min if needed; third dose of 12 mg may be given in 1–2 min (maximum 30 mg); follow all doses with 10-mL NS flush

Peds: 0.1 mg/kg (maximum 6 mg) rapid IV push; may repeat at 0.2 mg/kg (maximum 12 mg second dose); follow with 5-mL flush

Contraindicated: drug-induced ↑HR, second-/third-degree HB, VT.
Side effects: flushing, CP tightness, ↑HR, asystole
Precautions: a-fib/flutter (ineffective); avoid if Pt on dipyridamole

Albuterol (Ventolin) (Bronchodilator)

Bronchospasm: 2.5 mg nebulized in 3-mL NS, repeat prn

Peds: 0.15 mg/kg (0.3 mL/kg) nebulized in 3-mL NS, repeat prn

Contraindicated: hypersensitivity to adrenergic amines
Side effects: nervousness, restlessness, tremor, ↑HR, anxiety, N/V, HA, HTN, hyperglycemia

Precautions: tachydysrhythmias, cardiac disease, elderly

Alteplase (Activase, t-PA) (Fibrinolytic)

ACS (<12 hr old): 15-mg IV bolus; then 0.75 mg/kg (maximum 50 mg) IV over 30 min; then 0.5 mg/kg (maximum 35 mg) over 60 min; **Ischemic stroke (<3 hr old)**: 0.9 mg/kg (maximum 90 mg) IV over 60 min; give 10% of total dose as bolus over first minute, then remaining 90% over remaining hour
Contraindicated: see Ischemic CP Fibrinolytic Checklist in Tab 3
Side effects: ↓BP, reperfusion arrhythmias, HA, ↑bleeding time, hemorrhage, flushing, urticaria
Precautions: Pts with severe renal or hepatic disease

Aminophylline (Truphyllin) (Bronchodilator)

Bronchospasm: 250–500 mg IV infusion over 20–30 min
Peds: 6 mg/kg IV infusion over 20–30 min; maximum 12 mg/kg/day
Contraindicated: uncontrolled arrhythmias
Side effects: restlessness, HA, dizziness, arrhythmias, ↓BP, N/V
Precautions: HTN; too rapid infusion can cause cardiac arrest

Amiodarone (Cordarone) (Antiarrhythmic)

VF and pulseless VT: 300 mg IV, may repeat once with 150 mg in 3–5 min; maximum 2.2 g/24 hr
Recurrent life-threatening ventricular arrhythmias:

- **Rapid infusion**: 150 mg IV over 10 min (15 mg/min); may repeat every 10 min prn
- **Slow infusion**: 360 mg IV over 6 hr (1 mg/min)

EMS DRUGS

EMS DRUGS

- **Maintenance infusion**: 540 mg IV over 18 hr (0.5 mg/min); maximum cumulative dose 2.2 g IV/24 hr

Peds: refractory VF, pulseless VT: 5 mg/kg IV, IO
Perfusing SVT, VT: load 5 mg/kg IV, IO over 20–60 min; maximum single dose 300 mg or a total of 15 mg/kg/day

Contraindicated: ↓HR, cardiogenic shock, second- /third-degree HB
Side effects: ↓BP, prolonged QT interval
Precautions: avoid concurrent use with procainamide

Amyl Nitrite (Antidote to Cyanide)

Cyanide exposure: crushed ampule inhaled for 30 sec followed by 30 sec of oxygen; repeat prn

Peds: same as adults

Contraindicated: none in cyanide exposure
Side effects: HA, ↓BP, ↑HR, N/V
Precautions: effects diminish after approximately 20 min

Anistreplase (Eminase, APSAC) (Fibrinolytic)

AMI (<12 hr of onset of pain): 30 IU IV over 2–5 min
Contraindicated: see Ischemic CP Fibrinolytic Checklist in Tab 3
Side effects: bleeding, fever, N/V, allergic reaction
Precautions: may be ineffective if within 12 mo of Pt receiving anistreplase or streptokinase

Aspirin (Acetylsalicylic Acid) (Antiplatelet, Analgesic)

Acute coronary syndrome (ACS): 160–325 mg PO non-enteric–coated tablet (chewing preferred)
Contraindicated: hypersensitivity to aspirin
Side effects: gastric ulcer or irritation, GI bleed
Precautions: active ulcers, asthma

Atenolol (Tenormin) (Beta Blocker)

MI, UA, PSVT, a-fib, a-flutter, HTN: 5 mg slow IV (over 5 min); may repeat another 5 mg in 10 min
Contraindicated: ↓HR, ↓BP, second- /third-degree HB, cocaine use
Side effects: ↓BP, dizziness, ↓HR, HA, N/V
Precautions: concurrent use with calcium channel blockers can cause ↓BP; use caution in Pts with history of bronchospasm, heart failure, or conduction abnormalities

Atracurium (Tracrium) (Paralytic; Nondepolarizing)

RSI: 0.4–0.5 mg/kg IV

Peds: <2 yr: 0.3–0.4 mg/kg IV; **>2 yr:** same as adults

Contraindicated: known hypersensitivity to drug
Side effects: paralysis, ↓BP, ↓HR, ↑HR
Precautions: ensure intubation and suction equipment available, set up, and working
Onset: 2–2.5 min; **peak:** 5 min; **duration:** 30–40 min

EMS DRUGS

EMS DRUGS

Atropine Sulfate (Atropen) (Anticholinergic)

Bradycardia: 0.5–1 mg IV (may give via ET tube at double dose) every 3–5 min, maximum 0.04 mg/kg
Cardiac arrest: 1 mg every 3–5 min; maximum 3 mg
Organophosphate (OPP) exposure, nerve gas: 2–6 mg IV, IM depending on severity of symptoms; may repeat in 2-mg increments every 3 min titrated to relief of symptoms
Asthma: 0.4–2 mg nebulized in 3-mL NS

Peds: bradycardia: 0.02 mg/kg IV, IO (ET: 0.03 mg/kg); minimum single dose 0.1 mg, maximum single dose 1 mg); may double and repeat once; maximum pediatric total dose 1 mg, adolescent 2 mg
RSI: 0.01–0.02 mg/kg IV (minimum 0.1 mg, maximum 1 mg); IM dose is 0.02 mg/kg
OPP: 0.05 mg/kg IV, IM, IO

Contraindicated: tachycardia, a-fib, a-flutter, glaucoma
Side effects: ↑HR, HA, dry mouth, dilated pupils, VF/VT
Precautions: use caution in hypoxia; avoid using in hypothermic bradycardia and second-degree (Mobitz) type II HB

Bretylium (Bretylol) (Antiarrhythmic)

VF, pulseless VT: 5 mg/kg IV; may repeat 10 mg/kg every 15 min; maximum 30 mg/kg in 24 hr
VT with pulse: 5–10 mg/kg IV infused over 10 min
Maintenance drip: 1–2 mg/min

Peds: 5 mg/kg IV, IO; may repeat 10 mg/kg in 15–30 min

Contraindicated: none for life-threatening dysrhythmias
Side effects: ↓BP, N/V, CP, ↓HR
Precautions: digoxin toxicity, renal failure

Bumetanide (Bumex) (Diuretic)

CHF, pulmonary edema: 0.5–1 mg IV, IM over 1–2 min
Contraindicated: dehydration, pregnancy
Side effects: dizziness, HA, ↓BP, N/V
Precautions: dehydration, protect from light

Butorphanol (Stadol) (Synthetic Narcotic)

Moderate to severe pain: 1 mg IV; 2 mg IM
Contraindicated: head injury, undiagnosed abdominal pain
Side effects: HA, confusion, respiratory depression, N/V
Precautions: monitor RR, N/V, decreased LOC
Reversal: naloxone (see Naloxone this tab)

Calcium Chloride 10% (Mineral, Electrolytes)

Calcium channel blocker toxicity, hyperkalemia (also hypocalcemia and beta blocker OD): 500–1000 mg slow IV (over 5–10 min); may be repeated prn

Peds: 20 mg/kg (0.2 mL/kg) slow IV, IO; may be repeated

Contraindicated: hypercalcemia, VF, Pts receiving digoxin
Side effects: bradycardia, asystole, ↓BP, VF, N/V
Precautions: incompatible with sodium bicarbonate

Calcium Gluconate 10% (Mineral, Electrolyte)

Calcium channel blocker toxicity, hyperkalemia, hypocalcemia, hypermagnesemia: 500–1000 mg (5–10 mL) slow IV (over 5–10 min); may be repeated prn in 10 min

EMS DRUGS

Peds: 60–100 mg/kg slow IV, IO; may be repeated

Contraindicated: VF, hypercalcemia
Side effects: asystole, arrhythmias, N/V, syncope, ↓HR, tingling
Precautions: monitor BP, HR, ECG

Chlorpromazine (Thorazine) (Tranquilizer, Phenothiazine)

Acute psychosis, nausea: 25–100 mg IM

Peds: 0.5 mg/kg IM

Contraindicated: recent use of sedatives or hallucinogens
Side effects: drowsiness, AMS, orthostatic ↓BP
Precautions: may cause EPS, especially in pediatrics

Cimetidine (Tagamet®) (Histamine$_2$ Blocker)

Allergic reaction (EMS use): 300 mg IV, IO, IM, PO

Peds: 5–10 mg/kg IV, IO, IM, PO

Contraindicated: hypersensitivity
Side effects: HA, confusion, arrhythmias, hypotension
Precautions: hypotension from rapid IV infusion

Cyanide Antidote Kit (Cyanide Antidote)

Cyanide exposure: amyl nitrite: 1 ampule crushed and inhaled for 30 sec, repeat every minute until IV established, then **sodium nitrite:** 300 mg IV over 5 min, then **sodium thiosulfate:** 12.5 g IV over 5 min

Peds: amyl nitrite: same as adults; **sodium nitrite:** 10 mg/kg; **sodium thiosulfate:** 400 mg/kg

Contraindicated: some in cyanide exposure
Side effects: see individual drug
Precautions: see individual drug

Dalteparin (Fragmin) (Anticoagulant, LMW Heparin)

ACS: 120 IU/kg (maximum 10,000 IU) SQ every 12 hr (taken concurrently with aspirin)
Contraindicated: active bleeding or increased risk of bleeding
Side effects: bleeding, HA, dizziness, N/V, abdominal pain
Precautions: Pts receiving regional anesthesia

Dantrolene (Dantrium) (Skeletal Muscle Relaxant)

Malignant hyperthermia: 2.5 mg/kg rapid IV; repeat prn

Peds: same as adults

Contraindicated: none known for malignant hyperthermia
Side effects: drowsiness, muscle weakness, confusion, HA
Precautions: cardiac, pulmonary, or liver disease
Malignant Hyperthermia Association of the United States (MHAUS) Hotline: 1–800–644–9737

EMS DRUGS

EMS DRUGS

Dexamethasone (Decadron) (Glucocorticoid Steroid)

Anaphylaxis, cerebral edema, spinal trauma: 5–10 mg IV, IO, IM

Peds: 0.25–0.5 mg/kg IV, IO

Contraindicated: ulcer, infection, alcohol intolerance
Side effects: peptic ulceration, HTN, N/V
Precautions: tissue necrosis with infiltration

Dextrose 50% (Caloric Agent, Nutrient)

Hypoglycemic coma: 12.5–25 g slow IV; may repeat once

Peds: 0.5–1 g/kg IV
Note: D_{50}: 1–2 mL/kg; D_{25}: 2–4 mL/kg; D_{10}: 5–10 mL/kg

Contraindicated: CNS bleed, allergy to corn, hyperglycemia
Side effects: hyperglycemia, fluid overload
Precautions: IV route only (tissue necrosis with infiltration)

Diazepam (Valium) (Benzodiazepine, Anticonvulsant)

Seizures: 5–10 mg slow IV; may repeat every 10–15 min up to a maximum dose of 30 mg
Rectally: 0.2 mg/kg PR

Peds: 0.2 mg/kg slow IV every 2–5 min, maximum dose 5 mg (rectally: 0.3 mg/kg PR)

Contraindicated: head injury, coma, respiratory depression
Side effects: respiratory depression, AMS
Precautions: reduce dose by half in elderly Pts

Digoxin (Lanoxin) (Inotropic, Antiarrhythmic)

A-fib, a-flutter, CHF, pulmonary edema (may be used as alternative treatment for PSVT): loading dose 10–15 mcg/kg

Peds: consult OLMC

Contraindicated: uncontrolled ventricular arrhythmias, AV block, IHSS, constrictive pericarditis
Side effects: arrhythmias, fatigue, ↓HR, N/V, HA
Precautions: avoid electrical cardioversion of stable Pts; if unstable, use lower current settings (e.g., 10–20 J)

Digoxin Immune Fab (Digibind) (Digoxin Antidote)

Digoxin toxicity: dependent on serum digoxin levels; one 40-mg vial binds to approximately 0.6 mg digoxin; average is 10 vials (400 mg); mix each vial with 4 mL NS, and administer IV over 30 min using 0.22-mm membrane filter (may be administered as IV bolus if Pt unstable)

Digoxin Antidote Dosing Guidelines

If blood serum level known:	
Number of vials =	$\dfrac{\text{weight (kg)} \times \text{serum level (ng/mL)}}{100}$
If amount ingested or infused known:	
Number of vials =	(mg ingested or infused) × 0.8

EMS DRUGS

EMS DRUGS

Peds: same as adults

Contraindicated: hypersensitivity to drug
Side effects: increased serum digoxin levels
Precautions: allergies to sheep proteins

Diltiazem (Cardizem) (Calcium Channel Blocker)

A-fib, a-flutter, PSVT refractory to adenosine: 15–20 mg IV over 2 min (0.25 mg/kg); may repeat in 15 min at 20–25 mg IV over 2 min (0.35 mg/kg)
Infusion: start 5–15 mg/hr, titrate to HR
Contraindicated: second- or third-degree AV block, SBP <90 mm Hg, concurrent use of IV beta blockers, cardiogenic shock, sick sinus syndrome, drug- or toxin-induced tachycardia, wide-complex tachycardia of uncertain type, WPW syndrome
Side effects: ↓BP, dizziness, ↓HR, N/V
Precautions: incompatible with furosemide; flush IV line between doses of diltiazem and furosemide

Dimenhydrinate (Dramamine) (Antihistamine)

Adjunct to analgesia, N/V: 12.5–25 mg slow IV (50–100 mg IM)

Peds: 1.25 mg/kg IV, IM

Contraindicated: recent ingestion CNS depressants
Side effects: AMS, drowsiness, HA
Precautions: asthma, seizure disorders
Precautions: severe ↓BP in Pts on beta blockers

Diphenhydramine (Benadryl) (Antihistamine)

Allergic reaction, EPS: 25–50 mg IV, deep IM

Peds: (>10 kg) 1.25 mg/kg IV, deep IM

Contraindicated: asthma, pregnant, lactating
Side effects: dry mouth, drowsiness, ↓BP
Precautions: elderly, pregnancy

Dobutamine (Dobutrex) (Inotropic)

CHF, LV dysfunction: 2–20 mcg/kg/min IV infusion

Peds: same as adults

Contraindicated: allergy to drug, IHSS, BP <100 mm Hg
Side effects: dizziness, HA, ↓BP, VT, VF, N/V, AMS
Precautions: lower doses in renal failure, use caution with recent MI, arrhythmias, hypovolemia, sulfite allergies

Dopamine (Intropin) (Inotropic, Vasopressor)

Symptomatic hypotension (euvolemic), symptomatic bradycardia unresponsive to atropine: 2–20 mcg/kg/min
Note: Drop last number of Pt weight (in pounds) to determine gtt/min (e.g., 180-lb Pt = 18 gtt/min)

Peds: same as adults

Contraindicated: hypovolemic shock
Side effects: tachyarrhythmias, excessive vasoconstriction, extravasation can cause severe tissue necrosis
Precautions: avoid with sodium bicarbonate and furosemide
Extravasation: treat with phentolamine (see Phentolamine this tab)

EMS DRUGS

EMS DRUGS

Droperidol (Inapsine)
(Antiemetic, Major Tranquilizer)

Acute psychosis, N/V: 0.5–1.25 mg IV

Peds: >2 yr: 0.1 mg/kg IV

Contraindicated: hypersensitivity to drug
Side effects: ↑HR, ↓BP, drowsy, EPS, dizziness, restlessness
Precautions: FDA black box warning: prolongation of QT interval, VS, and ECG (12-lead) must be monitored

Enalaprilat (Vasotec)
(ACE Inhibitor, Antihypertensive)

ACS (HTN, LV dysfunction): 1.25 mg IV over 5 min
Contraindicated: STEMI, pregnancy, angioedema, ↓BP, serum potassium >5 mEq/L, volume-depleted
Side effects: dizziness, HA, cough, ↓BP
Precautions: reduce dose in renal failure; avoid in bilateral renal artery stenosis; generally not started until after reperfusion therapy completed and BP stabilized

Enoxaparin (Lovenox)
(Anticoagulant, LMW Heparin)

ACS: 1 mg/kg SC given with aspirin
Contraindicated: active bleeding or increased risk of bleeding
Side effects: Bleeding, HA, dizziness, N/V, abdominal pain, diarrhea, constipation, nose bleed
Precautions: severe liver and kidney disease, history of ulcers

Epinephrine (Adrenalin) (Sympathomimetic)

Cardiac arrest: 1 mg IV, IO (1:10,000) every 3–5 min; **anaphylaxis:** 0.5 mg SQ (1:1000); **asthma:** 0.3 mg SQ (1:1000); **refractory bradycardia and hypotension:** 2–10 mcg/min (1 mg of 1:1000 solution in 500 mL of saline, start at 1–5 mL/min)

Peds: IV/IO: 0.01 mg/kg (0.1 mL/kg of 1:10,000); **ET:** 0.1 mg/kg (0.1 mL/kg of 1:1000)

Contraindicated: hypersensitivity to adrenergic amines
Side effects: angina, HTN, ↑HR, VT, VF, nervousness, tremors
Precautions: tachydysrhythmias, cardiac disease, HTN, hyperthyroidism, glaucoma, DM, elderly, pregnancy

Epinephrine, Racemic (Micronefrin)

Laryngotracheobronchitis (croup): 0.25–0.75 mL of 2.25% solution nebulized in 2-mL NS

Peds: same as adults

Contraindicated: use controversial and contraindicated in some EMS jurisdictions for epiglottitis; follow local protocol
Side effects: angina, HTN, ↑HR, VT, VF, nervousness, tremors
Precautions: monitor VS regularly

Eptifibatide (Integrilin) (GP IIb/IIIa Platelet Inhibitor)

UA/NSTEMI (managed medically): 180 mcg/kg IV bolus over 1–2 min, then 2 mcg/kg/min IV infusion over 72–96 hr
UA/NSTEMI (with PCI): 180 mcg/kg IV bolus over 1–2 min, then 2 mcg/kg/min IV infusion, then repeat bolus in 10 min
Contraindicated: active internal bleeding, neurovascular event, major surgery or trauma within 1 mo, platelet count <150,000/mm³, concomitant use of another GB IIb/IIIa inhibitor

EMS DRUGS

Side effects: increased bleeding and bruising, GI irritation
Precautions: increased chance of bleeding, adjust dose if creatinine clearance <50 mL/min

Etomidate (Amidate) (Sedative, Hypnotic)

RSI: 0.2–0.6 mg/kg IV

Peds: 0.2–0.4 mg/kg IV

Contraindicated: hypersensitivity
Side effects: apnea, laryngospasm, myoclonic activity
Precautions: asthma, CV disease, ↓BP

Esmolol (Brevibloc) (Beta Blocker, Antiarrhythmic)

MI, UA, PSVT, a-fib, a-flutter, HTN: 0.5 mg/kg IV over 1 min followed by 50 mcg/kg infused over 4 min

Peds: 50 mcg/kg/min IV

Contraindicated: ↓HR, ↓BP, second- /third-degree HB, cocaine use
Side effects: ↓BP, dizziness, ↓HR, HA, N/V
Precautions: bronchospasm, CHF, dysrhythmias; concurrent use with calcium channel blockers can cause ↓BP

Fentanyl (Sublimaze) (Narcotic Analgesic)

Pain, RSI: induction: 2–10 mcg/kg IV; sedation: 3 mcg/kg IV

Peds: 0.5–1 mcg/kg IV, IO, IM every 3–5 min prn (maximum 4 mcg/kg)

Contraindicated: hypersensitivity, undiagnosed abdominal pain, shock, significant blood loss

Side effects: ↓RR, ↓BP, ↓HR, dizziness, AMS, N/V
Precautions: with ↓RR, ↓BP; **Caution:** rapid administration can cause chest-wall rigidity leading to respiratory distress

Flumazenil (Romazicon) (Benzodiazepine Antagonist)

Benzodiazepine toxicity: 0.2 mg IV, may repeat 0.3 mg in 30 sec, followed by 0.5 mg every min, maximum 3 mg/hr

Peds: 0.01 mg/kg IV, IO; maximum dose 0.2 mg; total maximum 1 mg

Contraindicated: TCA OD, seizures, ↑ICP, allergy to benzodiazepines.
Side effects: withdrawal symptoms, dizziness, seizures, N/V
Precautions: avoid using in multiple-drug OD; monitor for recurrent respiratory depression and withdrawal symptoms

Fosphenytoin (Cerebyx) (Anticonvulsant)

Status epilepticus: 15–20 mg PE/kg IV, IM

Peds: same as adults

Contraindicated: hypersensitivity
Side effects: ↓BP, dizziness, somnolence
Precautions: alcoholism, renal impairment, heart block

Furosemide (Lasix) (Diuretic, Distal Loop)

CHF with pulmonary edema, hypertensive crisis, increased ICP: 0.5–1 mg/kg slow IV over 1–2 min; may repeat once at 2 mg/kg slow IV over 1–2 min

Peds: 1 mg/kg slow IV, IO

EMS DRUGS

Contraindicated: ↓BP, dehydration, hypokalemia
Side effects: ↓BP, dehydration, hypokalemia
Precautions: monitor UO and electrolytes during therapy

Glucagon (Hormone)

Beta blocker OD, hypoglycemia: 1 mg IV, IO, IM; also used for **anaphylaxis** (same dose and route) for Pts unresponsive to epinephrine or who are taking beta blockers

Peds: <20 kg: 0.5 mg IV, IO, IM

Contraindicated: hypersensitivity
Side effects: ↑HR, N/V, hyperglycemia
Precautions: CV, renal disease

Haloperidol (Haldol) (Major Tranquilizer)

Acute psychosis: 2–5 mg IM
Contraindicated: using sedatives, Talwin-induced dysphoria
Side effects: AMS, EPS, orthostatic hypotension
Precautions: violent/aggressive Pt, hypotensive Pt

Heparin-Unfractionated (UFH) (Anticoagulant)

STEMI: initial bolus 60 IU/kg (maximum 4000 IU) IV; **NSTEMI:** initial bolus 60–70 IU/kg (maximum 5000 IU) IV; follow heparin protocol

Peds: Therapeutic anticoagulation: 50 IU/kg IV, IO

Contraindicated: pork allergy, bleeding, thrombocytopenia
Side effects: Bleeding, thrombocytopenia, itching
Precautions: history of gastric ulcers

Hydralazine (Apresoline) (Antihypertensive, Vasodilator)

Hypertensive crisis: 10–40 mg IV, IM

Peds: 0.1–0.2 mg/kg IV, IM

Contraindicated: CAD, mitral valve/rheumatic heart disease
Side effects: ↑HR, palpitations, HA, N/V, ↓BP
Precautions: monitor VS; may cause ECG changes

Hydrocortisone (Solu-Cortef) (Steroid)

Allergic reaction, anaphylaxis: 100–250 mg IV, IM

Peds: 4 mg/kg IV, IO, IM

Contraindicated: none in emergency setting
Side effects: GI bleed, suppression of natural steroids
Precautions: onset may be upward of 2–6 hr

Hydroxocobalamin (CyanoKit) (Cyanide Antidote)

Drug must be reconstituted with 100 mL NS, LR, D_5W
   Cyanide poisoning: 5 g IV infused over 15 min (may be repeated once for a total of 10 g)

Peds: 70 mg/kg IV infused over 15 min

Contraindicated: none known
Side effects: HTN, erythema, red-colored urine
Precautions: may cause significant HTN

EMS DRUGS

Hydroxyzine (Vistaril) (Antihistamine)

Anxiety; N/V: 25–100 mg deep IM

Peds: 1 mg/kg deep IM

Contraindicated: hypersensitivity
Side effects: somnolence, orthostatic hypotension
Precautions: hypotensive Pt

Ibutilide (Corvert) (Antiarrhythmic)

SVT, including a-fib, a-flutter: Pt ≥60 kg: 1 mg slow IV over 10 min; may repeat same dose in 10 min; **Pt <60 kg**: 0.01 mg/kg slow IV over 10 min; may repeat in 10 min.
Contraindicated: known or suspected low ejection fraction
Side effects: arrhythmias, torsades de pointes, HA, N/V
Precautions: CHF, LV dysfunction, pregnancy

Insulin (Humulin-R, Novolin-R) (Hypoglycemic)

DKA: bolus: 0.1–0.15 U/kg IV; *infusion: 0.05–0.1 U/kg/hr*

Peds: Infusion only: 0.05–0.1 U/kg/hr IV, IO

Contraindicated: unknown blood glucose level, hypoglycemia
Side effects: hypoglycemia
Precautions: reassess blood glucose level after administration; be prepared to manage hypoglycemia; never give U-500 IV

Inamrinone (Inocor) (Inotropic)

CHF: 0.75 mg/kg IV over 2–3 min (10–15 min if severe LV dysfunction); *infusion: 5–15 mcg/kg/min titrated to effect*

Peds: 0.75–1 mg/kg IV over 5 min; may be repeated twice; *infusion: 5–10 mcg/kg/min titrated to effect*

Contraindicated: hypersensitivity to drug or bisulfites
Side effects: ↑HR, ↓BP, thrombocytopenia, cardiac ischemia
Precautions: do not mix in dextrose or with other drugs

Ipecac Syrup (Emetic)

OD; poisoning: 15–30 mL PO followed by 3–4 glasses of water; may repeat 15 mL in 30 min if ineffective

Peds: *1–12 yr:* 5–15 mL PO; may repeat once in 20 min

Contraindicated: AMS; ingestion of strong acids, bases, or petroleum; TCA OD, antiemetic OD (phenothiazine)
Side effects: diarrhea, arrhythmias, sedation, N/V
Precautions: ipecac may complicate or worsen clinical management of OD or poisoning

Ipratropium 0.02% (Atrovent) (Bronchodilator)

Bronchospasm; COPD: 0.5 mg (2.5 mL) nebulized with albuterol

Peds: 25 mcg/kg nebulized

Contraindicated: hypersensitivity, peanut or soybean allergy
Side effects: HA, anxiety, nervousness, palpitations
Precautions: should not be used as primary treatment

Isoproterenol (Isuprel) (Inotropic)

Bradycardia: 2–10 mcg/min titrated to HR
Contraindicated: cardiac arrest, concurrent use with epinephrine, high dosages (except in beta-blocker OD).

Side effects: ↓BP, HA, VT, VF, ↑HR
Precautions: increases cardiac ischemia; consider Isuprel last

Kayexalate (Na Polystyrene Sulfonate) (Cation)

Hyperkalemia: 15 g PO water or sorbitol

Peds: 1 g/kg PO

Contraindicated: hyperkalemia, ileus, alcohol intolerance
Side effects: constipation, N/V, fecal impaction, gastric irritation, hypocalcemia, hypokalemia, sodium retention
Precautions: monitor ECG and electrolytes during therapy

Ketamine (Ketalar) (Anesthetic)

RSI: 2 mg/kg IV, IO

Peds: 1–2 mg/kg IV; 3–5 mg/kg IM

Contraindicated: severe HTN, ↑ICP, stroke
Side effects: HTN, laryngospasm, increased secretions
Precautions: hallucinations, emergence reactions

Ketorolac (Toradol) (NSAID, Nonopioid Analgesic)

Pain (moderate): 15–30 mg IV, IM
Contraindicated: lactation, pregnancy, alcohol intolerance
Side effects: drowsiness, GI bleed, N/V, HA, ↑bleeding time
Precautions: use half dose for Pt ≥65 yr, <50 kg, or with renal impairment; GI bleed, renal or CV disease

Labetalol (Normodyne, Trandate) (Beta Blocker)

MI, UA, PSVT, a-fib, a-flutter, HTN: 10 mg IV over 1–2 min; may repeat or double dose every 10 min to a maximum of 150 mg; *infusion: (after bolus) 2–8 mg/min IV*
Contraindicated: ↓HR, ↓BP, second- or third-degree HB, LV failure
Side effects: ↓BP, dizziness, ↓HR, HA, N/V
Precautions: concurrent use of calcium channel blockers can cause ↓BP; history of bronchospasm, heart failure, arrhythmias

Lidocaine (Xylocaine) (Antiarrhythmic, Anesthetic)

VF/pulseless VT, wide-complex tachycardia of uncertain type: 1–1.5 mg/kg IV (3–4 mg/kg ET); may repeat 0.5–0.75 mg/kg every 5–10 min, maximum 3 mg/kg; *infusion: 2–4 mg/min*

Peds: 1 mg/kg IV/IO (maximum 100 mg); *infusion: 20–50 mcg/kg/min*

Contraindicated: second- or third-degree HB, hypotension
Side effects: asystole, AMS, seizure, slurred speech
Precautions: ↓infusion if Pt >70 yr; CHF, shock, liver disease

Lisinopril (Prinivil) (ACE Inhibitor, Antihypertensive)

ACS: 5 mg PO within 24 hr of onset of symptoms
Contraindicated: STEMI, pregnancy, angioedema, hypotension, serum potassium <5 mEq/L, volume depleted
Side effects: dizziness, HA, cough, ↓BP
Precautions: reduce dose in renal failure; generally started after reperfusion therapy completed and BP stabilized

EMS DRUGS

EMS DRUGS

Lorazepam (Ativan)
(Benzodiazepine, Anticonvulsant)

Seizures, anxiety, sedation: 2–4 mg IV, IO, IM; may repeat in 10–15 min; maximum 8 mg; *for IV route, dilute in equal amount NS*

Peds: 0.05–0.1 mg/kg IV, IO, IM (over 2 min); maximum 4 mg

Contraindicated: narrow-angle glaucoma
Side effects: dizziness, drowsiness, apnea, asystole, N/V
Precautions: severe hepatic, renal, pulmonary impairment
Reversal: flumazenil (see Flumazenil this tab)

Magnesium Sulfate
(Electrolyte, Anticonvulsant)

Torsades de pointes: *cardiac arrest:* 1–2 g infused over 5–20 min; *noncardiac arrest:* 1–2 g infused over 5–60 min followed by 0.5–1 g/hr infusion; *eclampsia:* 1–4 g slow IV

Peds: *asthma, torsades de pointes:* 25–50 mg/kg IV, IO over 10–20 min; maximum 2 g

Contraindicated: hypermagnesemia, hypocalcemia, HB
Side effects: ↓BP; asystole; ↓RR; AMS; flushed, moist skin
Precautions: renal insufficiency

Mannitol (Osmitrol) (Diuretic [Osmotic])

Increased ICP: 0.5–1 g/kg IV over 5–10 min

Peds: 0.2–0.5 g/kg over 30–60 min

Contraindicated: intracranial bleeding, anuria, dehydration

Side effects: AMS, HA, blurred vision, N/V, ↑HR, ↓BP, CP, CHF
Precautions: elderly, CV and renal disease

Mark-I Kit (Cholinergic Antidote)

Nerve agent/OPP exposure: *atropine:* 2 mg IM followed by *pralidoxime (2-PAM):* 600 mg IM (1–2 g IV, IO route)

Peds: *atropine:* 0.02–0.05 mg/kg IM; *pralidoxime:* 20–50 mg/kg IV, IO over 15–30 min (same IM dose)

Contraindicated: none in nerve agent/OPP exposures
Side effects: ↑HR, ↑BP, N/V, weakness, laryngospasm
Precautions: do not mix with other drugs

Meperidine (Demerol) (Opioid Narcotic)

Pain (moderate to severe): 25–150 mg slow IV, IO, IM, SQ

Peds: 1–1.5 mg/kg slow IV, IO, IM, SQ

Contraindicated: cocaine use, concurrent MAO inhibitors, ↓RR
Side effects: ↓RR, ↓BP, confusion, sedation, seizure, N/V
Precautions: undiagnosed abdominal pain, head trauma
Reversal: naloxone (see Naloxone this tab)

Metaproterenol (Alupent) (Bronchodilator)

Bronchospasm: 0.3 mL 5% solution nebulized in 2.5-mL NS

Peds: >12 yr: 0.1–0.2 mL 5% solution nebulized in 3-mL NS

Contraindicated: hypersensitivity to adrenergic amines
Side effects: restlessness, ↑HR, anxiety, N/V, HA, HTN, tremor
Precautions: tachydysrhythmias, cardiac disease, elderly

EMS DRUGS

Methylprednisolone (Solu-Medrol) (Steroid)

Anaphylaxis: 40–125 mg IV, IO, IM
Spinal cord injury: 30 mg/kg IV (infusion: 5.4 mg/kg/hr)

Peds: 1–2 mg/kg IV, IO, IM

Contraindicated: hypersensitivity
Side effects: HA, hypokalemia, HTN, N/V, alkalosis
Precautions: diabetes, GI bleed

Metoclopramide (Reglan) (Antiemetic)

Nausea: 10–20 mg IV, IO

Peds: 1 mg/kg IV, IO

Contraindicated: hypersensitivity
Side effects: drowsiness, ↓BP, acute dystonia, seizures
Precautions: Parkinson's disease, epilepsy

Metoprolol (Lopressor, Toprol XL) (Beta Blocker)

A-fib, a-flutter, PSVT, HTN, MI, UA: 5 mg slow IV; repeat every 5 min for a total of 15 mg
Contraindicated: ↓HR, ↓BP, second- /third-degree HB, cocaine use
Side effects: ↓BP, dizziness, ↓HR, HA, N/V
Precautions: concurrent use with calcium channel blockers can cause ↓BP; use caution with history of bronchospasm

Midazolam (Versed)
(Benzodiazepine, Anticonvulsant)

RSI, sedation: 1–2.5 mg slow IV, IO, IM (maximum 0.1 mg/kg)

Peds: 0.05–0.2 mg/kg IV, IO, IM; *infusion:* 1–2 mcg/kg/min

Contraindicated: ↓BP, ↓RR, coma, alcohol, CNS depressants
Side effects: ↓BP, ↓RR, coma, N/V, HA, pain at IV site
Precautions: glaucoma (relative contraindication)
Reversal: Flumazenil (see Flumazenil this tab)

Milrinone (Primacor) (Inotropic)

Shock, CHF: load 50 mcg/kg IV, IO over 10 min
  Infusion: 0.375–0.75 mcg/kg/min IV, IO

Peds: load 25–50 mcg/kg IV, IO over 10–60 min; *infusion:* 0.5–0.75 mcg/kg/min IV, IO

Contraindicated: obstructive hypertrophic cardiomyopathy
Side effects: ↓BP, N/V
Precautions: shorter half-life than inamrinone; reduce dose in renal impairment; hemodynamic monitoring required

Morphine Sulfate (MS)
(Opioid, Narcotic Analgesic)

Pain, ACS (MONA): 2–4 mg slow IV every 5–30 min

Peds: 0.1–0.2 mg/kg slow IV, IO (maximum 15 mg)

Contraindicated: ↓BP/RR, abdominal pain, head injury, AMS
Side effects: ↓BP, ↓RR, ↓HR, AMS, N/V
Precautions: CHF, elderly, asthmatics, CNS-depressed Pt
Reversal: Naloxone (see Naloxone this tab)

EMS DRUGS

EMS DRUGS

Nalmefene (Revex)
(Opioid, Narcotic Antagonist)

Opioid, narcotic OD: 0.5–1 mg/70 kg; may repeat in 2–5 min
Contraindicated: hypersensitivity
Side effects: ↑HR, ↑BP, dysrhythmias, N/V, acute withdrawal
Precautions: avoid total narcotic reversal in addicted Pt; half-life may not be as long as narcotic half-life

Naloxone (Narcan)
(Opioid, Narcotic Antagonist)

Opioid, narcotic OD: 0.4–2 mg IV, IO, IM, SC (double ET dose) every 2 min; maximum 10 mg

Peds: 0.1 mg/kg IV, IO, IM, SC (double ET dose)

Contraindicated: hypersensitivity
Side effects: ↑HR, ↑BP, dysrhythmias, N/V, acute withdrawal
Precautions: avoid total narcotic reversal in addicted Pt; half-life may not be as long as narcotic half-life

Nicardipine (Cardene)
(Calcium Channel Blocker)

HTN: 5–20 mg/hr IV, IO
Contraindicated: aortic stenosis, ↓BP
Side effects: dizziness, HA, N/V, ↓BP, ↑HR, flushed skin
Precautions: hepatic dysfunction, renal failure; do not run LR

Nifedipine (Procardia) (Calcium Channel Blocker)

HTN, angina: 10 mg PO
Peds: 0.25–0.5 mg/kg SL (puncture capsule), PO; maximum 10 mg
Contraindicated: ↓BP, concomitant IV beta blockers, HB
Side effects: dizziness, HA, N/V, ↓BP, ↑HR, flushed skin
Precautions: hepatic dysfunction, renal failure

Nitroglycerin (Nitrostat) (Antianginal, Nitrate)

CP, CHF, HTN: tablet/spray: 0.4 mg SL every 5 min, maximum three doses; **paste**: 1–2 in topical (chest wall); **infusion**: 10–20 mcg/min; may increase by 5–10 mcg/min every 5–10 min
Contraindicated: ↓BP (<90), severe ↓HR, severe ↑HR, Viagra within 24 hr, RV infarction
Side effects: ↓BP, ↑HR, syncope, HA, flushed skin
Precautions: do not mix with other medications

Nitroprusside (Nipride, Nitropress) (Vasodilator)

Hypertensive crisis: 0.1 mcg/kg/min; titrate upward every 3–5 min to desired effect
Peds: ≤40 kg: 1–8 mcg/kg/min; >40 kg: 0.1–5 mcg/kg/min
Contraindicated: ↓BP (<90), severe ↓HR, severe ↑HR, Viagra within 24 hr
Side effects: thiocyanate toxicity, ↓BP, CO_2 retention
Precautions: protect from light; drug metabolizes into cyanide

EMS DRUGS

Nitrous Oxide + Oxygen (Nitronox) (Analgesic)

Pain, anxiety: inhalation titrated to relief of symptoms

Peds: same as adults

Contraindicated: AMS, head injury, abdominal pain, shock
Side effects: dizziness, N/V, apnea, cyanosis
Precautions: invert tank several times before and during use

Norepinephrine (Levophed) (Sympathomimetic)

Cardiogenic shock; hypotension: 0.5–1 mcg/min; titrate to desired BP; maximum 30 mcg/min

Peds: 0.1–2 mcg/kg/min

Contraindicated: hypovolemia
Side effects: ↑BP, end-organ ischemia, arrhythmias
Precautions: avoid mixing with NS only or alkaline solutions
Extravasation: Treat with phentolamine (see Phentolamine this tab)

Ondansetron (Zofran) (Antiemetic)

Nausea: 4 mg IV, IO, IM

Peds: ≤**40 kg:** 0.1 mg/kg IV, IO; >**40 kg:** 4 mg IV, IO, IM

Contraindicated: hypersensitivity
Side effects: HA, drowsiness, weakness, abdominal pain, EPS
Precautions: liver impairment, pregnancy, lactation

Oxytocin (Pitocin) (Hormone)

Postpartum hemorrhage: 3–10 U IM or 10–40 U in 1000-mL NS or LR infused at 10–40 U/min; titrate to effect
Contraindicated: hypersensitivity, incomplete delivery
Side effects: Dysrhythmias, HTN, seizure, coma, ↓BP
Precautions: evaluate for multiple births

Pancuronium (Pavulon) Paralytic (Nondepolarizing)

RSI: 0.15 mg/kg slow IV, IO; *infusion: 0.01 mg/kg/hr*

Peds: ≥1 yr: 0.15 mg/kg IV, IO; **<1 yr:** 0.1 mg/kg IV, IO

Contraindicated: neuromuscular disease
Side effects: apnea, ↑HR, ↓BP, HTN, arrhythmias, salivation
Precautions: have intubation equipment ready
Onset: 3–5 min; **peak:** 5 min; **duration:** 45–60 min

Phenobarbital (Luminal) (Anticonvulsant)

Seizures: 15–18 mg/kg IV

Peds: ≥1 mo: 15–18 mg/kg IV; **<1 mo:** 15–20 mg/kg IV

Contraindicated: respiratory disease, comatose, ↓CNS
Side effects: ↓BP, ↓RR, N/V, somnolence, coma
Precautions: hepatic or renal dysfunction, drug abuse, elderly

EMS DRUGS

Phentolamine (Regitine)
(Alpha-Adrenergic Blocker)

Extravasation of dopamine, norepinephrine, phenylephrine: 5–10 mg in 10–15 mL of NS infiltrated into area of extravasation
Cocaine-induced HTN: 2.5–5 mg IV; repeat every 10–15 min
Peds: 0.1–0.2 mg/kg (maximum 10 mg) infiltrated same as adults
cocaine-induced HTN: 0.1 mg/kg IV (up to 5 mg/dose)
Contraindicated: hypersensitivity
Side effects: minimal when limited to infiltration
Precautions: must be given within 12 hr of extravasation

Phenytoin (Dilantin)
(Anticonvulsant)

Seizures: load: 15–20 mg/kg slow (<50 mg/min) IV (maximum 1 g)
Peds: load: 10–20 mg/kg slow (<5 mg/kg/min) IV
Contraindicated: ↓HR, second-/third-degree HB, hypoglycemia
Side effects: ↓BP, ↑RR, ↑HR, N/V, ↑CNS; CV collapse (rapid IV)
Precautions: hepatic/CV/renal failure; do not mix with dextrose

Potassium Chloride
(Mineral, Electrolyte)

Hypokalemia (serum K+ <2.5 mEq/L): 20 mEq/day IV (maximum 10 mEq/hr); (serum K+ <2 mEq/L): 40 mEq/day IV (maximum 20 mEq/hr)
Peds: 0.3–0.5 mEq/kg/hr IV (maximum 1 mEq/kg/hr)

Contraindicated: hyperkalemia, severe renal impairment, untreated Addison's disease, severe tissue trauma
Side effects: arrhythmias, abdominal pain, N/V, diarrhea, confusion, restlessness, weakness, irritation at IV site
Precautions: monitor HR, BP, and ECG throughout infusion; pain and tissue necrosis with extravasation; use infusion pump

Pralidoxime (2-PAM) (Cholinesterase Antidote)

Nerve agent/OPP exposure: 600 mg IM (via auto-injector). *Infusion: 1–2 g IV, IO over 15–30 min*

Peds: 20–50 mg/kg IV, IO over 15–30 min (same IM dose)

Contraindicated: none in nerve agent or OPP exposures
Side effects: ↑HR, ↑BP, N/V, weakness, laryngospasm
Precautions: not recommended in carbamate poisoning

Procainamide (Pronestyl) (Antiarrhythmic)

VT, PSVT refractory to adenosine, rapid a-fib with WPW, stable wide-complex tachycardia of uncertain type: 20 mg/min (up to 50 mg/min) IV, IO (maximum 17 mg/kg); *infusion: 1–4 mg/min IV, IO*

Peds: 15 mg/kg IV, IO over 30–60 min

Contraindicated: second- or third-degree HB, torsade de pointes, lupus, myasthenia gravis, digoxin toxicity
Side effects: ↓BP, widening QT, asystole, HA, N/V, flushed skin, seizure, ventricular arrhythmias
Precautions: discontinue for ↓BP or widening QT interval

Promethazine (Phenergan) (Antiemetic)

Nausea: 12.5–25 mg deep IM, PR, PO

Peds: 0.25–0.5 mg/kg IV, IM, PR, PO

Contraindicated: narcotic or alcohol-induced CNS depression
Side effects: AMS, sedation, EPS, excitability, dizziness
Precautions: HTN, seizure history, pediatrics, sleep apnea

Propofol (Diprivan) (Sedative, Anesthetic)

RSI: 2–2.5 mg/kg IV, IO or may be given in 25–50-mg increments; *infusion: 100–200 mcg/kg/min*

Peds: 2–3 mg/kg IV, IO

Contraindicated: egg or soy allergy, labor and delivery
Side effects: apnea, ↓BP, ↑HR, dizziness, HA, N/V, pain at site
Precautions: lipid metabolism disorders, increased ICP; use half the dose for elderly and debilitated Pts
Onset: 40 sec; **peak:** <1 min; **duration:** 3–5 min

Propranolol (Inderal) (Beta Blocker)

MI, UA, PSVT, a-fib, a-flutter, HTN: 0.1 mg/kg divided into three equal doses and given at 2–3-min intervals (maximum 1 mg/min)
Contraindicated: ↑HR, ↓BP, second- /third-degree HB, cocaine use
Side effects: ↓BP, dizziness, ↑HR, HA, N/V
Precautions: ↓BP with concomitant calcium channel blockers, history of bronchospasm, heart failure, arrhythmias

Reteplase (Retavase) (Fibrinolytic)

ACS (<12 hr old): 10 U slow IV (over 2 min); repeat in 30 min; flush IV with NS before and after each bolus
Contraindicated: see Ischemic CP Fibrinolytic Checklist in Tab 3
Side effects: BP, reperfusion arrhythmias, HA, ↑bleeding time, hemorrhage, flushing, urticaria
Precautions: Pts with severe renal or hepatic disease

Rocuronium (Zemuron) (Paralytic) (Nondepolarizing)

RSI: 0.6–1.2 mg/kg IV

Peds: 0.6–1.2 mg/kg IV

Contraindicated: known hypersensitivity
Side effects: apnea, ↓BP, ↓HR, bronchospasm, hyperkalemia
Precautions: ensure intubation and suction equipment available
Onset: 0.5–1 min; **peak:** 1–2 min; **duration:** 40+ min

Sodium Bicarbonate 8.4% (Alkalizing Agent, Buffer)

Hyperkalemia, OD (TCA, ASA, cocaine, diphenhydramine), acidosis, prolonged out-of-hospital cardiac arrest: 1 mEq/kg IV, IO; repeat 0.5 mEq/kg IV in 10 min

Peds: same as adults

Contraindicated: metabolic alkalosis, hypocalcemia, renal failure, as antidote to ingestion of strong mineral acid
Side effects: hypokalemia, metabolic alkalosis
Precautions: ensure adequate ventilation; do not mix with other drugs; flush IV before and after administration

EMS DRUGS

Sodium Nitrite (Cyanide Antidote)

Cyanide exposure: 300 mg IV, IO; repeat 150 mg IV, IO prn every 30 min
Peds: 10 mg/kg IV, IO; repeat 5 mg/kg IV, IO prn every 30 min

Contraindicated: asymptomatic exposures
Side effects: ↓BP, ↑methemoglobinemia
Precautions: ↓BP with rapid IV administration

Sodium Thiosulfate ($Na_2S_2O_3$) (Cyanide Antidote)

Cyanide exposure: 12.5 g IV, IO; repeat 6.25 g IV, IO prn
 Commonly used to prevent cyanide toxicity in Pts receiving medications containing cyanide (e.g., nitroprusside)

Peds: 400 mg/kg IV, IO; repeat 200 mg/kg IV, IO prn

Contraindicated: none in cyanide exposure
Side effects: psychosis, N/V, joint pain
Precautions: none in cyanide exposure

Streptokinase (Streptase) (Fibrinolytic)

ACS (<12 hr old): 1.5 million U/hr IV
Contraindicated: see Ischemic CP Fibrinolytic Checklist in Tab 3
Side effects: ↓BP, reperfusion arrhythmias, HA, ↑bleeding time, hemorrhage, flushing, urticaria
Precautions: Pts with severe renal or hepatic disease

Succinylcholine (Anectine) (Paralytic) (Depolarizing)

RSI: 1–2 mg/kg IV (2–4 mg/kg IM)

Peds: children: 1–1.5 mg/kg IV; **infants:** 2 mg/kg (IM: double IV dose); pre-treat with atropine 0.01–0.02 mg/kg IV, IO (minimum dose 0.1 mg, maximum dose 1 mg); IM dose 0.02 mg/kg

Contraindicated: history of MH; avoid use in conditions that may cause hyperkalemia (e.g., burns >24 hr after injury, trauma, prolonged bed rest, closed head injuries)

Side effects: muscle fasciculation, increased intragastric pressure, increased intracranial pressure, increased intraocular pressure, ↓BP, ↓HR, apnea, bronchospasm, hyperkalemia, malignant hyperthermia

Precautions: ensure intubation and suction equipment available

Onset: 0.5–1 min; **peak:** 1–2 min; **duration:** 4–10 min

Tenecteplase (TNKase) (Fibrinolytic)

ACS (<12 hr old): 30–50 mg IV bolus (weight-adjusted)
Contraindicated: see Ischemic CP Fibrinolytic Checklist in Tab 3
Side effects: ↓BP, reperfusion arrhythmias, HA, ↑bleeding time, hemorrhage, flushing, urticaria
Precautions: Pts with severe renal or hepatic disease

Tetracaine (Pontocaine) (Ophthalmic Anesthetic) (Topical)

Eye pain/irrigation: 1–2 gtt (0.5% solution) in each eye

Peds: Same as adults

Contraindicated: open eye injury
Side effects: burning, irritation
Precautions: not recommended for prolonged use

Thiamine (Vitamin B₁) (Vitamin)

Alcoholism, malnutrition: 100 mg slow IV, IM (given with D_5W).
Peds: 10–25 mg slow IV, IM (not recommended pre-hospital)

Contraindicated: hypersensitivity, alcohol intolerance
Side effects: ↓BP, N/V, anxiety, diaphoresis
Precautions: not recommended for routine use in AMS Pts

Tirofiban HCl (Aggrastat) (GP IIb/IIIa Platelet Inhibitor)

UA/NSTEMI ACS: 0.4 mcg/kg/min IV for 30 min, then 0.1 mcg/kg/min IV infusion for 48–96 hr
Contraindicated: active internal bleeding, neurovascular event, major surgery or trauma within 1 month, platelet count <150,000/mm³, concomitant use of another GB IIb/IIIa inhibitor
Side effects: increased bleeding and bruising, GI irritation
Precautions: increased chance of bleeding, adjust dose if creatinine clearance <30 mL/min

Vasopressin (Pitressin) (Vasopressor)

Cardiac arrest: 40 U IV, IO one-time dose (alternative to epinephrine)
Contraindicated: pregnancy, epilepsy, heart failure, asthma, CAD, allergy to beef or pork protein, renal failure with ↑BUN
Side effects: dizziness, HA, N/V, MI, CP, cardiac ischemia
Precautions: monitor ECG throughout therapy

Vecuronium (Norcuron) (Paralytic) (Non-Depolarizing)

RSI: 0.1–0.2 mg/kg IV
Peds: 0.1–0.2 mg/kg IV, IM
Contraindicated: known hypersensitivity
Side effects: ↓BP, ↑HR, ↓HR, dyspnea, flushed skin, urticaria
Precautions: ensure intubation and suction equipment available
Onset: 2–3 min; **peak:** 3–5 min; **duration:** 30–90 min

Verapamil (Calan, Isoptin) (Calcium Channel Blocker)

PSVT, rapid a-fib, a-flutter: 2.5–5 mg slow IV (over 2 min); repeat 5–10 mg IV every 15–30 min (maximum 20 mg)
Contraindicated: a-fib/a-flutter with WPW, VT or wide-complex tachycardia of uncertain type, second- or third-degree HB, ↓BP
Side effects: ↓BP, exacerbation of CHF, asystole, ↓HR, HB
Precautions: Pt on oral beta blockers; may give prophylactic calcium chloride (8–16 mg/kg IV) to counteract secondary ↓BP

EMS DRUGS

Rx/OTC MEDS

Prescription and OTC Medications

BRAND NAME (CAPS); generic (lower case): class [common uses]

abacavir (ZIAGEN): antiviral [HIV, AIDS]
abatacept (ORENCIA): antirheumatic [RA]
ABILIFY (aripiprazole): **psychotropic** [schizophrenia]
acamprosate (CAMPRAL): inhibits alcohol [alcoholism]
acarbose (PRECOSE): oral **hypoglycemic** [DM]
ACCOLATE (zafirlukast): **bronchodilator** [asthma]
ACCUNEB (albuterol): **bronchodilator** [asthma, COPD]
ACCUPRIL (quinapril): **ACE inhibitor** [HTN, CHF]
ACCURETIC (quinapril, HCTZ): **ACE inhibitor, diuretic** [HTN]
ACCUTANE (isotretinoin): [acne]
acebutolol (SECTRAL): **beta blocker** [HTN, CP, arrhythmias]
ACEON (perindopril): **ACE inhibitor** [HTN]
APAP (TYLENOL): non-narcotic analgesic [pain]
acetazolamide (DIAMOX): **diuretic, anticonvulsant** [seizures]
acetylcysteine (MUCOMIST): mucolytic [asthma, APAP OD]
acetylsalicylic acid (aspirin): analgesic, antiplatelet [pain, ACS]
ACIPHEX (rabeprazole): ↓gastric acid [gastric ulcers]
ACLOVATE (alclometasone): topical steroid [allergic rash]
acrivastine (SEMPREX-D): pseudoephedrine, antihistamine
ACTHREL (corticorelin ovine triflutate): [Cushing's syndrome]
ACTICIN CREAM (permethrin): scabicide [scabies]
ACTIFED (triprolidine, pseudoephedrine): antihistamine [allergies]
ACTIGALL (ursodiol): bile acid [gallstones]
ACTIQ (fentanyl): oral transmucosal **narcotic** [CA pain]
ACTIVELLA (estradiol, norethindrone): HRT [menopause]
ACTONEL (risedronate): Ca^{++} regulator [Paget's disease]
ACTOS (pioglitazone): oral **hypoglycemic** [DM]
ACULAR (ketorolac): NSAID [allergic conjunctivitis]
acyclovir (ZOVIRAX): antiviral [herpes, shingles, chickenpox]
ADALAT (nifedipine): **Ca-channel blocker** [CP, HTN]
adapalene (DIFFERIN): antiacne [acne]
ADDERALL (amphetamines): CNS stimulant [ADHD]
ADIPEX-P (phentermine): appetite suppressant [weight control]

ADOXA (doxycycline): antibiotic [infection]
ADRENALIN (epinephrine): **bronchodilator** [asthma]
ADVAIR (fluticasone, salmeterol): **bronchodilator** [asthma]
ADVICOR (lovastatin): antihyperlipidemic [hyperlipidemia]
ADVIL (ibuprofen): NSAID analgesic [pain]
AEROBID (flunisolide): steroid inhaler [asthma, bronchitis]
AEROLATE (theophylline): **xanthine bronchodilator** [COPD]
agalsidase beta (FABRAZYME): enzyme [Fabry's disease]
AGENERASE (amprenavir): antiretroviral [AIDS, HIV]
AGGRENOX (ASA, dipyridamole): antiplatelet [↓CVA risk]
AGRYLIN (anagrelide): antiplatelet [thrombocythemia]
AHCHEW (chlorpheniramine, phenylephrine, methscopalamine): antihistamine, decongestant [cold/flu]
AKINETON (biperiden): antiparkinsonian [EPS]
ALAMAST (pemirolast): anti-inflammatory [conjunctivitis]
albendazole (ALBENZA): anthelmintic [tapeworm]
ALBENZA (albendazole): anthelmintic [tapeworm]
albuterol (PROVENTIL): **bronchodilator** [asthma, COPD]
ALDACTAZIDE (HCTZ, spironolactone): **diuretic** [HTN]
ALDACTONE (spironolactone): potassium-sparing **diuretic** [HTN]
ALDARA (imiquimod): immune modifier [genital warts]
ALDOCLOR (methyldopa, chlorothiazide): **diuretic** [HTN]
ALDOMET (methyldopa): **antihypertensive** [HTN]
ALDORIL (methyldopa, HCTZ): **antihypertensive** [HTN]
ALDURAZYME (laronidase): enzyme [mucopolysaccaridosis]
ALESSE (levonorgestrel, estradiol): contraceptive [birth control]
ALEVE (naproxen): NSAID analgesic [pain]
alglucosidase (MYOZYME): enzyme [Pompe disease]
aliskiren (TEKTURNA): **antihypertensive** [HTN]
ALKERAN (melphalan): anticancer [multiple myeloma, ovarian CA]
ALLEGRA (fexofenadine): antihistamine [seasonal allergies]
allopurinol (ZYLOPRIM): ↓serum uric acid [gout]
ALORA (estradiol): HRT [menopause]
alosetron (LOTRONEX): antidiarrheal [IBS]
alprazolam (XANAX): **benzodiazepine** [anxiety]
Alprostadil (CAVERJECT): vasodilator [ED, PDA, PAD/PVD]
ALTABAX (retapamulin) anti-infective [MRSA impetigo]
ALTACE (ramipril): **ACE inhibitor** [HTN]

Rx/OTC MEDS

Rx/OTC MEDS

ALTOCOR (lovastatin): antihyperlipidemic [high cholesterol]

ALUPENT (metaproterenol): **bronchodilator** [COPD, asthma]

aluminum hydroxide (MAALOX): atacid [heartburn]

amantadine (SYMMETREL): antiviral, antiparkinsonian [flu, EPS]

AMARYL (glimepiride): oral **hypoglycemic** [DM]

AMBIEN (zolpidem): hypnotic [insomnia]

AMBISOME (amphotericin B): antifungal [fungal infections]

amcinonide (CYCLOCORT): steroid [pruritus, inflammation]

AMERGE (naratriptan): antimigraine [migraine HA]

AMEVIVE (alefacept): immunosuppressive [protein [psoriasis]

amifostine (ETHYOL): [protects kidneys during chemotherapy]

amikacin (AMIKIN): antibiotic [infections]

AMIKIN (amikacin): antibiotic [infections]

amiloride (MIDAMOR): **diuretic** [CHF, HTN]

amino acid (NEPHRAMINE): nutrient [uremia]

aminobenzoate (POTABA): antifibrotic [scleroderma, Peyronie's disease]

aminophylline: **bronchodilator** [COPD, asthma]

aminosalicylic acid (PASER): antibiotic [TB]

amiodarone (CORDARONE): **antiarrhythmic** [arrhythmias]

AMITIZA (lubiprostone): laxatives [constipation]

amitriptyline (ELAVIL): TCA [depression]

amlodipine (LOTREL): **Ca-channel blocker** [HTN, CP]

ammonium lactate (LAC-HYDRIN): moisturizer [xerosis]

AMMONUL (sodium phenylacetate): [hyperammonemia]

amoxapine (ASENDIN): TCA [depression]

amoxicillin (AMOXIL): antibiotic [infections]

AMOXIL (amoxicillin): antibiotic [infections]

Amphetamine (ADDERALL): stimulant [ADHD]

AMPHOGEL (aluminum hydroxide): antacid [indigestion]

amphotericin-B (FUNGIZONE): antifungal [infections]

ampicillin (omnipen): antibiotic [infections]

amprenavir (AGENERASE): antiretroviral [AIDS, HIV]

amylase (ARCO-LASE): digestive enzyme [GI disorders]

amylolytic enzymes (ARCO-LASE): digestive enzymes [GI s/s]

ANADROL-50 (oxymetholone): steroid, androgen [anemia]

ANAFRANIL (clomipramine): TCA [depression]

anagrelide (AGRYLIN): ↑platelet numbers [thrombocythemia]

ANALPRAM-HC (pramoxine): topical anesthetic [itching, pain]
ANAPLEX-DM (non-narcotic form of Anaplex HD [cold/flu]
ANAPLEX-HD (hydrocodone, phenylephrine, chlorpheniramine): narcotic, antitussive, decongestant, antihistamine [cold/flu]
ANAPROX (naproxen): NSAID [pain]
anastrozole (ARIMIDEX): estrogen inhibitor [breast CA]
ANCOBON (flucytosine): antifungal [infections]
ANDRODERM (testosterone): androgen, steroid [hypogonadism]
ANEXSIA (hydrocodone, APAP): narcotic [pain]
anidulafungin (ERAXIS): antifungal [Candida]
ANOLOR-300 (butalbital, APAP, caffeine): sedative [pain]
ANTABUSE (disulfiram): inhibits alcohol [alcoholism]
anthralin (MICANOL): antipsoriatic [psoriasis, alopecia]
ANTIVERT (meclizine): antiemetic [vertigo]
ANUSOL-HC (hydrocortisone): steroid [inflammation]
ANZEMET (dolasetron): antiemetic, antiemetic [nausea]
APAP (acetaminophen): non-narcotic analgesic [pain]
APHRODYNE (yohimbine): alpha blocker [impotence]
APIDRA (insulin): hypoglycemic [DM]
APRI (desogrestel, estradiol): contraceptive [birth control]
AQUAMEPHYTON (phytonadione): Vit. K [coagulation disorder]
ARALEN (chloroquine): antimalarial [malaria]
ARAMINE (metaraminol): vasoconstrictor [hypotension]
ARANESP (darbepoetin): increases RBCs [anemia, chemo]
ARAVA (leflunomide): antiarthritic, anti-inflammatory [RA]
ARCO-LASE PLUS (digestive enzymes, hyoscyamine, atropine, phenobarbital): [digestive disorders]
arfomoterol (BROVANA): bronchodilator [COPD]
ARICEPT (donepezil): cholinergic enhancer [AD]
ARIMIDEX (anastrozole): estrogen inhibitor [breast CA]
aripiprazole (ABILIFY): psychotropic [schizophrenia]
ARISTOCORT (triamcinolone): steroid [inflammation]
ARMOUR THYROID (thyroid tablets): HRT [hypothyroid]
ARRANON (nelarabine): antineoplastic [leukemia]
ARTHROTEC (diclofenac, misoprostol): NSAID [arthritis]
ASA (aspirin): analgesic, antiplatelet [pain, ACS]
ASACOL (mesalamine): anti-inflammatory [UC]
ascorbic acid (Vit. C): Vit. [dietary supplement]

Rx/OTC MEDS

Rx/OTC MEDS

ASPART (insulin): **hypoglycemic** [DM]
ASTELIN (azelastine): antihistamine [allergic rhinitis]
ASTRAMORPH (morphine): **narcotic** [pain]
ATACAND (candesartan): **antihypertensive** [HTN]
ATARAX (hydroxyzine): **sedative, tranquilizer** [urticaria, anxiety]
atenolol (TENORMIN): **beta blocker** [HTN, arrhythmias]
atenolol + chlorthalidone: **beta blocker, diuretic** [HTN]
ATIVAN (lorazepam): **benzodiazepine**, anxiolytic [anxiety]
atomoxetine (STRATTERA): stimulant [ADHD]
atovaquone (MEPRON): antiprotozoal [pneumonia]
ATROVENT (ipratropium): **bronchodilator** [COPD]
AUGMENTIN (amoxicillin, clavulanate): antibiotic [infection]
AVALIDE (irbesartan, HCTZ): **antihypertensive** [HTN]
AVANDAMET (metformin): oral **hypoglycemic** [DM]
AVANDIA (rosiglitazone): oral **hypoglycemic** [DM]
AVAPRO (irbesartan): **antihypertensive** [HTN]
AVELOX (moxifloxacin): antibiotic [bronchitis, pneumonia]
AVIANE (levonorgestrel, estradiol): contraceptive [birth control]
AVINZA (morphine): **narcotic** [pain]
AVITA CREAM (tretinoin): antiacne [acne]
AVODART (dutasteride): inhibits testosterone [BPH]
AVONEX (interferon): antiviral [MS]
AXERT (almotriptan): antimigraine [migraines]
AXID (nizatadine): histamine$_2$ blocker [gastric ulcers]
AYGESTIN (norethindrone): HRT [amenorrhea, endometriosis]
AZACTAM (aztreonam): antibiotic [infection, UTI]
AZASAN (azathioprine): immunosuppressant [RA, antirejection]
azathioprine (IMURAN): immunosuppressant [RA, antirejection]
azelaic acid (AZELEX): antimicrobial [acne]
azelastine (OPTIVAR): antihistamine [allergic conjunctivitis]
AZELEX (azelaic acid): antiacne cream [acne]
AZILECT (rasagiline) MAO inhibitor [Parkinson's]
azithromycin (ZITHROMAX): antibiotic [infection]
AZMACORT (triamcinolone): steroid [asthma, bronchitis]
AZOPT (brinzolamide): ↓intraocular pressure [glaucoma]
AZT (zidovudine): antiviral [HIV, AIDS]
AZULADINE (sulfasatazine): anti-inflammatory [arthritis, UC]
B and O (belladonna, opium): **narcotic**, antispasmodic [pain]

bacitracin zinc: topical antibiotic [infection]
bacitracin (bacitracin): antibiotic [infantile pneumonia]
baclofen: (LIORESAL) muscle relaxant [MS]
BACTROBAN (mupirocin): topical antibiotic [skin infection]
BACTROBAN NASAL (mupirocin): antibiotic [infection]
balsalazide (COLAZAL): anti-inflammatory [UC]
Banana Pack: 1-L IV bag of NS that contains multivitamins (gives the distinctive yellow color), thiamine and folic acid.
BARACLUDE (entecavir): antiviral [hepatitis B]
basiliximab (SIMULECT): antirejection [transplant]
beclomethasone (BECONASE, QVAR): steroid [asthma]
BECONASE (beclomethasone): steroid [asthma]
BEELITH (magnesium, pyridoxine): magnesium, Vit. B$_6$
belladonna (BELLADENAL): antispasmodic [IBS]
BENADRYL (diphenhydramine): antihistamine [allergies]
BENEMID (probenecid): ↓uric acid [gout]
benicar (olmesartan): angiotensin-II blocker [HTN]
BENTYL (dicyclomine): antispasmodic [GI tract spasms]
BENYLIN (diphenhydramine): antihistamine [allergies]
BENZAMYCIN (erythromycin, benzoyl peroxide): [acne]
benzoic acid (PROSED DS): antibiotic, antifungal [UTI]
benzonatate (TESSALON): non-narcotic antitussive [cough]
benzoyl peroxide (PANOXYL): antibiotic [acne]
benztropine (COGENTIN): anticholinergic [Parkinson's]
betamethasone (CELESTONE): steroid [inflammation]
BETAPACE (sotalol): **beta blocker** [CP, arrhythmias, HTN]
BETASERON (interferon): immunological [MS]
betaxolol (KERLONE): **beta blocker** [HTN]
bethanechol (URECHOLINE): vagomimetic [urinary retention]
BETOPTIC (betaxolol): **beta-blocker** eyedrops [glaucoma]
BEXTRA (valdecoxib): COX-2 inhibitor [pain]
BIAXIN (clarithromycin) antibiotic [infection]
bicalutamide (CASODEX): antiandrogen [prostate CA]
BICILLIN (penicillin): antibiotic [infection]
BIDIL (hydralazine/isosorbide): vasodilator/**nitrate** [heart failure]
BILTRICIDE (praziquantel): anthelmintic [schistosomiasis, flukes]
biperiden (AKINETON): anticholinergic [Parkinson's, EPS]

Rx/OTC MEDS

Rx/OTC MEDS

bisacodyl (DULCOLAX): laxative [constipation]
bismuth subsalicylate (PEPTO-BISMOL): [antidiarrheal]
bisoprolol (ZEBETA): **beta blocker** [HTN]
bisoprolol, HCTZ: **beta blocker, diuretic** [HTN]
bitolterol (TORNALATE): **bronchodilator** [asthma]
bivalirudin (ANGIOMAX): anticoagulant [CP]
BLEPHAMIDE (sulfacetamide, prednisolone): antibiotic, steroid [ocular infections]
BLOCADREN (timolol): **beta blocker** [CP, HTN, arrhythmia]
BONTRIL-PDM (phendimetrazine): stimulant [obesity]
botulinum toxin type-A (BOTOX): paralytic [strabismus]
BRAVELLE (urofollitropin): FSH [infertility]
BRETHINE (terbutaline): **bronchodilator** [COPD, asthma]
BREVIBLOC (esmolol): **beta blocker** [tachycardia, HTN]
BREVICON: oral contraceptive [birth control]
BREVOXYL-4 (benzoyl peroxide): antibiotic [acne]
brimonidine (ALPHAGAN): alpha agonist [glaucoma]
brinzolamide (AZOPT): ↓intraocular pressure [glaucoma]
bromocriptine (PARLODEL): dopamine agonist [Parkinson's]
bromfenac (XIBROM): NSAID eyedrops [postoperative eye pain]
brompheniramine (BROMFED): antihistamine [allergies]
BROVANA (arformoterol): **bronchodilator** [COPD]
budesonide (RHINOCORT): corticosteroid [allergic rhinitis]
bumetanide (BUMEX): **diuretic** [edema, CHF]
BUPAP (butalbital, APAP): **sedative**/analgesic [HA]
BUPRENEX (buprenorphine): **narcotic** [pain]
buprenorphine (BUPRENEX): **narcotic** [pain]
bupropion (WELLBUTRIN): antidepressant [depression]
BUSPAR (buspirone): antianxiety [anxiety disorders]
busulfan (MYLERAN): anticancer [leukemia]
butabarbital (PYRIDIUM): **barbiturate sedative**, antispasmodic
butalbital (FIORINAL): **barbiturate** muscle relaxant, **sedative**
butalbital, APAP, caffeine (FIORICET): **sedative**, analgesic
butenafine (MENTAX): antifungal [athlete's foot, ringworm]
butoconazole (GYNAZOLE-1): antifungal [yeast infections]
butorphanol (STADOL-NS): **narcotic** [pain]
BYETTA (exenatide): **hypoglycemic** [DM]

cabergoline (DOSTINEX): dopaminergic [hyperprolactinemia]
Ca-DTPA (pentetate Ca tri-Na): radiation protectant [exposure]
caffeine: stimulant [HA]
CALAN (verapamil): Ca-channel blocker [CP, HTN, PSVT, HA]
CALCET: Ca++ supplement
CALCET PLUS: Ca++ supplement
CALCIBIND (cellulose phosphate): binds Ca++ [hypercalcemia]
calcifediol (CALDEROL): Vit. D [hypocalcemia, bone disease]
CALCIFEROL (ergocalciferol): Vit. D [hypocalcemia, hypoparathyroidism, rickets osteodystrophy]
CALCIJEX (calcitriol): Vit. D [hypocalcemia, hypoparathyroidism]
calcipotriene (DOVONEX): Vit. D [psoriasis]
calcitonin-salmon (MIACALCIN): bone resorption inhibitor hormone [hypercalcemia, Paget's disease, osteoporosis]
calcitriol (ROCALTROL): Vit. D [hypocalcemia, bone disease, hypoparathyroidism]
calcium (CALCET): Ca++ supplement
CALCIUM GLUCONATE TABS (Ca++): mineral [hypocalcemia]
CAMILA (norethindrone): oral contraceptive [birth control]
CAMPRAL (acamprosate): inhibits alcohol [alcoholism]
CANASA (mesalamine): anti-inflammatory [UC, proctitis]
candesartan cilexetil (ATACAND): antihypertensive [HTN]
capecitabine (XELODA): antineoplastic [breast CA]
CAPITAL, Codeine (APAP, codeine): narcotic [pain]
captopril (CAPOTEN): ACE inhibitor [HTN, CHF]
CARAFATE (sucralfate): antiulcer [gastric ulcers]
carbamazepine (TEGRETOL): anticonvulsant [seizures]
CARBATROL (carbamazepine): anticonvulsant [seizures]
carbenicillin (GEOCILLIN): antibiotic [UTI]
carbetapentane (RYNATUSS): antitussive [coughs]
carbidopa (SINEMET): antidyskinetic [Parkinson's]
carbinoxamine (RONDEC): antihistamine [cold]
CARDIZEM (diltiazem): Ca-channel blocker [CP, HTN, PSVT]
CARDURA (doxazosin): alpha blocker [HTN, BPH]
carisoprodol (SOMA): muscle relaxant [spasm]
CARNITOR (levocarnitine): [carnitine deficiency]
carvedilol (COREG): alpha/beta blocker [CP, CHF, HTN]
casanthranol (PERI-COLACE): laxative [constipation]

Rx/OTC MEDS

CASODEX (bicalutamide): anticancer [prostate CA]
caspofungin (CANCIDAS): antifungal [fungal infection]
CASTELLANI PAINT: antiseptic [wound care]
CATAFLAM (diclofenac): NSAID analgesic [pain]
CATAPRES (clonidine): **antihypertensive** [HTN]
CAVERJECT (alprostadil): vasodilator [ED]
CECLOR (cefaclor): antibiotic [infection]
CEDAX (ceftibuten): antibiotic [infection]
cefaclor (CECLOR): antibiotic [infection]
cefadroxil (DURICEF): antibiotic [infection]
cefazolin (ANCEF): antibiotic [infection]
cefdinir (OMNICEF): antibiotic [infection]
cefixime (SUPRAX): antibiotic [infection]
CEFIZOX (ceftizomine): antibiotic [infection]
CEFOBID (cefoperazone): antibiotic [respiratory infections]
cefoperazone (CEFOBID): antibiotic [respiratory infections]
cefotaxime (CLAFORAN): antibiotic [infection]
cefotetan (CEFOTAN): antibiotic [infection]
cefoxitin (MEFOXIN): antibiotic [infection]
cefpodoxime (VANTIN): antibiotic [infection]
cefprozil (CEFZIL): antibiotic [infection]
ceftazidime (CEPTAZ): antibiotic [infection]
ceftibuten (CEDAX): antibiotic [infection]
CEFTIN (cefuroxime): antibiotic [infection]
ceftizoxime (CEFIZOX): antibiotic [infection]
ceftriaxone (ROCEPHIN): antibiotic [infection]
cefuroxime (CEFTIN): antibiotic [infection]
CEFZIL (cefprozil): antibiotic [infection]
CELEBREX (celecoxib): NSAID analgesic [arthritis]
celecoxib (CELEBREX): NSAID analgesic [arthritis]
CELEXA (citalopram): antidepressant [depression]
celicept (mycophenolate): immunosuppressant [transplants]
cellulase (ARCOLASE): digestant [GI disorders]
CELONTIN (methsuximide): **anticonvulsant** [seizures]
CENESTIN (estrogens): HRT [menopause]
cephalexin (KEFLEX): antibiotic [infection]
CEREBYX (fosphenytoin): **anticonvulsant** [seizures]
CEREZYME (imiglucerase): enzyme [Gaucher's disease]

172

CERUBIDINE (daunorubicin): antibiotic, anticancer [leukemia]
CERVIDIL (dinoprostone): hormone [cervical ripening]
CESAMET (nabilone): antiemetics [nausea]
cetirizine (ZYRTEC): antihistamine [allergic rhinitis, urticaria]
cevimeline (EVOXAC): **cholinergic** [Sjögren's syndrome]
CHANTIX (varenicline): nicotine agonists [smoking cessation]
CHEMET: lead chelator [lead poisoning]
CHIBROXIN (norfloxacin): antibiotic [conjunctivitis]
chloral hydrate (SOMNOTE): **sedative**
chlorambucil (LEUKERAN): alkylating [CA]
chlordiazepoxide: **benzodiazepine**
chlorophyllin (CHLORESIUM): healing, wound deodorizer
chloroquine (ARALEN): antimalarial [malaria]
chlorothiazide (DIURIL): **antihypertensive diuretic** [HTN]
chloroxylenol (GORDOCHOM): antifungal [ringworm]
chlorpheniramine (NALEXA): antihistamine [cold and allergy]
chlorpromazine (THORAZINE): phenothiazine [psychosis]
chlorpropamide (DIABINESE): oral **hypoglycemic** [DM]
chlorthalidone (HYGROTON): **antihypertensive**, **diuretic**
cholestyramine (PREVALITE): antihyperlipidemic [↑cholesterol]
choline (MEGA B): nutrient [dietary supplement]
chondroitin (ARTHRIFLEX): dietary supplement [joint pain]
CIALIS (tadalafil): phosphodiesterase inhibitor [ED]
cicleonide (OMNARIS): corticosteroid [allergic rhinitis]
ciclopirox (LOPROX): antifungal [Candida]
cidofovir (VISTIDE): antiviral [cytomegalovirus in AIDS]
cilastatin (PRIMAXIN): antibiotic [infection]
cilostazol (PLETAL): vasodilator, platelet inhibitor [leg cramps]
cimetidine (TAGAMET): histamine$_2$ blocker [gastric ulcers]
ciprofloxacin (CIPRO): antibiotic [infection]
citalopram (CELEXA): antidepressant [depression]
CITRACAL (Ca^{++}): mineral [dietary supplement]
citric acid (BICITRA): systemic alkalinizer [alkalinizes urine]
cladribine (LEUSTATIN): antineoplastic [leukemia]
CLAFORAN (cefotaxime): antibiotic [infection]
CLARAVIS (isotretinoin): anti-inflammatory [psoriasis]
clarithromycin (BIAXIN): antibiotic [infection]
CLARITIN (loratadine): non-drowsy antihistamine [allergies]

Rx/OTC MEDS

Rx/OTC MEDS

CLARITIN-D (loratadine, pseudoephedrine): antihistamine, decongestant [allergic rhinitis]
clemastine (TAVIST): antihistamine [allergy]
CLEOCIN (clindamycin): antibiotic [acne]
CLEOCIN VAGINAL CREAM (clindamycin): antibiotic [vaginosis]
clofarabine (CLOLAR): antineoplastic [leukemia]
CLOLAR (clofarabine): antineoplastic [leukemia]
CUMARA (estradiol) HRT [menopause]
clindamycin (CLEOCIN): antibiotic [infection]
CLINDETS (clindamycin): antibiotic [acne]
CLINORIL (sulindac): NSAID analgesic [arthritis]
clobetasol (TEMOVATE): steroid [dermatoses]
CLOBEX (clobetasol): steroid [dermatoses]
clofibrate (ATROMID-S): ↓ serum lipids
CLOMID (clomiphene): ovulatory stimulant [infertility]
clomiphene (CLOMID): ovulatory stimulant [infertility]
clomipramine (ANAFRANIL): **TCA** [depression]
clonazepam (KLONOPIN): **anticonvulsant** [seizures, anxiety]
clonidine (CATAPRES): **antihypertensive** [HTN]
clopidogrel (PLAVIX): antiplatelet [ACS, AMI, stroke]
clorazepate (TRANXENE): **anticonvulsant** [seizures, anxiety]
CLORPACTIN (oxychlorosene): antiseptic, antibiotic [infection]
CLORPRES (clonidine, chlorthalidone): **diuretic** [HTN]
clotrimazole (MYCELEX): antifungal [*Candida*]
clozapine (CLOZARIL): **antipsychotic** [schizophrenia]
CLOZARIL (clozapine): **antipsychotic** [schizophrenia]
COCAINE (cocaine HCl): mucous membrane anesthetic
codeine: **narcotic**, antitussive [pain, cough]
COGENTIN (benztropine): antiparkinsonian [EPS]
COGNEX (tacrine): cholinesterase inhibitor [AD]
COLACE (docusate): stool softener [constipation]
COLAZAL (balsalazide): anti-inflammatory [UC]
colchicine (COLBENEMID): antigout [gout]
colesevelam (WELCHOL): antihyperlipidemic [hyperlipidemia]
COLESTID (colestipol): antihyperlipidemic [hyperlipidemia]
colestipol (COLESTID): antihyperlipidemic [hyperlipidemia]
colistimethate (COLY-MYCIN M): antibiotic [pseudomonas]
colistin (CORTISPORIN-TC): antibiotic [ear infections]

174

COLY-MYCIN-M (colistimethate): antibiotic [pseudomonas]
COMBIPATCH (estradiol, norethindrone): estrogen [menopause]
COMBIVENT (albuterol, ipratropium): **bronchodilator** [asthma]
COMBIVIR (lamivudine, zidovudine): antiviral [HIV, AIDS]
COMPAZINE (prochlorperazine): phenothiazine antiemetic [n/v]
COMTAN (entacapone): COMT inhibitor [Parkinson's]
CONCERTA (methylphenidate): stimulant [ADHD, narcolepsy]
CONDYLOX (podofilox): antimitotic [anogenital warts]
conivaptan (VAPRISOL): vasopressin antagonist [↓ sodium]
COPAXONE (glatiramer): neurologic [MS]
COPEGUS (ribavirin): antiviral [hepatitis C]
CORDARONE (amiodarone): **antiarrhythmic** [VF, VT]
CORDRAN (flurandrenolide): steroid [inflammation]
CORDYMAX (cordyceps sinensis): dietary supplement [fatigue]
COREG (carvedilol): alpha/**beta blocker** [HTN, CHF, CP]
CORMAX (clobetasol): steroid [dermatoses]
CORTEF (hydroxycortisone): steroid [inflammation]
CORTIC (chloroxylenol, pramoxine, hydrocortisone): antiseptic, antifungal, steroid ear drops [ear infection]
CORTIFOAM (hydrocortisone): steroid [proctitis]
CORTISOL (hydrocortisone): steroid [inflammation]
cortisone (CORTONE): steroid [inflammation]
CORTISPORIN-TC (neomycin, hydrocortisone): antibiotic, steroid [ear infection]
CORTISPORIN (neomycin, polymyxin, hydrocortisone): antibiotic, steroid [infection]
CORTONE (cortisone): steroid [inflammation]
CORTROSYN (cosyntropin): ACTH stimulator [diagnosis of adrenocortical insufficiency]
CORVERT (ibutilide): **antiarrhythmic** [a-fib, a-flutter]
CORZIDE (bendroflumethiazide, nadolol): **beta blocker**, **diuretic** [HTN]
COSOPT (timolol, dorzolamide): **beta blocker** [glaucoma]
COUMADIN (warfarin): anticoagulant [thrombosis prophylaxis]
COVERA-HS (verapamil): **Ca-channel blocker** [HTN, CP]
COZAAR (losartan): **antihypertensive** [HTN]
CREON-5, 10, 20 (pancrelipase): pancreatic enzyme replacement
CRINONE 4%, 8% (progesterone): [infertility, amenorrhea]

Rx/OTC MEDS

CRIXIVAN (indinavir): protease inhibitor antiviral [AIDS]
cromolyn (INTAL): antiallergenic [asthma prophylaxis]
CRYSELLE (norgestrel, estradiol): contraceptive [birth control]
CUMARA (estradiol): estrogen [menopause]
CUPRIMINE (penicillamine): chelator, anti-inflammatory
  [Wilson's disease, arthritis, heavy metal toxicity]
CUTIVATE (fluticasone): topical steroid [dermatoses]
cyanocobalamin (Vit. B_{12}): [anemia]
cyclobenzaprine (FLEXERIL): skeletal muscle relaxant
CYCLOCORT (amcinonide): steroid [dermatitis, pruritus]
cyclosporine (SANDIMMUNE): immunosuppressant [transplant]
CYLERT (pemoline): stimulant [ADHD]
CYCLESSA (desogestrel, estradiol): oral contraceptive
CYMBALTA (duloxetine): antidepressant [depression]
cyproheptadine (PERIACTIN): antihistamine [allergies]
CYSTOSPAZ-M (hyoscyamine): urinary tract antispasmodic
cytarabine (CYTOSAR-U): antineoplastic [CA, leukemia]
CYTOMEL (liothyronine): thyroid hormone [hypothyroid]
CYTOTEC (misoprostol): antiulcer [buffers NSAIDs]
CYTOVENE (ganciclovir): antiviral [HIV, AIDS]
D-FETA-II (pseudoephedrine, guaifenesin): decongestant, expec-
  torant [cold and allergy]
d4T stavudine (ZERIT): antiviral [HIV]
D-ALLERGY (chlorpheniramine, phenylephrine, meth-
  scopolamine): antihistamine, decongestant [allergies]
DACOGEN (decitabine): antineoplastic [hematologic CA]
DALMANE (flurazepam): anxiolytic [insomnia]
DANTRIUM (dantrolene): skeletal muscle relaxant [MH, MS, CP]
dantrolene (DANTRIUM): skeletal muscle relaxant [MH, MS, CP]
dapsone: antibiotic drug [leprosy, dermatitis herpetiformis]
DARANIDE (dichlorphenamide): anhydrase inhibitor
  [glaucoma]
DARAPRIM (pyrimethamine): antiparasitic [malaria]
darifenacin (ENABLEX): anticholinergic [UTI]
darunavir (PREZISTA): antiviral [HIV]
DARVOCET-N (propoxyphene, APAP): **narcotic** [pain]
DARVON (propoxyphene): **narcotic** [pain]
DARVON Comp (propoxyphene, ASA, caffeine) **narcotic** [pain]

dasatinib (SPRYCEL): antineoplastic [leukemia]
DAYPRO (oxaprozin): NSAID [arthritis]
DDAVP (desmopressin): ADH [nocturia, diabetes insipidus]
ddC (HIVID, zalcitabine): antiviral [AIDS]
DECADRON (dexamethasone): steroid [inflammation]
decitabine (DACOGEN): antineoplastic [hematologic CA]
DECLOMYCIN (demeclocycline): antibiotic [infection]
DEFEN-LA (pseudoephedrine, guaifenesin): decongestant, expectorant [cold/flu]
deferasirox (EXJADE): iron chelator [iron toxicity]
deferoxamine (DESFERAL): iron chelator [iron toxicity]
delavirdine (RESCRIPTOR): antiviral [HIV]
deltasone (prednisone): steroid [inflammation]
DEMADEX (torsemide): **diuretic** [CHF, HTN, edema]
demeclocycline (DECLOMYCIN): antibiotic [infection]
DEMEROL (meperidine): **narcotic** [pain]
DEMSER (metyrosine): **antihypertensive** [pheochromocytoma]
DEMULEN: oral contraceptive [birth control]
DENAVIR (penciclovir): antiviral [herpes, cold sores]
DEPACON (divalproex): **anticonvulsant** [seizures]
DEPADE (naltrexone): **narcotic antagonist** [narcotic addiction]
DEPAKENE (valproic acid): **anticonvulsant** [seizures]
DEPAKOTE (divalproex): **anticonvulsant** [migraines, seizures]
DEPO-MEDROL (methylprednisolone): steroid [inflammation]
DEPO-PROVERA (medroxyprogesterone): contraceptive, anticancer [endometrial and renal CA, birth control]
DEPRENYL (selegiline): MAO inhibitor [Parkinson's]
DERMA-SMOOTHE/FS (fluocinolone): steroid [dermatitis]
DESFERAL (deferoxamine): iron chelator [iron toxicity]
desipramine (NORPRAMIN): **TCA** [depression]
desmopressin (DDAVP): antidiuretic [diabetes insipidus]
DESOGEN (desogestrel, estradiol): contraceptive [birth control]
desogestrel (DESOGEN): oral contraceptive [birth control]
desonide (DESOWEN): steroid [inflammation]
desoximetasone (TOPICORT): steroid [dermatitis]
DESOXYN (methamphetamine): stimulant
DETROL (tolterodine): antispasmodic [overactive bladder]
dexamethasone (DECADRON): steroid [edema, cerebral]

Rx/OTC MEDS

DEXEDRINE (dextroamphetamine): stimulant [ADHD]
dexmethylphenidate (FOCALIN): stimulant [ADHD]
dextroamphetamine (ADDERALL): stimulant [ADHD]
dextroamphetamine (DEXEDRINE): stimulant [ADHD]
dextromethorphan (DELSYM): cough suppressant [cold/flu]
dextrose (GLUCOSE): nutrient [hypoglycemia]
DEXTROSTAT (dextroamphetamine): stimulant [ADHD]
DIABETA (glyburide): oral **hypoglycemic** [DM]
DIABINESE (chlorpropamide): oral **hypoglycemic** [DM]
DIAMOX (acetazolamide): **diuretic**, **anticonvulsant** [glaucoma, CHF, seizures, mountain sickness]
diazepam (VALIUM): anxiolytic [anxiety, seizure]
DIBENZYLINE (phenoxybenzamine): alpha blocker [HA]
dichloralphenazone (MIDRIN): **sedative** [HA]
dichlorphenamide (DARANIDE): ↓ ocular pressure [glaucoma]
diclofenac (VOLTAREN): NSAID, analgesic [arthritis]
dicyclomine (BENTYL): anticholinergic [IC]
didanosine (VIDEX): antiviral [AIDS, HIV]
DIDRONEL (etidronate): bone metabolism regulator [Paget's disease]
diethylpropion (TENUA-TE): appetite suppressant [obesity]
difenoxin (MOTOFEN): antidiarrheal [diarrhea]
DIFFERIN (adapalene): topical retinoid [acne]
diflorasone (PSORCON): steroid [dermatoses]
DIFLUCAN (fluconazole): antifungal [yeast infection]
diflunisal (DOLOBID): NSAID analgesic
DIGITEK (digoxin): inotrope, **antiarrhythmic** [CHF, a-fibrillation]
digoxin (LANOXIN): cardiac glycoside [CHF, dysrhythmias]
dihydrocodeine (SYNALGOS-DC): **narcotic** [pain]
DILANTIN (phenytoin): **anticonvulsant**
DILATRATE SR (isosorbide): **nitrate** [CP]
DILAUDID (hydromorphone): **narcotic** [pain]
diltiazem (CARDIZEM): **Ca-channel blocker** [CP, HTN, PSVT]
dimenhydrinate (DRAMAMINE): antihistamine [allergies]
DIOCTYL (docusate): stool softener [constipation]
DIOVAN (valsartan): angiotensin II inhibitor [HTN]
DIOVAN-HCT (valsartan, HCTZ): Diovan with a **diuretic** [HTN]

DIPENTUM (olsalazine): anti-inflammatory [UC]
diphenhydramine (BENADRYL): antihistamine
diphenoxylate (LOMOTIL): anticholinergic [diarrhea]
diphenylhydantoin (DILANTIN): anticonvulsant [seizures]
dipotassium phosphate (URO-KP-NEUTRAL): urinary acidifier, antiurolithic [UTI, kidney stones]
DIPROLENE (betamethasone): steroid [dermatoses]
dipyridamole (PERSANTINE): vasodilator [CP]
dirithromycin (DYNABAC): antibiotic [infection]
disodium phosphate (URO-KP-NEUTRAL): urinary acidifier, antiurolithic [UTI, kidney stones]
disopyramide (NORPACE): antiarrhythmic [PVCs]
disulfiram (ANTABUSE): inhibits alcohol [alcoholism]
DITROPAN-XL (oxybutynin): anticholinergic, antispasmodic [dysuria, incontinence, urinary frequency]
DIURIL (chlorothiazide): antihypertensive, diuretic [HTN]
divalproex (DEPAKOTE): anticonvulsant [seizures]
docusate (DIALOSE): stool softener [constipation]
dolasetron (ANZEMET): antiemetic [nausea and vomiting]
DOLOBID (diflunisal): NSAID analgesic [pain]
DOLOPHINE (methadone): narcotic [pain]
donepezil (ARICEPT): cholinergic [AD]
DONNATAL (phenobarbital, belladonna): barbiturate sedative, antispasmodic [ulcers]
DOPRAM (doxapram): respiratory stimulant [COPD]
dornase alfa (PULMOZVME): lytic enzyme [cystic fibrosis]
DORYX (doxycycline): antibiotic [infection]
dorzolamlde (TRUSOPT): anhydrase inhibitor [glaucoma]
DOSTINEX (cabergoline): dopaminergic [hyperprolactinemia]
DOVONEX (calcipotriene): Vit. D [psoriasis]
doxazosin (CARDURA): alpha blocker [HTN, BPH]
doxepin (SINEQUAN): TCA [depression]
DOXIL (doxorubicin): antineoplastic [AIDS-related tumors]
doxorubicin (DOXIL): antineoplastic [AIDS-related tumors]
doxycycline (VIBRAMYCIN): antibiotic [infection]
doxylamine (UNISOM): antihistamine sedative [insomnia]
DRAMAMINE (dimenhydrate): antiemetic [nausea]
dronabinol (MARINOL): appetite stimulant [chemo, AIDS]

Rx/OTC MEDS

drotrecogin (XIGRIS) anti-infective [sepsis]
DTIC-DOME (dacarbazine): anticancer [melanomas, Hodgkin's]
duloxetine (CYMBALTA): antidepressant [depression]
DUONEB (ipratropium, albuterol): **bronchodilator** [COPD]
DURAGESIC (fentanyl): **narcotic** [pain]
DURAMORPH (morphine): **narcotic** [pain]
DURATUSS AM/PM PACK GP (guaifenesin, pseudoephedrine): decongestant, expectorant [cold/flu]
DURATUSS-G (guaifenesin): expectorant [cold/flu]
DYAZIDE (HCTZ, triamterene): **antihypertensive, diuretic** [HTN]
DYNABAC (dirithromycin): antibiotic [infection]
DYNACIN (minocycline): antibiotic [infection]
DYNACIRC CR (isradipine): **Ca-channel blocker** [HTN, CP]
DYRENIUM (triamterene): **diuretic,** potassium-sparing [CHF]
EC-NAPROSYN (naproxen): NSAID analgesic [arthritis, pain]
ECOTRIN (BAYOR): enteric-coated ASA, NSAID analgesic [pain]
eculizumab (SOLIRIS) hemostatic [nocturnal hemoglobinuria]
EDECRIN (ethacrynic acid): **diuretic** [CHF]
edrophonium (ENLON): anticholinesterase [myasthenia gravis]
EES (erythromycin): antibiotic [infection]
efavirenz (SUSTIVA): antiviral [HIV]
EFFEXOR (venlafaxine): antidepressant
ELAPRASE (idursulfase): enzyme [Hunter's syndrome]
ELDEPRYL (selegiline): MAO inhibitor [Parkinson's]
ELIMITE (permethrin): topical scabicidal [scabies, lice]
ELMIRON (pentosan): urinary tract analgesic [cystitis]
ELOCON (mometasone): topical steroid [inflammation]
Eloxatin (oxaliplatin): antineoplastic [colorectal CA]
ELSPAR (asparginase): antineoplastic [leukemia, sarcoma]
EMCYT (estramustine): anticancer [prostate CA]
EMGEL (erythromycin): antibiotic [infection]
EMLA (lidocaine, prilocaine): topical anesthetic
EMSAM (selegiline TD): MAO inhibitor [major depression]
EMTRIVA (emtricitabine): antiviral [HIV, AIDS]
ENABLEX (darifenacin): anticholinergic [UTI]
enalapril (VASOTEC): **ACE inhibitor** [HTN, CHF]
enalaprilat (VASOTEC): **ACE inhibitor** [HTN, CHF]

ENDOCET (oxycodone, APAP): **narcotic** [pain]
ENDODAN (hydrocodone, APAP): **narcotic** [pain]
ENJUVIA (plant-derived estrogen): HRT [menopause]
ENLON (edrophonium): anticholinesterase [myasthenia gravis]
ENLON-PLUS (edrophonium, atropine): anticholinesterase [myasthenia gravis]
ENPRESSE (levonorgestrel, ethinyl estradiol): contraceptive
entacapone (COMTAN) [Parkinson's]
entecavir (BARACLUDE): antiviral [hepatitis B]
ENTOCORT-EC (budesonide): steroid [inflammation]
ephedrine (RYNATUSS): **bronchodilator** [asthma, COPD]
EPIFOAM (hydrocortisone, pramoxine): anti-inflammatory, antipruritic, local anesthetic [dermatosis]
epinephrine (PRIMATENE MIST): **bronchodilator** [asthma]
EPIPEN (epinephrine): **bronchodilator** [anaphylaxis]
EPIVIR (lamivudine): antiviral [HIV]
EPIVIR HBV (lamivudine): antiviral [hepatitis B]
epoetin alfa (EPOGEN): increases RBC production [anemia]
EPOGEN (epoetin alfa): increases RBC production [anemia]
ERAXIS (anidulafungin): antifungal [*Candida*]
ERGAMISOL (levamisole): immunomodulator [colon CA]
ergocalciferol (CALCIFEROL): Vit. D [hypocalcemia, rickets, hypoparathyroidism, osteodystrophy]
erlotinib (TARCEVA): antineoplastic [lung CA]
ERRIN (norethindrone): oral contraceptive [birth control]
ERYC (erythromycin): antibiotic [infection]
ERYGEL (erythromycin): antibiotic [infection, acne]
ERYPED (erythromycin): antibiotic [infection]
ERY-TAB (erythromycin): antibiotic [infection]
erythromycin (EES): antibiotic [infection]
ESGIC (APAP, caffeine, butalbital): analgesic, **barbiturate** [HA]
ESKALITH (lithium): **tranquilizer** [mania, depression]
estazolam (PROSOM): **sedative/hypnotic** [insomnia]
ESTRACE (estradiol): estrogen [menopause]
ESTRADERM (estradiol): topical estrogen [menopause]
estradiol (CUMARA, EVAMIST): estrogen [menopause]
estramustine (EMCYT): antineoplastic [prostate CA]
ESTRATEST (estrogens, methyltestosterone): HRT [menopause]

Rx/OTC MEDS

ESTRING (estrogen): HRT [urogenital symptoms d/t menopause]

estrogens (ESTRATEST, methyltestosterone): HRT [menopause]

estropipate (ORTHO-EST): estrogens [menopause]

ESTROSTEP FE/21 (norethindrone): contraceptive [birth control]

eszopiclone (LUNESTA): **sedative/hypnotic** [insomnia]

ethacrynate (EDECRIN): **diuretic** [pulmonary edema]

ethacrynic acid (EDECRIN): **diuretic** [pulmonary edema]

ethinyl estradiol (ORTHO-NOVUM): contraceptive [birth control]

ethionamide (TRECATOR SC): antibiotic [TB]

ethosuximide (ZARONTIN): **anticonvulsant** [absence seizure]

etidronate (DIDRONEL): bone metabolism regulator [Paget's disease]

etodolac (LODINE): NSAID analgesic [arthritis]

etonorgestrel (IMPLANON): contraceptive [birth control]

etoposide (VEPESID): antineoplastic [testicular CA, lung CA]

EULEXIN (flutamide): antiandrogenic, anticancer [prostate CA]

EVAMIST (estradiol): estrogen [menopause]

EVISTA (raloxifene): [prevention of osteoporosis]

EVOXAC (cevimeline): **cholinergic** [Sjögren's syndrome (dry mouth)]

EXELON (rivastigmine): cholinesterase inhibitor [AD]

exenatide (BYETTA): **hypoglycemic** [DM]

EXJADE (deferasirox): iron chelator [iron toxicity]

EXTENDRYL (phenylephrine, methscopolamine, chlorpheniramine): decongestant, antihistamine [allergies]

EXUBERA (insulin inhalation powder): antidiabetic [DM]

FABRAZYME (agalsidase beta) enzyme [Fabry's disease]

FACTIVE (gemifloxacin): antibiotic [infection]

famciclovir (FAMVIR): antiviral [herpes]

famotidine (PEPCID): H_2 blocker, ↓gastric acid [gastric ulcers]

FAMVIR (famciclovir): antiviral [herpes]

FARESTON (toremifene): antiestrogen [breast CA, menopause]

felbamate (FELBATOL): **anticonvulsant** [seizures]

FELBATOL (felbamate): **anticonvulsant** [seizures]

FELDENE (piroxicam): NSAID analgesic

felodipine (PLENDIL): **Ca-channel blocker** [HTN, CP]

FEMARA (letrozole): estrogen inhibitor [breast CA]
FEMHRT (norethindrone, estradiol): HRT [osteoporosis]
fenofibrate (TRICOR): antihyperlipidemic [hyperlipidemia]
fenoprofen (NALFON): NSAID analgesic
fentanyl (DURAGESIC, FENTORA): narcotic [pain]
FENTORA (fentanyl): narcotic [pain]
FEROSOL: iron supplement [iron deficiency]
FERRLECIT (sodium ferric gluconate): hematinic [anemia]
ferrous fumarate (CHROMAGEN): iron supplement [anemia]
ferrous gluconate: iron supplement [iron deficiency]
ferrous sulfate: iron supplement [iron deficiency]
FERTINEX (urofollitin): follicle-stimulating hormone [infertility]
fexofenadine (ALLEGRA): antihistamine [allergies]
filgrastim (NEUPOGEN): white blood cell stimulator [CA, bone marrow transplant, chemotherapy]
finasteride (PROPECIA): dihydrotestosterone inhibitor [hair loss]
FLORICET (butalbital, APAP, caffeine): sedative, analgesic
FLAGYL (metronidazole): antimicrobial [infection]
flavocoxid (LIMBREL): nonopioid analgesic [osteoarthritis]
flecainide (TAMBOCOR): antiarrhythmic [PSVT, a-fib, VT]
FLEXERIL (cyclobenzaprine): skeletal muscle relaxant
FLOLAN (epoprostenol): vasodilator [pulmonary HTN]
FLOMAX (tamsulosin): alpha₁ blocker [enlarged prostate]
FLONASE (fluticasone): steroid [allergic rhinitis]
FLORICAL (fluoride, Ca^{++}): mineral supplement
FLOVENT (fluticasone): steroid [asthma]
FLOXIN (ofloxacin): antibiotic [infection]
floxuridine (FUDR): antineoplastic [GI/liver CA]
fluconazole (DIFLUCAN): antifungal [*Candida*]
flucytosine (ANCOBON): antifungal [*Candida*]
FLUDARA (fludarabine): antiviral, antimetabolite [leukemia]
fludarabine (FLUDARA): antiviral, antimetabolite [leukemia]
FLUMADINE (rimantadine): antiviral [influenza A]
flumazenil (ROMAZICON): benzodiazepine antagonist [benzodiazepine OD]
flunisolide (AEROBID): steroid [asthma]
fluocinolone (CAP EX): steroid [pruritis]
fluocinonide (LIDEX): steroid [pruritus]

Rx/OTC MEDS

Rx/OTC MEDS

FLUOROPLEX (fluorouracil): antineoplastic [CA]
fluorouracil (EFUDEX) [CA]
fluoxetine (PROZAC): antidepressant [depression, OCD]
fluphenazine: antipsychotic [schizophrenia, hallucinations]
flurandrenolide (CORDRAN): steroid [dermatosis]
flurazepam (DALMANE): sedative/hypnotic [insomnia]
flurbiprofen: NSAID analgesic [arthritis]
flutamide (EULEXIN): antiandrogenic; anticancer [prostate CA]
fluticasone (FLONASE): steroid [allergies]
fluvastatin (LESCOL): antihyperlipidemic [hyperlipidemia]
fluvoxamine (LUVOX): antidepressant [depression]
FOCALIN (dexmethylphenidate): stimulant [ADHD]
folic acid (VITAFOL-OB): vitamin coenzyme [anemia]
follitropin beta (FOLLISTIM): fertility hormone [ovulation]
FORTAMET (metformin): oral hypoglycemic [DM]
FORTAZ (ceftazidime): antibiotic [infection]
FORTOVASE (saquinavir): antiviral [HIV]
FOSAMAX (alendronate): bone loss inhibitor [osteoporosis]
foscarnet (FOSCAVIR): antiviral [herpes]
FOSCAVIR (foscarnet): antiviral [herpes]
fosfomycin (MONUROL): antibiotic [UTI]
FOSFREE (Ca++, iron): minerals [dietary supplement]
fosinopril (MONOPRIL): ACE inhibitor [HTN]
fosphenytoin (CEREBYX): anticonvulsant [seizures]
FOSRENOL (lanthanum): phosphate binders [renal failure]
FROVA (frovatriptan): antimigraine [migraine HA]
FUNGOID (clotrimazole): antifungal [fungal infection]
furosemide (LASIX): diuretic [CHF, HTN]
FUZEON (enfuvirtide): antiviral [HIV, AIDS]
gabapentin (NEURONTIN): anticonvulsant/analgesic [seizures, postherpetic neuralgia, herpes zoster, shingles]
GABITRIL (tiagabine): anticonvulsant [seizures]
galsufase (NAGLAZYME): enzyme [mucopolysaccharidosis VI]
ganciclovir (CYTOVENE): antiviral [HIV, AIDS]
GAVISCON (magnesium, aluminum): antacid, laxative
gemfibrozil (LOPID): antihyperlipidemic [hyperlipidemia]
GEMZAR (gemcitabine): antineoplastic [lung, pancreatic CA]

GENGRAF (cyclosporine): immunosuppressive [prevention of organ transplant rejection, RA, psoriasis]
GENOTROPIN (somatropin): growth stimulator [AIDS, growth disorders, wasting syndrome]
gentamicin (GARAMYCIN): antibiotic [infection]
GEOCILLIN (carbenicillin): antibiotic [infection]
GEODON (ziprasidone): **antipsychotic** [schizophrenia]
ginkgo (YINHSING): antiplatelet, CNS stimulant [various uses]
glatiramir (COPAXONE): modifies immune response [MS]
GLEEVEC (imatinib): anticancer [leukemia, GI CA]
GLIADEL WAFER (polifeprosan): oncolytic [malignant glioma]
glimepiride (AMARYL): oral **hypoglycemic** [DM]
glipizide (GLUCOTROL): oral **hypoglycemic** [DM]
glucagon (GLUCAGEN): hormone, glycogenolytic [hypoglycemia, Ca-channel and beta blocker OD]
GLUCOPHAGE (metformin): oral **hypoglycemic** [DM]
glucosamine (COSAMIN-DS): cartilage growth stimulator
GLUCOTROL (glipizide): oral **hypoglycemic** [DM]
GLUCOVANCE (glyburide, metformin): oral **hypoglycemic**
GLULISINE (insulin): **hypoglycemic** [DM]
glyburide (DIABETA): oral **hypoglycemic** [DM]
glycopyrrolate (ROBINUL): anticholinergic [gastric ulcers]
GLYNASE (glyburide): oral **hypoglycemic** [DM]
GLYSET (miglitol): oral **hypoglycemic** [DM]
GOLYTELY (polyethylene glycol, electrolytes): bowel preparation, laxative [GI procedures, acute iron OD in children]
GORDOCHOM (chloroxylenol): antifungal [ringworm]
goserelin (ZOLADEX): antineoplastic [prostate CA]
granisetron (KYTRIL): antiemetic [chemotherapy, n/v]
GRANULEX (trypsin, balsam of Peru, castor oil): [decubitus ulcers]
GRIFULVIN-V (griseofulvin): antifungal [ringworm]
gris-PEG (griseofulvin): antifungal [ringworm]
griseofulvin (FULVICIN): antifungal [ringworm]
guaifenesin (HYCOTUSS): expectorant [colds, bronchitis]
guanfacine (TENEX): **antihypertensive** [HTN]
GYNAZOLE-I (butoconazole): antifungal [yeast infections]
GYNODIOL (estradiol): HRT [menopause, osteoporosis]

Rx/OTC MEDS

HALCION (triazolam): **benzodiazepine** [insomnia]
HALDOL (haloperidol): **antipsychotic** [psychosis, hyperactivity]
halobetasol (ULTRAVATE): steroid [pruritus]
haloperidol (HALDOL): **antipsychotic** [psychosis, hyperactivity]
HCTZ (hydrochlorothiazide): **antihypertensive, diuretic** [HTN]
HEMOCYTE (iron): iron supplement [anemia]
HEP-FORTE (protein, vitamins, minerals): dietary supplement
hesperidin (PERIDIN-C): antioxidant [dietary supplement]
HEXALEN (altretamine): anticancer [ovarian CA]
HIVID (zalcitabine): antiviral [AIDS]
HUMALOG (insulin): **hypoglycemic** [DM]
HUMATROPE (somatropin): human growth hormone
HUMULIN N, HUMULIN R (insulin): **hypoglycemic** [DM]
HURRICAINE TOPICAL (benzocaine): topical anesthetic
HYCAMTIN (topotecan): antineoplastic [ovarian, hepatic CA]
HYCODAN (hydrocodone, homatropine): **narcotic** antitussive
HYCOMINE COMPOUND (hydrocodone, chlorpheniramine, APAP, caffeine, phenylephrine): **narcotic** antitussive, antihistamine, decongestant [colds, URI]
HYCOTUSS (hydrocodone, guaifenesin): **narcotic** antitussive, expectorant [cold/flu]
HYDRA-ZIDE (hydralazine, HCTZ): **diuretic** [HTN]
hydralazine (APRESOLINE): **antihypertensive** [HTN]
hydralazine/isosorbide (BIDIL): vasodilator/**nitrate** [heart failure]
hydrochlorothiazide (HCTZ): **antihypertensive, diuretic** [HTN]
hydrocodone: **narcotic** antitussive [cold/flu]
hydrocodone, APAP: **narcotic** [pain]
hydrocortisone (COATEF): steroid [inflammation]
HYDROCORTONE (hydrocortisone): steroid [inflammation]
HYDRODIURIL (HCTZ): **antihypertensive, diuretic** [HTN, edema]
hydromorphone (DILAUDID): **narcotic** [pain, cough]
HYDROQUINONE (MELANEX): [pigmentation disorders]
HYDROSTAT-IR (hydromorphone): **narcotic** [pain, cough]
hydroxychloroquine (PLAQUENIL): antimalarial [malaria]
hydroxypropyl (LACRISERT): ophthalmic lubricant [dry eyes]
hydroxyureas: anticancer, elastogenic [melanoma, leukemia, ovarian CA, sickle cell anemia]

hydroxyzine (ATARAX): **sedative, tranquilizer**, antihistamine
HYLAFORM (hyaluronic acid): antiwrinkle [facial wrinkles]
hylan (SYNVISC): artificial joint fluid [osteoarthritis]
hyoscyamine (CYSTOSPAS): antispasmodic [GI, urinary spasm]
HYTRIN (terazosin): **antihypertensive** [HTN]
HYZAAR (losartan/HCTZ): **antihypertensive** [HTN]
IBERET (iron, vitamins, mineral): vitamin, mineral supplement
ibuprofen (ADVIL): NSAID, analgesic [pain]
ibutilide (CORVERT): **antiarrhythmic** [a-fib, a-flutter]
idursulfase (ELAPRASE): enzyme [Hunter's syndrome]
ILETIN (insulin preparations): **hypoglycemic** [DM]
iloprost (VENTAVIS): **vasodilator** [pulmonary HTN]
imatinib (GLEEVEC): anticancer [leukemia, GI CA]
imipenem (PRIMAXIN): antibiotic [infection]
imipramine (TOFRANIL): **TCA** [depression]
imiquimod (ALDARA): immune system modifier [genital warts]
IMITREX (sumatriptan): [migraine HA]
IMODIUM AD (loperamide): antidiarrheal [diarrhea]
IMPLANON (etonorgestrel): contraceptive [birth control]
IMURAN (azathioprine): immunosuppressant [RA, antirejection]
INCRELEX (mecasermin): growth hormone [growth failure]
indapamide (LOZOL): **antihypertensive, diuretic** [HTN]
INDERAL (propranolol): **beta blocker** [dysrhythmias, HTN]
INDOCIN SR (indomethacin): NSAID analgesic [arthritis]
indomethacin (INDOCIN): NSAID analgesic [arthritis]
INFASURF (caltactant): surfactant [respiratory distress syndrome in premature infants]
INFERGEN (interferon alfacon$_1$): antiviral [hepatitis C]
infliximab (REMICADE): [Crohn's disease]
INH (isoniazid): antibiotic [TB]
INSPRA (eplerenone): aldosterone blocker [HTN]
insulin (HUMULIN): **hypoglycemic** [DM]
insulin inhalation powder (EXUBERA): antidiabetic [DM]
INTAL (cromolyn): anti-inflammatory [asthma]
INVEGA (paliperidone): **antipsychotic** [schizophrenia]
INVERSINE (mecamylamine): **antihypertensive**
INVIRASE (saquinavir): protease inhibitor antiviral [HIV, AIDS]
iodoquinol (YODOXIN): amebicide [intestinal infections]

Rx/OTC MEDS

IONAMIN (phentermine): stimulant [appetite suppression]
ipratropium (ATROVENT): **bronchodilator**
irbesartan (AVAPRO): **antihypertensive** [HTN]
isoniazid (RIFAMATE): antibiotic [TB]
isoproterenol (ISUPREL): sympathomimetic [bradycardia]
ISOPTIN-SR (verapamil): **Ca-channel blocker** [CP, HTN, PSVT]
isosorbide (ISORDIL): long-acting **nitrate** [CP]
ISUPREL (isoproterenol): sympathomimetic [bradycardia]
itraconazole (SPORANOX): antifungal [infection]
JANUVIA (sitagliptin) **antidiabetic** [DM]
JE-VAX (Japanese encephalitis vaccine) vaccine [encephalitis]
JOUVETTE (norethindrone): contraceptive [birth control]
JUNEL (norethindrone, estradiol): contraceptive [birth control]
K-DUR (potassium chloride): potassium supplement
K-PHOS (potassium phosphate): urinary acidifier [kidney
    stones]
K-TAB (potassium chloride): potassium supplement
KADIAN (morphine): **narcotic** [pain]
KALETRA (lopinavir, ritonavir): antiviral [HIV, AIDS]
kaolin, pectin (KAOPECTATE): stool binder [diarrhea]
KAOPECTATE (kaolin, pectin): stool binder [diarrhea]
KARIVA (desogrestel, estradiol): contraceptive [birth control]
kava-kava (YAGONA): **sedative/hypnotic** [anxiety]
KEFLEX (cephalexin): antibiotic [infection]
KEPIVANCE (palifermin): cytoprotective [adjunct to
    chemotherapy]
KEPPRA (levatiracetam): **anticonvulsant** [seizures]
KERLONE (betaxolol): **beta blocker** [HTN]
KETEK (telithromycin): antibiotic [bronchitis, pneumonia]
ketoconazole (NIZORAL): antifungal [infection]
ketoprofen (ORUDIS): NSAID [arthritis]
ketorolac (TORADOL): NSAID analgesic [pain, inflammation]
ketotifen (ZADITOR): antihistamine [allergic conjunctivitis]
kineret (anakinra): DMARD, interleukin$_1$ blocker [RA]
KIONEX (sodium polystyrene): [hyperkalemia]
KLARON (sulfacetamide): antibiotic [infection]
KLONOPIN (clonazepam): **benzodiazepine** [seizures]

KLOR-CON (KCl): potassium supplement
KOGENATE (antihemophilic factor viii) [hemophilia]
KRISTALOSE (lactulose): stool softener [constipation]
KRONOFED-A (pseudoephedrine, chlorpheniramine): decongestant, antihistamine [cold and allergy]
kunecatechins (VEREGEN): catechins [genital warts]
KUTRASE (digestive enzymes, hyoscamine, phenyltoloxamine): antispasmodic, sedative [indigestion]
KU-ZYME (digestive enzymes): [indigestion]
KWELL (lindane): parasiticide [lice, scabies]
KYTRIL (granisetron): antinauseant/antiemetic
labetalol (NORMODYNE): beta blocker [HTN, CP]
LAC-HYDRIN (ammonium lactate): moisturizer [xerosis]
lactulose (KRISTALOSE): laxative [constipation]
LAMICTAL (lamotrigine): anticonvulsant [seizures]
LAMISIL (terbinafine): antifungal [fungal infections]
lamivudine (EPIVIR): antiviral [HIV]
lamotrigine (LAMICTAL): anticonvulsant [seizures]
LANOXICAPS (digoxin): cardiac glycoside [CHF, dysrhythmias]
LANOXIN (digoxin): cardiac glycoside [CHF, dysrhythmias]
lansoprazole (PREVACID): ↓gastric acid [gastric ulcers]
lanthanum (FOSRENOL): phosphate binders [renal failure]
LANTUS (insulin): hypoglycemic [DM]
lapatinib (TYKERB) antineoplastic [breast CA]
LARIAM (mefloquine): antimalarial [malaria]
LASIX (furosemide): diuretic [HTN, CHF]
latanoprost (XALATAN): prostaglandin agonist [glaucoma]
leflunomide (ARAVA): antiarthritic, anti-inflammatory [RA]
lenalidomide (REVLIMID): antianemic [anemia]
LENTE, ULTRA LENTE (insulin): hypoglycemic [DM]
LESCOL (fluvastatin): antihyperlipidemic
LESSINA (levonorgestrel, ethinyl estradiol): contraceptive
LEUKERAN (chlorambucil): anticancer [leukemia, lymphoma]
leuprolide (LUPRON): HRT [endometriosis]
levalbuterol (XOPENEX): bronchodilator [COPD, asthma]
levamisole (ERGAMISOLE): immunostimulant [colon CA]
LEVAQUIN (levofloxacin): antibiotic [pneumonia]
levetiracetam (KEPPRA): anticonvulsant [seizures]

Rx/OTC MEDS

LEVATOL (penbutolol): **beta blocker** [HTN]
LEVBID (hyoscyamine): antispasmodic [gastric ulcers]
LEVEMIR (insulin detemir): **hypoglycemic** [DM]
LEVITRA (vardenafil): phosphodiesterase inhibitor [ED]
LEVLEN (levonorgestrel, estradiol): contraceptive [birth control]
levocetirizine (XYZAL): antihistamine [allergies]
levodopa (SINEMET): antidyskinetic [Parkinson's]
levofloxacin (LEVAQUIN): antibiotic [pneumonia]
levonorgestrel (NORPLANT): contraceptive [birth control]
LEVORA (levonorgestrel, estradiol): contraceptive [birth control]
levorphanol (LEVO-DROMORAN): **narcotic** [pain]
LEVOTHROID (levothyroxine): thyroid hormone [hypothyroid]
levothyroxine (SYNTHROID): thyroid hormone [hypothyroid]
LEVOXYL (levothyroxine): thyroid hormone
LEVSIN (hyoscyamine): antispasmodic [gastric ulcers]
LEXAPRO (escitalopram): SSRI antidepressant [depression]
LEXXEL (enalapril, felodipine): **Ca-channel blocker** [HTN]
LIBRIUM (chlordiazepoxide): anxiolytic, **sedative** [anxiety]
LIDEX (fluocinonide): steroid [pruritus]
LIFEPAK (multivitamins, minerals): dietary supplement
LIMBREL (flavocoxid): nonopioid analgesic [osteoarthritis]
LINCOCIN (lincomycin): antibiotic [infection]
lindane (KWELL): parasiticide [scabies]
LIORESAL (baclofen): muscle relaxant [MS]
liothyronine (CYTOMEL): thyroid hormone
liotrix (THYROLAR): thyroid hormone
LIPITOR (atorvastatin): antihyperlipidemic [hyperlipidemia]
lisdexamfetamine (VYVANSE): CNS stimulant [ADHD]
lisinopril (ZESTRIL): **ACE inhibitor** [HTN, CHF, AMI]
lisinopril, HCTZ (ZESTORETIC): **ACE inhibitor** [HTN, CHF, MI]
LISPRO (insulin): **hypoglycemic** [DM]
lithium (LITHOBID): antimanic [depression, mania]
LITHOBID (lithium): antimanic [depression, mania]
LO/OVRAL 28: oral contraceptive [birth control]
LOCOID (hydrocortisone): steroid [inflammation]
LODRANE (brompheniramine, pseudoephedrine): antihistamine, decongestant [cold/flu]

LOESTRIN 21, FE (norethindrone, estradiol): oral contraceptive
LOMOTIL (diphenoxylate, atropine): anticholinergic [diarrhea]
LONITEN (minoxidil): vasodilator, **antihypertensive** [HTN]
LONOX (diphenoxylate, atropine): anticholinergic [diarrhea]
loperamide (IMODIUM): antidiarrheal [diarrhea]
LOPID (gemfibroxil): antihyperlipidemic [hyperlipidemia]
lopinavir (KALETRA): antiviral [HIV, AIDS]
LOPRESSOR (metoprolol): **beta blocker** [HTN]
LOPROX (ciclopirox): antifungal [ringworm, *Candida*]
LORABID (loracarbef): antibiotic [sinusitis]
loratadine (CLARITIN): non-drowsy antihistamine [allergies]
lorazepam (ATIVAN): **benzodiazepine** [anxiety, seizure]
LORCET (hydrocodone, APAP): **narcotic** [pain]
LORTAB (hydrocodone, APAP): **narcotic** [pain]
losartan (COZAAR): **antihypertensive** [HTN]
LOTENSIN (benazepril): **ACE inhibitor** [HTN, CHF]
LOTREL (amlodipine, benazepril): **Ca-channel blocker** [HTN]
LOTRIMIN (clotrimazole): antifungal [infection]
LOTRISONE (clotrimazole, betamethasone): topical antifungal, steroid [infection, inflammation]
LOTRONEX (alosetron): antidiarrheal [IBS]
lovastatin (MEVACOR): antihyperlipidemic [hyperlipidemia]
loxapine (LOXITANE): **antipsychotic** [schizophrenia]
LOW-OGESTREL 28 (norgestrel, estradiol): oral contraceptive
LOXITANE (loxapine): **tranquilizer**
lubiprostone (AMITIZA): laxatives [constipation]
LUCENTIS (ranibizumab): ocular agent [macular degeneration]
LUMIGAN (bimatoprost): ↓ocular pressure [glaucoma]
LUNESTA (eszopiclone): **sedative/hypnotic** [insomnia]
LUPRON DEPOT (leuprolide): HRT [endometriosis]
MACROBID (nitrofurantoin): antibiotic [UTI]
MACRODANTIN (nitrofurantoin): antibiotic [UTI]
MACUGEN (pegaptanib): ocular agent [macular degeneration]
MAG-OX (magnesium): mineral, dietary supplement
magnesium chloride (SLOW-MAG): dietary supplement
MAGONATE (magnesium gluconate): [asthma, HTN]
MALARONE (atovaquone, proguanil): antimalarial [malaria]
malathion (OVIDE): organophosphate insecticide [head lice]

Rx/OTC MEDS

MARINOL (dronabinol): appetite stimulant [AIDS, chemo]
MATULANE (procarbazine): antineoplastic [Hodgkin's]
MAVIK (trandolapril): **ACE inhibitor** [HTN]
MAXAIR (pirbuterol): B² stimulant [asthma, COPD]
MAXALT (rizatriptan): antimigraine [migraine HA]
MAXIDEX (dexamethasone): steroidal eyedrops
MAXIDONE (hydrocodone, APAP): **narcotic** [pain]
MAXZIDE (triamterene, HCTZ): **antihypertensive, diuretic** [HTN]
MEBARAL (mephobarbital): **anticonvulsant** [seizures, anxiety]
mecasermin (INCRELEX): growth hormone [growth failure]
mechlorethamine (MUSTARGEN): antineoplastic [Hodgkin's]
meclizine (ANTIVERT): antiemetic [vertigo]
meclofenamate: NSAID [arthritis, pain, dysmenorrhea]
medroxyprogesterone: HRT [amenorrhea, endometriosis]
MEFOXIN (cefoxitin): antibiotic [infection]
MEGADOSE: vitamin, mineral complex
megestrol (MEGACE): appetite stimulant, antineoplastic [anorexia with AIDS, breast and endometrial CA]
melatonin (BEVITAMEL): sleep hormone [insomnia]
MELLARIL (thioridazine): **antipsychotic** [schizophrenia]
MENEST (estrogens): HRT [breast/prostatic CA, menopause]
MENTAX (butenafine): antifungal [ringworm, athlete's foot]
meperidine (DEMEROL): **narcotic** [pain]
MEPHYTON (Vit. K₁): [coagulation disorders]
meprobamate (MILTOWN): **tranquilizer**
MEPRON (atovaquone) antibiotic [*Pneumocystis carinii,* AIDS]
MERIDIA (sibutramine): stimulant [obesity]
mesalamine (ASACOL, CANASA, PENTASA, ROWASA): GI anti-inflammatory [UC]
MESTINON (pyridostigmine): anticholinesterase [myasthenia gravis]
METADATE-CD, ER (methylphenidate): stimulant [ADHD]
METAGLIP (glipizide, metformin): oral **hypoglycemic** [DM]
metaproterenol (ALUPENT): **bronchodilator** [COPD, asthma]
metformin (GLUCOPHAGE): oral **hypoglycemic** [DM]
methadone (DOLOPHINE): **narcotic** [pain]

METHADOSE (methadone): **narcotic** [pain]
methamphetamine (DESOXYN): stimulant [ADHD, obesity]
methazolamide: lowers intraocular pressure [glaucoma]
methenamine (URISED): antiseptic [UTI, cystitis]
methimazole (TAPAZOLE): antithyroid [hyperthyroidism]
methocarbamol (ROBAXIN): muscle relaxant [muscle spasm]
methotrexate: anticancer [psoriasis, RA]
methsuximide (CELONTIN): **anticonvulsant** [seizure]
methyclothiazide (AQUATENSEN): **diuretic** [HTN]
methyl aminolevulinate (METVIX): antineoplastic [keratosis]
methyldopa (ALDOMET): **antihypertensive** [HTN]
methylphenidate (RITALIN): stimulant [ADHD, narcolepsy]
methylprednisolone (MEDROL): steroid [inflammation]
metoclopramide (REGLAN): gastric emptying [heartburn, ulcers]
metolazone (ZAROXOLYN): **antihypertensive, diuretic** [HTN]
metoprolol (TOPROL-XL): **beta blocker** [CP, HTN, arrhythmias]
metronidazole (FLAGYL): antimicrobial [diarrhea]
METVIX (methyl aminolevulinate): antineoplastic [keratosis]
MEVACOR (lovastatin): antihyperlipidemic [hyperlipidemia]
mexiletine (MEXITIL): **antiarrhythmic** [arrhythmias]
MIACALCIN (calcitonin-salmon): hormone, bone resorption inhibitor [hypercalcemia, Paget's disease, osteoporosis]
micafungin (MYCAMINE): antifungal [*Candida*]
MICARDIS (telmisartan): **ACE inhibitor** [HTN]
miconazole (MONISTAT): antifungal [candidiasis]
MICRONASE (glyburide): oral **hypoglycemic** [DM]
MICROZIDE (HCTZ): thiazide **antihypertensive, diuretic** [HTN]
MIDAMOR (amiloride): potassium-sparing **diuretic** [HTN]
midazolam (VERSED): **benzodiazepine** [sedation, anxiety]
midodrine (PROAMATINE): vasopressor [postural hypotension]
MIDRIN (isomethoptene, dichloralphenazone, APAP): vasoconstrictor, **sedative**, analgesic [HA]
miglitol (GLYCET): oral **hypoglycemic** [DM]
milrinone (PRIMACOR): inotrope, vasodilator [CHF]
MINIPRESS (prazosin): alpha₁ blocker [HTN]
MINITRAN (transdermal nitroglycerin): **nitrate** [CP]
MINIZIDE (prazosin, polythiazide): **antihypertensive** [HTN]

Rx/OTC MEDS

Rx/OTC MEDS

MINOCIN (minocycline): antibiotic [infection]

minocycline (MINOCIN): antibiotic [infection]

minoxidil: **antihypertensive,** vasodilator [baldness, HTN]

MIRALAX (polyethylene glycol): laxative [constipation]

MIRAPEX (pramipexole): dopaminergic [Parkinson's]

mirtazapine (REMERON): antidepressant [depression]

misoprostol (CYTOTEC): antiulcer [gastric ulcers d/t NSAIDs]

MOBAN (molindone): **tranquilizer**

MOBIC (meloxicam): NSAID analgesic

modafinil (PROVIGIL): promotes wakefulness [narcolepsy]

MODURETIC (amiloride, HCTZ): **antihypertensive, diuretic** [HTN]

moexipril (UNIVASC): **ACE inhibitor** [HTN]

mometasone (ELOCON): topical steroid [inflammation]

MONOCAL (fluoride, Ca^{++}): mineral supplement

MONODOX (doxycycline): antibiotic [infection]

MONOKET (isosorbide mono**nitrate**): **nitrate** [CP]

MONOPRIL (fosinopril): **ACE inhibitor** [HTN]

MONUROL (fosfomycin): antibiotic [UTI]

morphine sulfate: **narcotic** [pain]

MOTOFEN (difenoxin, atropine): **narcotic,** antidiarrheal

MOTRIN (ibuprofen), NSAID [pain]

moxifloxacin (AVELOX): antibiotic [bronchitis, pneumonia]

MS CONTIN (morphine): **narcotic** [pain]

MS-IR (morphine): **narcotic** [pain]

MUSE URETHRAL SUPP. (alprostadil): vasodilator [ED]

MYCAMINE (micafungin): antifungal [*Candida*]

MYCOBUTIN (rifabutin): antibiotic [AIDS]

mycophenolate (CELLCEPT): immunosuppressant [transplant]

MYKROX (metolazone): **antihypertensive, diuretic** [HTN]

MYLANTA (Al, Mg, simethicone): antacid, antigas [indigestion]

MYLERAN (busulfan): anticancer [leukemia]

MYOZYME (alglucosidase): enzyme [Pompe's disease]

nabilone (CESAMET): antiemetics [nausea]

nabumetone (RELAFEN): NSAID [arthritis]

nadolol (CORGARD): **beta blocker** [HTN, CP, arrhythmias]

nafarelin (SYNAREL): gonadotropin-releasing hormone [endometriosis, precocious puberty, ↓gonadal steroids]

194

naftifine (NAFTIN): topical antifungal [fungal infections]
NAFTIN (naftifine): topical antifungal [fungal infections]
NAGLAZYME (galsulfase): enzyme [mucopolysaccharridosis]
nalbuphine (NUBAINE): **narcotic** [pain]
NALEX-A (chlorpheniramine, phenyltoloxamine, phenylephrine): antihistamine, **sedative**, decongestant [colds]
nalmefene (REVEX): narcotic antagonist [narcotic OD]
naloxone (NARCAN): narcotic antagonist [narcotic OD]
naltrexone (REVIA, VIVITROL): **narcotic** antagonist [alcoholism]
NAMENDA (memantine): NMDA antagonist [AD]
nandrolone (DECA-DURABOLIN): anabolic steroid, androgenizing hormone [anemia, breast CA]
naphazoline (NAPHCON): steroid [itchy, congested eyes]
NAPHCON-A (pheniramine, naphazoline): antihistamine, steroid [itchy, irritated eyes]
NAPRELAN (naproxen): NSAID analgesic [pain]
NAPROSYN (naproxen): NSAID analgesic [pain]
naproxen (EC-NAPROSYN): NSAID analgesic [pain]
naratriptan (AMERGE): antimigraine [migraine HA]
NARCAN (naloxone): narcotic antagonist [narcotic OD]
NARDIL (phenelzine): MAO inhibitor [depression, bulimia]
NASACORT-AO (triamcinolone): steroid [allergies]
NASAREL (flunisolide): steroid [rhinitis]
NASATAB-LA (guaifenesin, pseudoephedrine): expectorant, decongestant [cold/flu]
NASCOBAL (cyanocobalamin): Vit. B_{12} [anemia]
NASONEX (mometasone): steroid [allergic rhinitis]
NAVANE (thiothixene): **antipsychotic** [schizophrenia]
NAVELBINE (vinorelbine): antineoplastic [breast CA, Hodgkin's]
NECON (norethindrone, estradiol): contraceptive [birth control]
nedocromil (TILADE): anti-inflammatory [asthma]
nefazodone (SERZONE): antidepressant [depression]
nelarabine (ARRANON): antineoplastic [leukemia]
nelfinavir (VIRACEPT): protease inhibitor antiviral [HIV]
NEMBUTAL (pentobarbital): **anticonvulsant** [seizures]
NEODECADRON (neomycin, dexamethasone): antibiotic, steroid [infection, inflammation]

Rx/OTC MEDS

Rx/OTC MEDS

neomycin (NEOSPORIN): antibiotic [infection]

NEORAL (cyclosporine): immunosuppressant [organ transplant]

NEOSPORIN (polymyxin, bacitracin, neomycin): antibiotic ointment [infection]

NEPHROCAPS (vitamins): supplement [uremia, renal failure]

NEPTAZANE (methazolamide): ↓aqueous humor [glaucoma]

NESACAINE (chloroprocaine): local anesthetic [pain]

NESTABS CBF (multivitamins): vitamin supplement

NEUPRO (rotigotine TD): antiparkinson [Parkinson's]

NEURONTIN (gabapentin): **anticonvulsant** [see gabapentin]

nevirapine (VIRAMUNE): antiviral [HIV, AIDS]

NEXAVAR (sorafenib): antineoplastic [renal cell carcinoma]

NEXIUM (esomeprazole): ↓gastric acid [ulcers, esophagitis]

niacin (Vit. B-3): antihyperlipidemic [hyperlipidemia]

NIACOR (niacin): Vit. B_3 [hyperlipidemia, B_3 deficient]

NIASPAN (niacin): Vit. B_3 [hyperlipidemia, B_3 deficient]

nicardipine (CARDENE): **Ca-channel blocker** [CP, HTN]

NICODERM (nicotine): [smoking cessation]

NICOMIDE (vitamins, minerals): [acne]

NICORETTE (nicotine chewing gum): [smoking cessation]

nicotine (NICOTROL NS): [smoking cessation]

nicotinic acid (niacin): Vit. B_3 [hyperlipidemia]

NICOTROL PATCH (nicotine): [smoking cessation]

nifedipine (PROCARDIA): **Ca-channel blocker** [CP, HTN]

NIFEREX-150 (iron): mineral [anemia]

NILANDRON (nilutamide): antiandrogen [prostate CA]

nilutamide (NILANDRON): antiandrogen [prostate CA]

nimodipine (NIMOTOP): **Ca-channel blocker** [migraine HA]

NIMOTOP (nimodipine): **Ca-channel blocker** [migraine HA]

NIPENT (pentostatin): chemotherapeutic [leukemia]

nisoldipine (SULAR): **Ca-channel blocker** [HTN]

NITRO-DUR (nitroglycerin): long-acting **nitrate** [CP]

nitrofurantoin (FURADANTIN): antibiotic [UTI]

nitroglycerin (NITROSTAT): vasodilator [CP]

NITROLINGUAL SPRAY (nitroglycerin): **nitrate** [CP]

NITROSTAT (nitroglycerin): vasodilator [CP]

NIX (permethrin): parasiticide [head lice]

nizatidine (AXID): histamine₂ blocker [gastric ulcers]
NIZORAL (ketoconazole): antifungal [yeast infection]
NOLVADEX (tamoxifen): anticancer [breast CA]
NORCO C-III (hydrocodone, APAP): **narcotic** [pain]
NORDETTE: oral contraceptive [birth control]
NORDITROPIN (somatropin): growth hormone [growth failure]
norethindrone (NORINYL): contraceptive [birth control]
NORFLEX (orphenadrine): non-narcotic analgesic [pain]
norfloxacin (NOROXIN): antibiotic [UTI]
NORGESIC (orphenadrine): non-narcotic analgesic [pain]
norgestimate (ORTHO-CYCLEN 21): contraceptive [birth control]
norgestrel (LO/OVRAL): oral contraceptive [birth control]
NORINYL: oral contraceptive [birth control]
NORITRATE (metronidazole): antibiotic [rosacea, acne]
NORMODYNE (labetalol): **beta blocker** [HTN, CP]
NOROXIN (norfloxacin): antibiotic [UTI]
NORPACE (disopyramide): **antiarrhythmic** [PVCs]
NORPLANT (levonorgestrel): contraceptive [birth control]
NORPRAMIN (desipramine): **TCA** [depression]
NOR-QD (norethindrone): contraceptive [birth control]
NORTREL (norethindrone, ethinyl): contraceptive [birth control]
nortriptyline (PAMELOR): **TCA** [depression]
NORVASC (amlodipine): **Ca-channel blocker** [HTN, CP]
NORVIR (ritonavir): protease inhibitor antiviral [HIV]
NOVANTRONE (mitoxantrone): antineoplastic [prostate CA, MS]
NOVOLIN (insulin): **hypoglycemic** [DM]
NOVOLOG (insulin): **hypoglycemic** [DM]
NOXAFIL (posaconazole): antifungals [*Candida*]
NPH (insulin): **hypoglycemic** [DM]
NUBAIN (nalbuphine): **narcotic** [pain]
NULEV (hyoscyamine): antispasmodic [gastric ulcers]
NUMORPHAN (oxymorphone): **narcotic** [pain]
NUPRIN (ibuprofen): NSAID analgesic [pain]
nystatin (MYCOSTATIN): antifungal [infection]
NYSTOP (nystatin): antifungal [*Candida*]
OBEGYN: vitamins, minerals [prenatal supplement]
octreotide (SANDOSTATIN): antidiarrheal, growth inhibitor [carcinoid tumor, acromegaly, intestinal tumors, diarrhea]

Rx/OTC MEDS

OCUFLOX (of loxacin): opthalmic anti-infective [conjunctivitis]
ofloxacin (FLOXIN): antibiotic [infection]
olanzapine (ZYPREXA): **antipsychotic** [psychosis]
olopatadine (PATANOL): antihistamine [conjunctivitis]
olsalazine (DIPENTUM): salicylate [UC]
OMACOR (omega-3-acid): antihyperlipidemia [hyperlipidemia]
omalizumab (XOLAIR): **bronchodilator** [COPD, asthma]
omega-3-acid (OMACOR): antihyperlipidemia [hyperlipidemia]
omeprazole (PRILOSEC): ↓gastric acid [gastric ulcers, GERD]
OMNICEF (cefdinir): antibiotic [pneumonia, bronchitis]
OMNIHIST LA (chlorpheniramine, phenylephrine, methsco-
    polamine): antihistamine, decongestant [cold]
ONCASPAR (pegaspargase): oncolytic [leukemia]
ondansetron (ZOFRAN): antiemetic [n/v]
ONTAK (denileukin diftitox): antineoplastic [T-cell lymphoma]
OPANA (oxymorphone): **narcotic** [pain]
oprelvekin (NEUMEGA): platelet factor [thrombocytopenia]
OPTICROM (cromolyn): antihistamine [conjunctivitis, keratitis]
OPTIVAR (azelastine): antihistamine [allergic conjunctivitis]
ORAMORPH-SR (morphine sulfate): **narcotic** [pain]
ORAP (pimozide): **antipsychotic** [motor and phonic tics]
ORENCIA (abatacept): antirheumatic [RA]
ORINASE (tolbutamide): oral **hypoglycemic** [DM]
Orlistat (XENICAL): lipase inhibitor [obesity]
Orphenadrine (NORFLEX): analgesic, anticholinergic [pain]
ORPHENGESIC (orphenadrine, ASA, caffeine): analgesic [pain]
ORTHO EVRA (norelgestromin): contraceptive [birth control]
ORTHO TRI-CYCLEN-21, 28: oral contraceptive [birth control]
ORTHO-CEPT 21, 28: oral contraceptive [birth control]
ORTHO-CYCLEN-21, 28: oral contraceptive [birth control]
ORTHO-EST (estropipate): estrogen [menopause, osteoporosis]
ORTHO-NOVUM: oral contraceptive [birth control]
OS-CAL: Ca⁺⁺, Vit. D supplement [dietary supplement]
OVCON: oral contraceptive [birth control]
OVIDE (malathion): **OPP** insecticide [head lice]
OVRAL: oral contraceptive [birth control]
OVRETTE (norgestrel): oral contraceptive [birth control]

198

oxandrolone (OXANDRIN): anabolic steroid [osteoporosis]
oxaprozin (DAYPRO): NSAID [arthritis]
oxazepam (SERAX): **benzodiazepine** [ETOH withdrawl]
oxcaribazepine (TRILEPTAL): **anticonvulsant** [seizures]
oxiconazole (OXISTAT): antifungal [fungal skin infections]
OXISTAT (oxiconazole): topical antifungal [fungal infection]
OXSORALEN (methoxsalen): photosensitizer [repigmenting]
oxybutynin (DITROPAN): anticholinergic [urinary incontinence]
oxycodone (PERCODAN): **narcotic** [pain]
oxycodone w/APAP (TYLOX): **narcotic** [pain]
oxycodone/ASA: **narcotic**, aspirin [pain]
OXYCONTIN (oxycodone): **narcotic** [pain]
OXYFAST (oxycodone): **narcotic** [pain]
OXYTROL (oxybutynin): antispasmodic [urinary incontinence]
OXYIR (oxycodone): **narcotic** [pain]
oxymetholone (ANADROL-50): anabolic steroid [anemia]
oxymorphone (OPANA, NUMORPHAN): **narcotic** [pain]
oxytetracycline (TERRAMYCIN): antibiotic [infection]
PACERONE (amiodarone): **antiarrhythmic** [arrhythmias]
palifermin (KEPIVANCE): cytoprotective [adjunct to chemo]
paliperidone (INVEGA): **antipsychotic** [schizophrenia]
paclitaxel (TAXOL): anticancer [ovarian CA]
palivizumab (SYNAGIS): antiviral [respiratory syncytial virus]
PALLADONE (hydromorphone): **narcotic** [pain, cough]
pamabrom (WOMEN'S TYLENOL): analgesic, **diuretic** [PMS]
PAMELOR (nortriptyline): **TCA** [depression]
pancrelipase (CREON-5): digestive enzyme [pancreatitis, CF]
PANHEMATIN (hemin): porphyrin inhibitor [porphyria]
panitumumab (VECTIBIX): antineoplastic [colorectal CA]
pantoprazole (PROTONIX): ↓gastric acid [gastric ulcers]
papain (ACCUZYME): débriding [ulcers, burns]
PARAPLATIN (carboplatin): anticancer [ovarian CA]
paricalcitrol (ZEMPLAR): Vit. D [hyperparathyroidism]
PARLODEL (bromocriptine): dopamine agonist [Parkinson's]
PARNATE (tranylcypromine): MAO inhibitor [depression]
paroxetine (PAXIL): SSRI antidepressant [depression, PTSD]
PASER (aminosalicylic acid): bacteriostatic [TB]

Rx/OTC MEDS

Rx/OTC MEDS

PATANOL (olopatadine): [allergic conjunctivitis]
PAXIL (paroxetine): SSRI antidepressant [depression]
PCE (erythromycin): antibiotic [infection]
PEDI-DRI (nystatin): antifungal antibiotic [fungal infection]
PEDIAFLOR (fluoride): mineral [osteoporosis, dental caries]
PEDIAPRED (prednisolone): steroid [allergies, arthritis, MS]
PEDIAZOLE: antibiotic [infection]
PEGANONE (ethotoin): **anticonvulsant** [seizures]
pegaptanib (MACUGEN): ocular agent [macular degeneration]
pegaspargase (ONCASPAR): oncolytic [leukemia]
PEGASYS (peginterferon alfa-2a): antiviral [hepatitis C]
pemirolast (ALAMAST): anti-inflammatory [conjunctivitis]
pemoline (CYLERT): stimulant [ADHD, narcolepsy]
penbutolol (LEVATOL): **beta blocker** [HTN, CP]
penciclovir (DENAVIR): antiviral [herpes, cold sores]
penicillamine (CUPRIMINE): chelator, antirheumatic [arthritis,
   heavy metal poisoning, cystinuria, Wilson's disease]
penicillin: antibiotic [infection]
PENTASA (mesalamine): GI anti-inflammatory [UC]
pentazocine (TALWIN): **narcotic** [pain]
pentazocine/APAP: **narcotic** [pain]
pentazocine, Naloxone (TALWIN NX): **narcotic** [pain]
pentetate Ca tri-Na (Ca-DTPA): radiation protectant [exposure]
pentetate Zn tri-Na (Zn-DTPA): radiation protectant [exposure]
pentobarbital (NEMBUTAL): **sedative/hypnotic** [insomnia]
pentosan (ELMIRON): urinary tract analgesic [bladder pain]
pentostatin (NIPENT): chemotherapy, antibiotic [leukemia]
pentoxifylline (TRENTAL): hemorrheologic [PVD]
PEPCID (famotidine): H_2 blocker, ↓gastric acid [gastric ulcers]
PERCOCET (oxycodone, APAP): **narcotic** [pain]
PERCODAN (oxycodone, ASA): **narcotic** [pain]
PERDIEM (psyllium): bulk-forming laxative [constipation]
pergolide (PERMAX): dopamine receptor stimulation
   [Parkinson's]
PERI-COLACE (casanthranol, docusate): laxative [constipation]
PERIACTIN (cyproheptadine): antihistamine [allergies]
PERIDIN C (vitamins, antioxidants): dietary supplement

perindopril (ACEON): **ACE inhibitor** [HTN]
PERIOSTAT (doxycycline): antibiotic [infection]
PERMAX (pergolide): dopamine receptor stimulation [Parkinson's]
permethrin lotion (ELI MITE): parasiticide [head lice]
perphenazine (TRILAFON): phenothiazine, major **tranquilizer**
PERSANTINE (dipyridamole): vasodilator [CVA, CP]
PFIZERPEN (penicillin): antibiotic [infection]
phenazopyridine (PYRIDIUM): analgesic [bladder pain]
phenelzine (NARDIL): MAO inhibitor [depression, bulimia]
PHENERGAN (promethazine): antiemetic, **sedative** [n/v]
pheniramine (NAPHCON-A): antihistamine [irritated eyes]
phenobarbital: **barbiturate sedative**, **anticonvulsant** [seizures]
phenoxybenzamine (DIBENZVUNE): α-blocker [HTN, sweating]
phentermine (ADIPEX-P): amphetamine [obesity]
phenyl salicylate (PROSED): analgesic [UTI, cystitis, urethritis]
phenylephrine (NEO-SYNEPHRINE): decongestant [colds]
PHENYTEK (phenytoin): **anticonvulsant** [seizures]
phenytoin (DILANTIN): **anticonvulsant** [seizures]
phosLo (Ca^{++}): phosphate reducer [renal failure]
PHOTOFRIN (porfimer): antineoplastic [esophageal, lung CA]
PHRENILIN (butalbital, APAP): **barbiturate** analgesic [pain]
phytonadione (AQUAMEPHYTON): Vit. K [coagulation disorders]
pilocarpine (SALAGEN): **cholinergic** [dry mouth, Sjögren's syndrome]
PIMA (potassium iodide): expectorant [asthma, bronchitis]
pimozide (ORAP): **antipsychotic** [Tourette's syndrome]
pindolol (VISKEN): **beta blocker** [HTN, CP]
pioglitazone (ACTOS): oral **hypoglycemic** [DM]
piperacillin (PIPERACIL): antibiotic [infection]
pirbuterol (MAXAIR): **bronchodilator** [asthma, COPD]
piroxicam (FELDENE): NSAID analgesic [arthritis]
PLAN-B TABS (levonorgestrel): contraceptive [birth control]
PLAQUENIL (hydroxychloroquine): antimalarial [malaria]
PLAVIX (clopidogrel): platelet inhibitor [MI, atherosclerosis]
PLENDIL (felodipine): **Ca-channel blocker** [HTN, CP]
PLETAL (cilostazol): vasodilator, platelet inhibitor [leg cramps]

Rx/OTC MEDS

plicamycin (MITHRACIN): antineoplastic [testicular tumors]
PNEUMOTUSSIN (guaifenesin, hydrocodone): expectorant, **narcotic** antitussive [cold/flu]
PODOCON-25 (podophyllin): cytotoxic [venereal warts]
podofilox (CONDYLOX): destroys warts [anogenital warts]
podophyllin (PODOCON-25): cytotoxic [genital warts]
polymyxin (NEOSPORIN): antibiotic ointment [infection]
polythiazide (RENESE): **antihypertensive**, **diuretic** [CHF, HTN]
POLYTRIM (trimethoprim, polymyxin): antibiotic [infection]
PONSTEL (mefenamic acid): NSAID analgesic [pain]
porfimer (PHOTOFRIN): cytotoxic [esophageal CA, lung CA]
PORTIA (levonorgestrel): oral contraceptive [birth control]
posaconazole (NOXAFIL): antifungals [*Candida*]
POTABA (aminobenzoate): antifibrotic [scleroderma]
potassium bicarbonate (KLOA-CON/EF): potassium supplement
potassium chloride (K-TAB): potassium supplement
potassium citrate (UROCIT-K): ↑urinary pH [kidney stones]
potassium iodide (chelated mineral): iodine supplement
potassium phosphate (K-PHOS): urinary acidifier [kidney stones]
pramipexole (MIRAPEX): dopamine agonist [Parkinson's]
pramlintide (SYMLIN): **hypoglycemic** [DM]
PRAMOSONE (hydrocortisone, pramoxine): steroid [dermatosis]
pramoxine (ANALPRAM-HC): topical anesthetic [itching, pain]
PRANDIN (repaglinide): oral **hypoglycemic** [DM]
PRAVACHOL (pravastatin): antihyperlipidemic [hyperlipidemia]
pravastatin (PRAVACHOL): antihyperlipidemic [hyperlipidemia]
PRAVIGARD (pravastatin, ASA): statin antihyperlipidemic, antiplatelet [hyperlipidemia plus ASA therapy]
PRAX (pramoxine): topical anesthetic [itching, pain]
praziquantel (BILTRICIDE): antiparasitic [liver flukes]
prazosin (MINIPRESS): alpha$_1$ blocker, vasodilator [HTN]
PRECOSE (acarbose): delays digestion of carbohydrates [DM]
prednisolone (ORAPRED): steroid [inflammation, allergy]
prednisone (DELTASONE): steroid [inflammation, allergy]
PREFEST (estradiol, norgestimate): HRT [menopause]

202

PRELONE SYRUP (prednisolone): steroid [inflammation]
PRELU-2 (phendimetrazine): amphetamine [obesity]
PREMARIN: estrogens [menopause]
PREMPHASE (estrogens): HRT [menopause, osteoporosis]
PREMPRO (estrogens): HRT [menopause]
PRENATE (vitamins): prenatal vitamins [dietary supplement]
PREPIDIL (dinoprostone): cervical ripening [induction of labor]
PREVACID (lansoprazole): ↓gastric acid [gastric ulcers]
PREVALITE (cholestyramine): antihyperlipidemic [hyperlipidemia]
PREVPAC (lansoprazole, amoxicillin, clarithromycin): inhibits gastric secretion, antibiotic [duodenal ulcers]
PREZISTA (darunavir): antiviral [HIV]
PRIALT (ziconotide): Ca-channel blocker, analgesic [pain]
PRIFTIN (rifapentine): antibiotic [TB]
prilocaine (EMLA): local anesthetic [analgesia]
PRILOSEC (omeprazole): ↓gastric acid [gastric ulcers]
PRIMATENE MIST (epinephrine): bronchodilator [asthma]
PRIMATENE TABS (theophylline, ephedrine, phenobarbital): xanthine bronchodilator [asthma]
PRIMAXIN (imipenem, cilastatin): antibiotic [infection]
Primidone (MYSOLINE): anticonvulsant [seizures]
PRINIVIL (lisinopril): ACE inhibitor [HTN, CHF]
PRINZIDE (lisinopril, HCTZ): antihypertensive [HTN]
PROAMATINE (midodrine): vasopressor [hypotension]
Pro-Banthine (propantheline): anticholinergic [gastric ulcers]
probenecid (BENEMID): ↑uric acid secretion [gout]
procainamide (PROCANBID): antiarrhythmic [PVCs]
PROCANBID (procainamide): antiarrhythmic [PVCs]
procarbazine (MATULANE): antineoplastic [Hodgkin's]
PROCARDIA XL (nifedipine): Ca-channel blocker [CP, HTN]
prochlorperazine (COMPAZINE): phenothiazine antiemetic [n/v]
PROCOMIL (yohimbine): adrenergic antagonist [ED]
PROCRIT (epoetin alfa): ↑RBC production [anemia, renal failure]
PROCTOCORT (hydrocortisone): steroid [inflammation, itching]

Rx/OTC MEDS

PROCTOCREAM, FOAM (hydrocortisone): [see Proctocort]

progesterone (CRINONE): fertility hormone

PROGRAF (tacrolimus): immunosuppressant [transplants]

PROLASTIN: alpha$_1$ proteinase inhibitor [emphysema]

promethazine (PHENERGAN): **sedative**, antiemetic [n/v]

PROMETRIUM (progesterone): fertility hormone [infertility, amenorrhea, endometrial hyperplasia]

propafenone (RYTHMOL): **beta blocker** [PSVT, a-fib]

propantheline (Pro-Banthine): anticholinergic [gastric ulcers]

PROPECIA (finasteride): dihydrotestosterone inhibitor [baldness]

propoxyphene (DARVON): **narcotic** [pain]

propranolol (INDERAL): **beta blocker** [HTN, dysrhythmias]

PROSCAR (finasteride): [BPH]

PROSEDIDS (methenamine, phenyl salicylate, methylene blue, benzoic acid, atropine, hyoscyamine): bactericidic [UTI]

PROSOM (estazolam): hypnotic [insomnia]

PROSTIN-E2 (dinoprostone): oxytocic [benign hydatiform mole]

protease (ARCO-LASE): digestive enzyme [poor digestion]

PROTONIX (pantoprazole): PPI [gastric ulcers]

protriptyline (VIV ACTIL): **TCA** [depression]

PROVENTIL (albuterol): **bronchodilator** [asthma]

PROVERA (medroxyprogesterone): HRT [amenorrhea]

PROVIGIL (modafinil): promotes wakefulness [narcolepsy]

PROZAC (fluoxetine): heterocyclic antidepressant [depression]

pseudoephedrine (HALOTUSSIN): decongestant [colds]

PSORCON E (diflorasone): steroid [dermatoses]

psyllium (METAMUCIL): fiber laxative [constipation]

PULMICORT (budesonide): steroid [asthma]

PULMOZYME (domase alfa or DNase): lytic enzyme [CF]

PURINETHOL (mercaptopurine): antileukemia [leukemia]

pyrazinamide (RIFATER): antibiotic [TB]

PYRIDIUM (phenazopyridine): analgesic [bladder pain]

pyridostigmine (MESTINON): anticholinesterase [myasthenia gravis]

pyridoxine (Vit. B$_6$): vitamin [dietary supplement, INH poisoning, sideroblastic anemia, neonatal seizures]

pyrilamine (ATROHIST): antihistamine [colds, allergies]
pyrimethamine (DARAPRIM): antiparasitic [malaria]
quetiapine (SEROQUEL): **antipsychotic** [psychosis]
quinapril (ACCUPRIL): **ACE inhibitor** [HTN, CHF]
quinapril (Quinaretic): **ACE inhibitor**, **diuretic** [HTN]
QUINARETIC (quinapril-HCTZ): ACE inhibitor, **diuretic** [HTN]
QUINIDEX (quinidine): **antiarrhythmic** [dysrhythmias]
quinidine gluconate, sulfate: **antiarrhythmic** [dysrhythmias]
quinine: antimalarial [malaria]
quinupristin, dalfopristin (SYNERCID): antimicrobials [infection]
QUIXIN (levofloxacin): ocular anti-infective [conjunctivitis]
QVAR (beclomethasone): steroid anti-inflammatory [asthma]
raloxifene (EVISTA): [prevention of osteoporosis]
ramelteon (ROZEREM): **sedative/hypnotic** [insomnia]
ramipril (ALTACE): **ACE inhibitor** [HTN]
RANEXA (ranolazine): antianginal [angina]
ranibizumab (LUCENTIS): ocular agent [macular degeneration]
ranitidine (ZANTAC): histamine$_2$ blocker [gastric ulcers]
ranolazine (RANEXA): antianginal [angina]
RAPAMUNE (sirolimus): immunosuppressant [antirejection]
rasagiline (AZILECT) MAO inhibitor [Parkinson's]
REBETROL (ribavirin): antiviral [hepatitis C]
REBETRON (interferon-α, ribavirin): antiviral [hepatitis C]
rebif (interferon-β$_{1a}$): antiviral [MS]
RECOMBINATE (factor VIII): clotting [hemophilia]
REGLAN (metoclopramide): [heartburn, gastric ulcers]
REHYDRALYTE (glucose, sodium, potassium): oral electrolytes
RELAFEN (nabumetone): NSAID [arthritis]
RELENZA (zanamivir) antiviral [influenza]
RELPAX (eletriptan): antimigraine [migraine HA]
REMERON (mirtazapine): antidepressant [depression]
REMICADE (infliximab): [Crohn's disease]
REMINYL (galantamine): acetylcholinesterase inhibitor [AD]
RENACIDIN antiurolithic [urinary tract stones]
RENAGEL (sevelamer): phosphate binder [renal failure]
RENESE (polythiazide): **antihypertensive, diuretic** [CHF, HTN]
RENOVA (tretinoin): antiacne [acne]

Rx/OTC MEDS

repaglinide (PRANDIN): stimulates release of insulin [DM]
REPRONEX (mentropins): fertility drug [infertility]
REQUIP (ropinirole): dopaminergic [Parkinson's]
RESCRIPTOR (delavirdine): antiviral [HIV, AIDS]
RESTASIS (cyclosporine): immunosuppressant [dry eyes]
RESTORIL (temazepam): **benzodiazepine**
RESTYLANE (hyaluronan): anti-inflammatory [facial wrinkles]
retapamulin (ALTABAX) anti-infective [MRSA impetigo]
RETIN-A (tretinoin): antiacne [acne, facial wrinkles]
RETROVIR (zidovudine): antiviral [HIV, AIDS]
REVIA (Naltrexone): narcotic antagonist [alcoholism]
REVLIMID (lenalidomide): antianemic [anemia]
REYATAZ (atazanavir): protease inhibitor, antiviral [HIV, AIDS]
RHINOCORT (budesonide): corticosteroid [allergic rhinitis]
ribavirin (REBETROL): antiviral [viral infections]
riboflavin (Vit. B_2): Vit. supplement
RIFADIN (rifampin): antibiotic [TB, meningitis]
RIFAMATE (rifampin, isoniazid): antibiotic [TB]
rifampin (RIFADIN): antibiotic [TB, meningitis]
rifapentine (PRIFTIN): antibiotic [TB]
RIFATER (isoniazid, rifampin, pyrazinamide): antibiotic [TB]
rifaximin (XIFAXAN): anti-infective [traveler's diarrhea, *E. coli*]
RILUTEK (riluzole): [amyotrophic lateral sclerosis]
RIMACTANE (rifampin): antibiotic [TB, meningitis]
risedronate (ACTONEL): bone stabilizer [Paget's disease]
RISPERDAL (risperidone): **antipsychotic** [schizophrenia]
risperidone (RISPERDAL): **antipsychotic** [schizophrenia]
RITALIN (methylphenidate): stimulant [ADHD, narcolepsy]
ritonavir (NORVIR): antiviral [HIV, AIDS]
rivastigmine (EXELON): cholinesterase inhibitor [AD]
R-MS (morphine sulfate): **narcotic** suppository [pain]
ROBAXIN (methocarbamol): **sedative** [muscle spasm, pain]
ROBINUL (glycopyrrolate): anticholinergic [gastric ulcers]
ROBITUSSIN (guaifenesin): expectorant [cough, cold]
ROCALTROL (calcitriol): Vit. D [hypocalcemia, bone disease]
ROCEPHIN (ceftriaxone): antibiotic [infection]
ROFERON-A (interferon): [AIDS, Kaposi's sarcoma, leukemia]
ROGAINE (minoxidil): topical hair growth [baldness]

ROMAZICON (flumazenil): benzodiazepine antagonist [benzodiazepine OD]
ropinirole (REQUIP): dopaminergic [Parkinson's]
rosiglitazone (AVANDIA): oral **hypoglycemic** [DM]
rotigotine TD (NEUPRO): antiparkinson [Parkinson's]
ROWASA (mesalamine): anti-inflammatory [UC, proctitis]
ROXANOL-100 (morphine): **narcotic** [pain]
ROXICET (oxycodone, APAP): **narcotic** [pain]
ROXICODONE (oxycodone): **narcotic** [pain]
ROZEREM (ramelteon): **sedative/hypnotic** [insomnia]
ROZEX (metronidazole): antibiotic, antiprotozoal [rosacea]
RUM-K (potassium): potassium supplement
RYNATAN (phenylephrine, chlorpheniramine, pyrilamine): antihistamine, decongestant [cold/flu]
RYNATUSS: antitussive, antihistamine [cold/flu]
RYTHMOL (propafenone): **antiarrhythmic** [VT, a-fib]
SAIZEN (somatropin): growth hormone
SALAGEN (pilocarpine): parasympathomimetic [glaucoma]
salicylic acid (SAL-ACID): removes warts [warts]
salmeterol (SEREVENT): **bronchodilator** [asthma, COPD]
SALPLANT Gel (salicylic acid): removes warts [warts]
SANDIMMUNE (cyclosporine): immunosuppressant [transplant]
SANDOSTATIN (octreotide): antidiarrheal [diarrhea]
saquinavir (FORTOVASE): antiviral [HIV, AIDS]
SARAFEM (fluoxetine): antidepressant [premenstrual dysphoric disorder, depression, panic disorder, bulemia]
SARAPIN (pitcher plant): analgesic [sciatica, neuritis, neuralgia]
scopolamine (DONNATAL): antispasmodic, **sedative** [n/v]
SEASONALE (levonorgestrel, estradiol): oral contraceptive
SEDAPAP (butalbital, APAP): **sedative**/analgesic [tension HA]
selegiline (ELDEPRYL): MAO inhibitor [Parkinson's]
selegiline TD (EMSAM): MAO inhibitor [major depression]
selenium (SELSUN BLUE): mineral [seborrhea, dandruff]
SEMPREX-D (acrivastine, pseudoephedrine): antihistamine
senna extract (SENOKOT): laxative [constipation]
SENOKOT (senna fruit extract): laxative [constipation]
SENOKOT-S (senna, docusate): laxative [constipation]

Rx/OTC MEDS

Rx/OTC MEDS

SENOKOT XTRA (senna extract): laxative [constipation]
SEPTRA (trimethoprim, sulfamethoxazole): antibiotic [infection]
SERENTIL (mesoridazine): **tranquilizer**
SEREVENT (salmeterol): **bronchodilator** [asthma, COPD]
SEROPHENE (clomiphene): induces ovulation [infertility]
SEROQUEL (quetiapine): **antipsychotic** [schizophrenia]
SEROSTIM (somatropin): HRT [end-stage AIDS]
sertraline (ZOLOFT): antidepressant [depression, OCD]
SERZONE (nefazodone): antidepressant [depression]
sildenafil (VIAGRA): phosphodiesterase inhibitor [ED]
SILVADENE (silver sulfadiazine): topical antimicrobial [burns]
SIMPLY COUGH (dextromethorphan): antitussive [cough]
SINEMET (carbidopa, levodopa): antidyskinetic [Parkinson's]
SINEQUAN (doxepin): **TCA** [depression]
SINGULAIR (montelukast): [asthma]
SINUVENT (phenylpropanolamine, guaifenesin): decongestant, expectorant [cold/flu]
sitagliptin (JANUVIA) **antidiabetic** [DM]
SKELAXIN (metaxalone): **sedative**, analgesic [pain, anxiety]
SLO-NIACIN (niacin): antihyperlipidemic [hyperlipidemia]
sodium oxybate (XYREM): promotes wakefulness [narcolepsy]
sodium phenylacetate (AMMONUL): [hyperammonemia]
solifenacin (VESICARE): anticholinergic [overactive bladder]
SOLIRIS (eculizumab) hemostatic [nocturnal hemaglobinuria]
SOMA (carisoprodol): **sedative**, antispasmodic [muscle pain]
somatropin (NORDITROPIN): growth hormone [growth failure]
SOMNOTE (chloral hydrate): **sedative**
SONATA (zaleplon): **sedative/hypnotic** [insomnia]
sorafenib (NEXAVAR): antineoplastic [renal cell carcinoma]
SORIATANE (acitretin): retinoid [psoriasis]
sotalol (BETAPACE): **beta blocker** [HTN, CP, arrhythmias]
SPECTAZOLE (econazole): antifungal [infection]
SPECTRACEF (cefditoren): antibiotic [infection]
spironolactone, HCTZ: **diuretic** [HTN]
spironolactone (ALDACTONE): potassium-sparing **diuretic**
SPAINTEC (norgestimate, estradiol): oral contraceptive
SPORANOX (itraconazole): antifungal [infection]

SPRYCEL (dasatinib): antineoplastic [leukemia]
SSKI (potassium iodide): expectorant [asthma, bronchitis]
STADOL-NS (butorphanol): **narcotic** [pain]
STAGESIC (hydrocodone, APAP): **narcotic** [pain]
STALEVO (levodopa, carbidopa, entacapone): [Parkinson's]
STATUSS (hydrocodone, phenylephrine, pseudoephedrine, pyrilamine, chlorpheniramine): **narcotic**, antitussive [cold/flu]
STATUSS-DM (non-narcotic version of STATUSS)
stavudine (ZERIT): antiviral [HIV]
STELAZINE (trifluoperazine): **tranquilizer**
STRATTERA (atomoxetine): stimulant [ADHD]
streptomycin: antibiotic [infection]
STRIANT (testosterone): androgen [hypogonadism]
STROMECTOL (ivernectin): antiparasitic [intestinal nematodes]
SUBOXONE (buprenorphine, naloxone): **narcotic**, narcotic antagonist [narcotic addiction]
SUBUTEX (buprenorphine): **narcotic** [narcotic addiction]
sucralfate (CARAFATE): antiulcer [duodenal ulcers]
sufentanil: **narcotic**, anesthetic [pain, sedation]
SULAR (nisoldipine): **Ca-channel blocker** [HTN]
sulfamethoxazole (SEPTRA): bacteriostatic [UTI]
sulfanilamide (AVC): anti-infective [*Candida*]
sulfisoxazole (PEDIAZOLE): bacteriostatic [UTI]
sulindac (CLINORIL): NSAID analgesic [arthritis]
sumatriptan (IMITREX): [migraine HA]
sunitinib (SUTENT): antineoplastic [CA]
SUPRAX (cefixime): broad-spectrum antibiotic [infection]
SURMONTIL (trimipramine): **TCA** [depression]
SUSTIVA (efavirenz): antiviral [HIV, AIDS]
SUTENT (sunitinib): antineoplastic [CA]
SYMBYAX (olanzapine, fluoxetine) **psychotropic** [depression]
SYMLIN (pramlintide): **hypoglycemic** [DM]
SYMMETREL (amantadine): antiparkinsonian [Parkinson's]
SYNAGIS (palivizumab): antiviral, antibody [RSV]
SYNALGOS-DC (dihydrocodeine, ASA, codeine): **narcotic** [pain]

SYNAREL (naferelin): gonadotropin-releasing hormone [endometriosis, precocious puberty, dysmenorrheal]

SYNTHROID (levothyroxine): thyroid hormone [HRT]

SYPRINE (trientine): copper chelator [Wilson's disease]

TABLOID (thioguanine): purine analog [leukemia]

tadalafil (CIALIS): phosphodiesterase inhibitor [ED]

TAGAMET (cimetidine): ↓gastric acid [gastric ulcers]

TALWIN NX (pentazocine, naloxone): **narcotic** [pain]

TAMBOCOR (flecainide): **antiarrhythmic** [PSVT, a-fib, VT]

TAMIFLU (oseltamivir) antiviral [influenza]

tamoxifen (NOLVADEX): anticancer [breast CA]

TAO (troleandomycin): antibiotic [pneumonia, URI]

TAPAZOLE (methimazole): antithyroid [hyperthyroidism]

TARCEVA (erlotinib): antineoplastic [lung CA]

TARKA (trandolapril, verapamil): **Ca-channel blocker** [HTN]

TASMAR (tolcapone): [Parkinson's]

TEGRETOL (carbamazepine): **anticonvulsant** [seizures]

TEKTURNA (aliskiren): **antihypertensive** [HTN]

telbivudine (TYZEK): antiviral [hepatitis B]

telmisartan (MICARDIS): **ACE inhibitor** [HTN]

temazepam (RESTORIL): **benzodiazepine**

TEMOVATE (clobetasol): steroid [inflammation]

TENORMIN (atenolol): **beta blocker** [CP, dysrhythmias, HTN]

TENUATE (diethylpropion): stimulant [obesity]

TEQUIN (gatifloxacin) antibiotic [infection]

terazosin (HYTRIN): alpha$_1$ blocker **antihypertensive**

terbinafine (LAMISIL): antifungal [nail fungus, ringworm]

TERRA-CORTRIL (hydrocortisone, oxytetracycline): steroid, antibiotic [ocular infections]

TESSALON (benzonatate): non-narcotic cough suppressant

testosterone (ANDRODERM): androgenizing hormone

TESTRED (methyltestosterone): androgenizing hormone

tetracycline (HELIDAC): antibiotic [infection]

TEVETEN (eprosartan); angiotensin II inhibitor [HTN]

thalidomide (THALOMID): immunosuppressant [HIV, leprosy]

THALOMID (thalidomide): immunosuppressant [HIV, leprosy]

THEO-24 (theophylline): **bronchodilator** [asthma, COPD]
THEOLAIR (theophylline): **bronchodilator** [asthma, COPD]
theophylline (UNIPHYL): **bronchodilator** [asthma, COPD]
THERA-GESIC (salicylate): topical NSAID analgesic [arthritis]
thiabendazole (MINTEZOL): antiparasitic [pinworm, trichinosis]
thiamine (Vit. B_1): Vit. supplement [malnutrition]
thioguanine (TABLOID): anticancer [leukemia]
THIOLA (tiopronin): cysteine-depletor [kidney stone prevention]
thioridazine (MELLARIL): **antipsychotic** [schizophrenia]
thiothixene (NAVANE): **antipsychotic** [schizophrenia]
THORAZINE (chlorpromazine): phenothiazine [psychosis]
thyroid tabs (ARMOUR THYROID TABS): thyroid hormone
THYROLAR (liotrix): thyroid hormone
tiagabine (GABITRIL): **anticonvulsant** [seizures]
TIAZAC (diltiazem): **Ca-channel blocker** [HTN, CP, PSVT]
ticarcillin (TIMENTIN): antibiotic [infection]
TICE: inflammatory mycobacterium [bladder CA]
TICLID (ticlopidine): platelet inhibitor [stroke prophylaxis]
TIGAN (trimethobenzamide): antiemetic [n/v]
tigecycline (TYGACIL): anti-infective [skin infections]
TIKOSYN (dofetilide): **antiarrhythmic** [a-fib]
TILADE (nedocromil): anti-inflammatory [asthma]
TIMENTIN (ticarcillin, clavulanate): antibiotic [infection]
TIMOLIDE (timolol, HCTZ): **beta blocker, diuretic** [HTN]
timolol (BLOCADREN) **beta blocker** [HTN, CP, arrhythmias]
TIMOPTIC (timolol): **beta blocker** [glaucoma]
tizanidine (ZANAFLEX): alpha blocker [spasticity]
TOBI inhalation (tobramycin): antibiotic [cystic fibrosis]
TOBRADEX (tobramycin, dexamethasone): antibiotic, steroid [infection, inflammation]
TOFRANIL (imipramine): **tricydic antidepressant** [depression]
tolazamide: oral **hypoglycemic** [DM]
tolbutamide: oral **hypoglycemic** [DM]
tolmetin: NSAID analgesic [pain]
tolterodine (DETROL): antispasmodic [overactive bladder]

Rx/OTC MEDS

Rx/OTC MEDS

TOPAMAX (topiramate): **anticonvulsant** [seizures]
TOPROL XL (metoprolol): **beta blocker** [HTN, CP, arrhythmias]
TORADOL (ketorolac): NSAID analgesic [pain, inflammation]
TRACLEER (bosentan): [pulmonary HTN]
tramadol (ULTRAM): analgesic [pain]
TRANDATE (labetalol): **beta blocker** [HTN]
TRANSDERM-SCOP (scopolamine): anticholinergic [n/v]
TRANXENE (clorazepate): **benzodiazepine** [anxiety, seizures]
TRAUMEEL: anti-inflammatory [arthritis]
trazodone (DESYREL): antidepressant [depression]
TRECATOR-5C (ethionamide): bacteriostatic [TB]
TRELSTAR Depot (triptorelin): antineoplastic [prostate CA]
TRENTAL (pentoxifylline): hemorrheologic [PVD]
tretinoin (RETIN-A): antiacne, antiwrinkle [acne, wrinkles]
TREXALL (methotrexate): anticancer [breast CA, RA]
TRI-LEVLEN: oral contraceptive [birth control]
TRI-NORINYL-28: oral contraceptive [birth control]
triamcinolone (AZMAGORT): steroid [asthma]
triamterene, HCTZ (DYAZIDE): **antihypertensive,
    diuretic** [HTN]
triazolam (HALCION): **benzodiazepine** [insomnia]
TRICOR (fenofibrate): antihyperlipidemic [hyperlipidemia]
trientine (SYPRINE): copper chelator [Wilson's disease]
trifluoperazine (STELAZINE): **tranquilizer**
trihexyphenidyl (ARTANE): antispasmodic [Parkinson's]
TRILEPTAL (oxcarbazepine): **anticonvulsant** [seizures]
TRILISATE (salicylate): anti-inflammatory, analgesic [pain]
trimethoprim, sulfamethoxazole (ZOTRIM): antibiotic
    [infection]
trimethoprim (SEPTRA): antibiotic [infection]
TRINSICON (vitamins): antianemic [anemia]
TRIOVAN (trovafloxacin): antibiotic [infection]
TRIPHASIL (levonorgestrel): contraceptive [birth control]
TRISENOX (arsenic): suppresses bone marrow [leukemia]
TRIZIVIR (abacavir, lamivudine, zidovudine): antiviral [HIV]
TRUSOPT (dorzolamide): anhydrase inhibitor [glaucoma]

TUSSAFED HC (hydrocodone, phenylephrine, guaifenesin): **narcotic** antitussive, decongestant, expectorant [cold/flu]
TUSSIONEX (hydrocodone, chlorpheniramine): **narcotic** antitussive, antihistamine [cold/flu]
TYGACIL (tigecycline): anti-infective [skin infections]
TYKERB (lapatinib) antineoplastic [breast CA]
TYLENOL (APAP, acetaminophen): analgesic [pain, fever]
TYLENOL w/Codeine (APAP, codeine): **narcotic** [pain]
TYZEK (telbivudine): antiviral [hepatitis B]
ULTRABROM, PD (brompheniramine, pseudoephedrine): antihistamine [cold/flu]
ULTRACET (tramadol, APAP): **narcotic** [pain]
ULTRALENTE (insulin): **hypoglycemic** [DM]
ULTRAM (tramadol): analgesic [pain]
ULTRASE: pancreatic enzymes [cystic fibrosis, pancreatitis]
ULTRAVATE (halobetasol): steroid [pruritus]
URIMAX (methenamine, salicylate, methylene blue, hyoscyamine): urinary tract antiseptic, antispasmodic [UTI]
UNIPHYL (theophylline): **bronchodilator** [asthma, COPD]
UNIQUE E (Vit. E): vitamin [dietary supplementation]
UNIRETIC (moexepril, HCTZ): **ACE inhibitor, diuretic** [HTN]
UNISOM (doxylamine): antihistamine, **sedative** [insomnia]
UNIVASC (moexipril): **ACE inhibitor** [HTN]
urea (ACCUZYME): débriding ointment [pressure ulcers]
URECHOLINE (bethanechol): ↑bladder tone [urinary retention]
URISED (methenamine, methylene blue, salicylate, atropine, hyoscyamine): antiseptic, analgesic, antispasmodic [UTI]
UROAXTRAL (alfuzosin): smooth muscle relaxer [BPH]
URO-KP-NEUTRAL (dipotassium phosphate): [UTI, kidney stones]
URO-MAG (magnesium): magnesium [hypomagnesemia]
UROCIT-K (potassium citrate): urinary alkalinizer [kidney stones]
UROQID ACID (methenamine): bactericide [UTI]
Ursodiol (ACTIGALL): bile acid [gall stones]
valacyclovir (VALTREX): antiviral [herpes, shingles]
VALCYTE (valganciclovir): antiviral [cytomegalovirus]
VALIUM (diazepam): **benzodiazepine** [anxiety, sedation]

Rx/OTC MEDS

valproic acid (DEPAKENE): **anticonvulsant** [seizures]
valrubicin (VALSTAR): anticancer [bladder CA]
valsartan (DIOVAN): angiotensin II inhibitor [HTN]
VALTREX (valaciclovir): antiviral [herpes, shingles]
VANCENASE, AQ (beclomethasone): steroid [allergies]
VANCOCIN (vancomycin): antibiotic [infection]
vancomycin (VANCOCIN): antibiotic [UC]
VANIQA Cream (eflomithine): facial hair growth inhibitor
VANTIN (cefpodoxime): antibiotic [infection]
VAPRISOL (conivaptan): vasopressin antagonist [↓sodium]
VAQTA (hepatitis A vaccine): vaccine [prevention of hepatitis A]
vardenafil (LEVITRA): phosphodiesterase inhibitor [ED]
varenicline (CHANTIX): nicotine agonists [smoking cessation]
VASERETIC (enalapril, HCTZ): **antihypertensive, diuretic** [HTN]
VASOTEC (enalaprilat): **ACE inhibitor** [HTN, CHF]
VECTIBIX (panitumumab): antineoplastic [colorectal CA]
VELOSULIN (insulin): **hypoglycemic** [DM]
venlafaxine (EFFEXOR): antidepressant [depression]
VENTAVIS (iloprost): **vasodilator** [pulmonary HTN]
VENTOLIN (albuterol): **bronchodilator** [asthma, COPD]
verapamil (ISOPTIN): **Ca-channel blocker** [CP, PSVT, HTN]
VEREGEN (kunecatechins): catechins [genital warts]
VERELAN, -PM (verapamil): **Ca-channel blocker** [CP, HTN, PSVT]
VERMOX (mebendazole): anthelminthic [intestinal worms]
VESANOID (tretinoin): anticancer [leukemia]
VESICARE (solifenacin): anticholinergic [overactive bladder]
V-FEND (voriconazole): antifungal [fungal infection]
VIAGRA (sildenafil): phosphodiesterase inhibitor [ED]
VIBRA-TABS (doxycycline): antibiotic [infection]
VIBRAMYCIN (doxycycline): antibiotic [infection]
VICODIN HP, -ES (hydrocodone, APAP): **narcotic**, antitussive
VICODIN TUSS (hydrocodone, guaifenesin): **narcotic**, antitussive expectorant [cold/flu]
VICON FORTE (vitamins [vitamin supplementation]
VICOPROFEN (hydrocodone, ibuprofen): **narcotic** [pain]

214

VIDEX (didanosine): antiviral [HIV, AIDS]
VIOKASE: pancreatic enzyme [cystic fibrosis, pancreatitis]
VIRACEPT (nelfinavir): protease inhibitor antiviral [HIV, AIDS]
VIRAMUNE (nevirapine): antiviral [HIV, AIDS]
VIRAZOLE (ribavirin): antiviral [hepatitis C]
VIREAD (tenofovir): nucleoside analog antiviral [HIV, AIDS]
VIRILON (methyltestosterone): androgen [breast CA]
VISTARIL (hydroxyzine): antiemetic, **sedative** [nausea]
VITAFOL-OB: multivitamins and minerals [prenatal supplement]
vitamin A (MEGADOSE): vitamin [vitamin A deficiency]
VITORIN (simvastatin): antihyperlipidemic [hyperlipidemia]
VIVACTIL (protriptyline): **TCA** [depression]
VIVELLE (estradiol) [osteoporosis, menopause]
VIVITROL (naltrexone): narcotic antagonist [alcoholism]
VOLMAX (albuterol): **bronchodilator** [asthma, COPD]
VOLTAREN (diclofenac): NSAID analgesic [pain]
vorinostat (ZOLINZA): antineoplastic [T-cell lymphoma]
VOSPIRE (albuterol): **bronchodilator** [asthma, COPD]
VYVANSE (lisdexamfetamine): CNS stimulant [ADHD]
WOMEN'S TYLENOL (pamabrom): analgesic, **diuretic** [PMS]
XALATAN (latanoprost): prostaglandin agonist [glaucoma]
XANAX (alprazolam): **benzodiazepine** [anxiety]
XELODA (capecitabine): antineoplastic [breast CA]
XENICAL (orlistat): lipase inhibitor [obesity]
XIBROM (bromfenac): NSAID eyedrops [post-op eye pain]
XYFAXAN (rifaximin): anti-infective [traveler's diarrhea, E. coli]
XIGRIS (drotrecogin) anti-infective [sepsis]
XOLAIR (omalizumab): **bronchodilator** [COPD, asthma]
XOPENEX (levalbuterol): **bronchodilator** [COPD, asthma]
XYREM (sodium oxybate): promotes wakefulness [narcolepsy]
XYZAL (levocetirizine): antihistamine [allergies]
YAGONA (kava kava): **sedative/hypnotic** [anxiety]
YASMIN (estradiol/drospirenone): contraceptive [birth control]
YINHSING (ginkgo): antiplatelet, CNS stimulant [various uses]
YODOXIN (iodoquinol): amebicide [intestinal infections]
yohimbine (PROCOMIL): adrenergic antagonist [ED]

Rx/OTC MEDS

Rx/OTC MEDS

ZADITOR (ketotifen): antihistamine, anti-inflammatory [allergies]

zalcitabine (HIVID): antiviral, [HIV, AIDS]

zaleplon (SONATA): **sedative/hypnotic** [insomnia]

ZANAFLEX (tizanidine): muscle relaxant [muscle spasms]

ZANTAC (ranitidine): histamine₂ blocker [gastric ulcers]

ZARONTIN (ethosuximide): **anticonvulsant** [seizures]

ZAROXOLYN (metolazone): **antihypertensive, diuretic** [HTN]

ZEBETA (bisoprolol): **beta blocker, antihypertensive** [HTN]

ZELNORM (tegaserod): stimulates peristalsis [constipation, IBS]

ZEMPLAR (paricalcitol): Vit. D analog [hyperparathyroidism]

ZERIT (stavudine d4T): antiviral [HIV, AIDS]

ZESTORETIC (lisinopril, HCTZ): **ACE inhibitor, diuretic** [HTN]

ZESTRIL (lisinopril): **ACE inhibitor** [HTN, CHF]

ZETIA (ezetimibe): antihyperlipidemic [hyperlipidemia]

ZIAC (bisoprolol, HCTZ): **antihypertensive, diuretic** [HTN]

ZIAGEN (abacavir): antiviral [HIV, AIDS]

ziconotide (PRIALT): **Ca-channel blocker**, analgesic [pain]

zidovudine (AZT-RETROVIR): antiviral [HIV, AIDS]

ZINACEF (cefuroxime): antibiotic [infection]

ZINECARD (dexrazoxane): cardioprotective [cardiomyopathy]

ZITHROMAX (azithromycin): antibiotic [infection]

Zn-DTPA (pentetate Zn tri-Na): radiation protectant [exposure]

ZOCOR (simvastatin): antihyperlipidemic [hyperlipidemia]

ZOFRAN (ondansetron): antiemetic [nausea]

ZOLADEX (goserelin) [endometriosis]

ZOLINZA (vorinostat): antineoplastic [T-cell lymphoma]

ZOLOFT (sertraline): antidepressant [depression]

zolpidem (AMBIEN): hypnotic [insomnia]

ZOMIG (zolmitriptan): [migraine HA]

ZONEGRAN (zonisamide): **anticonvulsant** [seizures]

ZOTRIM (trimethoprim, sulfamethoxazole): antibiotic [infection]

ZOVIRAX (acyclovir): antiviral [herpes, shingles]

Z-TUSS Expectorant (hydrocodone, pseudoephedrine, chlorpheniramine, guaifenesin): **narcotic**, antitussive, decongestant, antihistamine, expectorant [cold/flu]

Z-TUSS (hydrocodone, pseudoephedrine. guaifenesin): **narcotic** antitussive, decongestant, expectorant [cold/flu]
ZYBAN (buproprion): antidepressant [smoking cessation]
ZYDONE (APAP, hydrocodone): **narcotic** [pain]
ZYFLO (zileuton): bronchospasm inhibitor [asthma]
ZYLOPRIM (allopurinol): ↓serum uric acid [gout]
ZYPREXA ZYDIS (olanzapine) **psychotropic** [schizophrenia]
ZYRTEC (cetirizine): antihistamine [allergy, hives, asthma]
ZYVOX (linezolid): antibiotic [pneumonia, skin infections]

Rx/OTC MEDS

EMS TOOLS

Run Report

Unit # _____ EMT/Medic Name _____

Code _____ Priority _____ Destination _____ ETA _____

Age ____ Sex ____ Chief Complaint _____

Mechanism of injury _____

Nature of illness _____

Hx of current illness/injury _____

_____

Allergies _____

Medication _____

PMH _____

_____

LOC _____ AVPU _____ GCS _____

Rhythm _____ HR ____ RR ____ BP _____ Sat ___ % on _____

Neurological _____

HEENT/skin _____

Heart _____

Lungs _____

Chest/back _____

Abdomen/pelvis _____

Extremities _____

Treatment _____

Notes

Wong-Baker FACES Pain Rating Scale*

Spanish Numerical Pain Scale

0	2	4	6	8	10
Cero	Dos	Cuatro	Seis	Ocho	Diez
Ningún dolor (no pain) →				(much pain) Mucho dolor ←	

Referred Pain

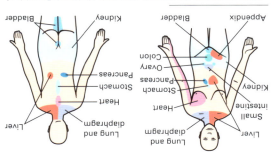

*From Hockenberry MJ, Wilson D, Winkelstein ML: Wong's Essentials of Pediatric Nursing, ed. 7, St. Louis, 2005, p. 1259. Used with permission. Copyright, Mosby.

Dermatomes

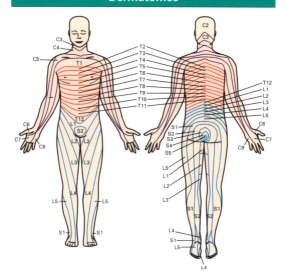

Criteria for Determination of Death

- Traumatic cardiac arrest associated with asystole in two leads
- Decomposition or decapitation
- Obvious signs of rigor mortis (stiffness)

> **EMS TOOLS**

- Obvious signs of lividity (rigor mortis/venous pooling)
- Incineration of the torso and/or head
- Massive crush injury and/or penetrating injury with evisceration or total destruction of vital organs
- Gross dismemberment of torso

Contraindications

- Pt in ventricular fibrillation
- Victim of electrocution, lightning, or drowning
- Associated hypothermia

Physician On Scene

EMTs and paramedics may act only within their scope of practice and as directed by local EMS protocol.
The following minimum criteria must be satisfied for a licensed, on-scene physician to take over Pt care:

- OLMC must be contacted to authorize transfer of Pt care
- Physician must accompany Pt to hospital in ambulance and complete/sign Pt care report
- EMTs and paramedics may follow orders from on-scene physician only after being authorized to do so by OLMC
- Conflicts between physician orders and EMS protocol must be settled by OLMC
- Follow EMS protocol when OLMC cannot be reached

Situations Requiring Mandatory Reporting

- Abuse and/or neglect (spousal, child, elder)
- Rape or sexual assault
- Gunshot or stab wounds
- Animal bites
- Communicable diseases (hepatitis, HIV, meningitis, TB, etc.)

Crime Scenes and Evidence Preservation

Note: Pt care takes precedence over preservation of evidence.

- Do not enter crime scene until cleared by law enforcement
- Always attempt to enter/exit scene using same path
- Position vehicle away from tire tracks, skid marks, and debris
- Do not touch or move anything at a crime scene unless it is necessary to deliver medical care
- Avoid walking through blood and other fluids
- Document original location of any items moved by EMS, and advise law enforcement if items are removed
- When removing Pt clothing, do not cut through gunshot or knife holes, and leave as much clothing intact as possible
- Law enforcement may accompany Pt en route to hospital
- Document statements made by Pt or bystanders
- Inform receiving hospital of any special circumstances
- If Pt is pronounced dead at scene, consult OLMC, and as much as possible avoid touching body

Refusal of Service

- Inform OLMC of Pt refusal of medical care
- Request law enforcement if Pt has impaired decision-making capacity (under the influence, combative, AMS)
- Thoroughly document refusal, and have Pt sign refusal form

Key points to document

- Pt alert, oriented, competent
- No influence of drugs or alcohol
- Consequences of refusing medical care clearly explained
- Benefits of transport and further evaluation explained
- Pt left in care of friend or family (if applicable)
- Advised Pt of follow-up care or to call 911 if needed

EMS TOOLS

EMS TOOLS

Patient Abandonment

- Improper termination of Pt care by EMS provider
- Transfer of care to personnel, on scene or at hospital, not qualified to meet medical needs of Pt

Metric Equivalents

lbs	kg	lbs	kg	lbs	kg
325	148	150	68	40	18
300	136	140	64	30	14
275	125	130	59	25	11
250	114	120	55	20	9
225	102	110	50	15	7
210	96	100	46	10	4.5
200	91	90	41	5	2.3
190	86	80	36		
180	82	70	32	*Quick Convert*	
170	77	60	27	(lb ÷ 2) − 10%	
160	73	50	23		

Volume	Mass
1 tsp . . . . .5 mL	1 mg . . . . .1000 mcg
1 tbsp . . . . .15 mL	1 kg . . . . .1000 gram
1 oz . . . . .30 mL	1 gram . . . . .1000 mg
1 cc . . . . .1 mL	1 grain . . . . .60 mg
1 cup . . . . .240 mL	1/150 grain . . . . .4 mg
1 pint . . . . .473 mL	1 kg . . . . .2.2 lb
1 quart . . . . .946 mL	1 litevr . . . . .1 kg
1 liter . . . . .960 oz	1 oz . . . . .28 g

Frequently Used Phone Numbers

Dispatch _____

County Control _____

911 Dispatch Center _____

Field Supervisor _____

Online Medical Control _____

Level 1 Trauma Center _____

PCI Center _____

Stroke Center _____

Burn Center _____

Hyperbaric Center _____

Station # _____

Station # _____

Hospital _____

Hospital _____

EMS Office/Director _____

Interpretation Services _____

Poison Control (National)	800-222-1222
Chemtrec (HazMat; 24-hr)	800-424-9300
CDC (biological; 24-hr)	770-488-7100
DAN (Divers Alert Network)	919-684-8111
USAMRIID (biological)	888-872-7443
REAC/TS (radiation)	423-576-3131

EMS TOOLS

EMS TOOLS

Basic English-to-Spanish Translation

English Phrase • [pro-**nun**-ci-**a**-tion] • *Spanish Phrase*
Introductions—Greetings
Hello [**oh**-lah] *Hola*
Good morning [**bweh**-nohs dee-ahs] *Buenos días*
Good afternoon [**bweh**-nohs **tahr**-dehs] *Buenos tardes*
Good evening [**bweh**-nahs **noh**-chehs] *Buenas noches*
My name is [meh **yah**-moh] *Me llamo*
I am a medic [soy lah/el **meh**-di-co] *Soy la/el medico*
I am a nurse [soy oon/oona **en**-fehr-**meh**-ro/ra] *Soy un/una enfermero/ra*
What is your name? [**koh**-moh seh **yah**-mah **oo**-sted?] *¿Cómo se llama usted?*
How are you? [**koh**-moh eh-**stah oo**-stehd?] *¿Como esta usted?*
Very well [mwee **b'yehn**] *Muy bien*
Thank you [**grah**-s'yahs] *Gracias*
Yes, No [see, noh] *Sí, No*
Please [pohr fah-**vohr**] *Por favor*
You're welcome [deh **nah**-dah] *De nada*
Assessment—Areas of the Body
Head [kah-**beh**-sah] *Cabeza*
Eye [**oh**-hoh] *Ojo*
Ear [oh-**ee**-doh] *Oído*
Nose [nah-**reez**] *Nariz*
Throat [gahr-**gahn**-tah] *Garganta*
Neck [**kweh**-yoh] *Cuello*
Chest, heart [**peh**-choh, **koh**-rah-sohn] *Pecho, corazón*
Back [eh-**spahl**-dah] *Espalda*
Abdomen [ahb-doh-mehn] *Abdomen*
Stomach [eh-**stoh**-mah-goh] *Estómago*
Rectum [**rehk**-toh] *Recto*
Penis [**peh**-neh] *Pene*
Vagina [vah-**hee**-nah] *Vagina*
Arm [**brah**-soh] *Brazo*
Hand [**mah**-noh] *Mano*

Leg [p'**yehr**-nah] *Pierna*
Foot [p'**yeh**] *Pie*
Assessment—History
Do you have... [T'**yeh**-neh oo-stehd...] *¿Tiene usted...*

- Difficulty breathing? [di-fi-kul-**tad pah**-reh reh-spee-**rahr**] *¿Dificultad para respirar?*
- Chest pain? [doh-**lorh** en el **peh**-chow] *¿Dolor en el pecho?*
- Abdominal pain? [doh-**lorh** ab-**do**-minahl] *¿Dolor abdominal?*
- Diabetes? [dee-ah-**beh**-tehs] *¿Diabetes?*

Are you... [¿**ehs**-tah...] *¿Esta...*

- Dizzy? [¿mar-eh-**a**-dho(dha)] *¿Mareado(a)?*
- Nauseated? [¿kohn **now**-say-as] *¿Con nauseas?*
- Pregnant? [¿ehm-bah-rah-**sah**-dah?] *¿Embarazada?*

Are you allergic to any medications? [¿ehs ah-**lehr**-hee-koh ah ahl-**goo**-nah meh-dee-**see**-nah?] *¿Es alergico a alguna medicina?*
Assessment—Pain
Do you have pain? [T'**yeh**-neh oo-stehd doh-**lorh**?] *¿Tiene usted dolor?* [(0) cero, (1) uno, (2) dos, (3) tres, (4) cuatro, (5) cinco, (6) seis, (7) siete, (8) ocho, (9) nueve, (10) diez]
Where does it hurt? [**dohn**-deh leh **dweh**-leh?] *¿Donde le duele?*
Is the pain... [es oon doh-**lor**...] *¿Es un dolor...*

- Dull? [**Leh**-veh] *¿Leve?*
- Aching? [kans-**tan**-teh] *¿constante?*
- Crushing? [ah-plahs-**tan**-teh?] *¿Aplastante?*
- Sharp? [ah-**goo**-doh?] *¿Agudo?*
- Stabbing? [ah-poo-nya-**lawn**-teh] *¿Apuñalante?*
- Burning? [Ahr-d'**yen**-teh?] *¿Ardiente?*

Does it hurt when I press here? [Leh **dweh**-leh kwahn-doh leh ah-pree-**eh**-toh ah-**kee**?] *¿Le duele cuando le aprieto aqui?*
Does it hurt to breathe deeply? [S'**yen**-teh oo-**sted** doh-**lor** kwahn-doh reh-**spee**-rah pro-**foon**-dah-men-teh?] *¿Siente usted dolor cuando respira profundamente?*
Does it move to another area? [El doh-**lor** zĕh moo-**eh**-veh a oh-tra ah-**ri**-ah] *¿El dolor se mueve a otra area?*
Is the pain better now? [c-n-teh al-**goo**-nah me-horr-**i**-ah] *¿Siente alguna mejoria?*

EMS TOOLS

EMS TOOLS

Symbols and Abbreviations

$\bar{a}$ before
α alpha
β beta
@ at
# pound, quantity (number of)
" inch
® right
Ⓛ left
Ⓑ bilateral
↑ increase
↓ decrease
ψ psychiatric
∅ none, no
Δ change
/ per, divided by
< less than
> greater than
° degrees
Rx treatment, prescription
μ micro
AAA abdominal aortic aneurysm
ABC automated blood count (airway, breathing, circulation)
ABD abdominal (dressing)
ABG arterial blood gas
AC before meals (a.m.), antecubital
ACE angiotensin-converting enzyme
ACLS advanced cardiac life support
ACS acute coronary syndrome

ACTH adrenocorticotropic hormone
AD right ear, Alzheimer's disease
ADA American Diabetic Association
ADH antidiuretic hormone
ADHD attention deficit hyper-activity disorder
ADL activity of daily living
ADR adverse drug reaction
AED automated external defibrillator
AHA American Heart Association
AIDS acquired immunodefi-ciency syndrome
AKA above-the-knee amputation
ALOC altered level of consciousness
ALS advanced life support, amyotrophic lateral sclerosis
AMI acute myocardial infarction
AMPLE see SAMPLE
AMS altered mental status, acute mountain sickness
AP anterior to posterior
APAP acetaminophen, Tylenol
APGAR appearance, pulse, grimace, activity, respiration
aPTT activated partial thromboplastin time

228

AS left ear
ASA aspirin
AU both ears
AV atrioventricular
AVB atrioventricular block
AVM arteriovenous malformation
AVPU alert, verbal, painful, unresponsive
BBB bundle branch block
BCC, BCCa basal cell carcinoma
BE barium enema, base excess
b.i.d. twice a day
BKA below-the-knee amputation
BM bowel movement
BMI body mass index
BP blood pressure
BPH benign prostatic hyperplasia
BPM beats per minute
BS blood sugar, bowel sounds
BSA body *or* burn surface area
BUN blood urea nitrogen
BVM bag-valve mask
$\bar{c}$ with
°C degrees Celsius, centigrade
C&S, CS culture and sensitivity
Ca^{++} calcium
CA cancer
CAD coronary artery disease
CBC complete blood count
CBG chemical blood glucose
CDC Centers for Disease Control and Prevention
CF cystic fibrosis
CHB complete heart block
CHF congestive heart failure
CI cardiac index
Cl$^-$ chloride
CNS central nervous system
CO carbon monoxide, cardiac output
CO$_2$ carbon dioxide
COPD chronic obstructive pulmonary disease
CP chest pain, cerebral palsy
CPAP continuous positive airway pressure
CPR cardiopulmonary resuscitation
CSF cerebrospinal fluid
CSM circulation sensory and motor
CT computed tomography
CV cardiovascular
CVA cerebrovascular accident
CVC central venous catheter
CVP central venous pressure
CX circumflex coronary artery
D$_5$W 5% dextrose in water
DBP diastolic BP
DC discontinue, direct current
DIC disseminated intravascular coagulopathy
DKA diabetic ketoacidosis
dL deciliter
DM diabetes mellitus
DOPE dislodgement, obstruction, pneumothorax, equipment

EMS TOOLS

EMS TOOLS

DT delirium tremens
DTS distance, time, shielding
DVT deep vein thrombosis
DZ, Dz disease
ECG, EKG electrocardiogram
ED erectile dysfunction, emergency department (ER)
EFM electronic fetal monitoring
EMS emergency medical services
EPS extrapyramidal symptoms
ESR erythrocyte sedimentation rate

ET endotracheal
EtOH alcohol
ETT endotracheal tube
°F degrees Fahrenheit
Fe iron
FFP fresh-frozen plasma
FHR fetal heart rate
Fr, fr French
GCS Glasgow Coma Scale
GI gastrointestinal
gtt drop
GU genitourinary
H&H hemoglobin & hematocrit
H+ hydrogen ion
HA headache
HACE high-altitude cerebral edema
HAPE high-altitude pulmonary edema
HAZMAT hazardous material
HB heart block

HCl hydrogen chloride
HCO₃ carbonic acid
Hct hematocrit
HCTZ hydrochlorothiazide
HELLP hemolysis, elevated liver enzymes, low platelets
Hgb hemoglobin
HHNS hyperglycemic, hyperosmolar, nonketotic syndrome
HIV human immunodeficiency virus
HOB head of bed
hr, h hour
HRT hormone replacement therapy
HS hour of sleep (nighttime)
HTN hypertension
HVS hyperventilation syndrome
IBC iron-binding capacity
IBD irritable bowel disease
IBS irritable bowel syndrome
IBW ideal body weight
IC incident commander
ICP intracranial pressure
ICS intercostal space
ID intradermal
IDDM insulin-dependent diabetes mellitus
IHSS idiopathic hypertrophic subaortic stenosis
IM intramuscular
IN intranasal
INH isoniazid
INR international ratio
IO intraosseous
I/O intake & output

IV intravenous
IVC inferior vena cava
IVF IV fluid
IVP IV push
IVPB IV piggyback
J joule
JVD jugular vein distention
K⁺ potassium
KB knife blade (scalpel)
KCl potassium chloride
kg kilogram
LAD left anterior descending
LAT lateral
LBBB left bundle branch block
LLQ left lower quadrant
LMA laryngeal mask airway
LNMP last normal menstrual period
LOC level of consciousness
LPM liters per minute
LR lactated Ringer's
LTC left to count
LUQ left upper quadrant
mA milliampere
MAP mean arterial pressure
MAR medication administration record
MAST military antishock trousers
MCA motorcycle accident
mcg microgram
MCI mass casualty incident
MCL modified chest lead
mEq milliequivalent
mg milligram
Mg⁺⁺ magnesium
MgSO₄ magnesium sulfate
MH malignant hyperthermia
MI myocardial infarction
min minute, minimum
mL milliliter
mm millimeter
mm Hg millimeter of mercury
MOA monoamine oxidase
MRI magnetic resonance imaging
MRSA methicillin-resistant *Staphylococcus aureus*
MS morphine, multiple sclerosis, musculoskeletal
MSO₄ morphine sulfate
MVA motor vehicle accident
Na⁺ sodium
NAD no apparent/acute distress
NaHCO₃ sodium bicarbonate
NG nasogastric
NGT nasogastric tube
NI nasointestinal
NIDDM noninsulin-dependent diabetes mellitus
NPA nasopharyngeal airway
NPO nothing by mouth
NRB non-rebreather
NS normal saline
NSAID nonsteroidal anti-inflammatory drug
NSR normal sinus rhythm
NTG nitroglycerin
NTP nitroglycerin paste
N/V nausea and vomiting
O₂ oxygen
OCD obsessive-compulsive disorder
OD overdose, right eye
OLMC online medical control

EMS TOOLS

OPA oropharyngeal airway
OPP organophosphate
OPQRST onset, provocation, quality, radiation, severity, timing
OS left eye
OT occupational therapy
OTC over the counter
OU both eyes
oz ounce
p̄ after
PAC premature atrial complex
PAD peripheral artery disease
Pao$_2$ partial pressure of oxygen in arterial blood
PAP pulmonary artery pressure
PASG pneumatic antishock garment
PCI percutaneous intervention
PCW pulmonary capillary wedge pressure
PDA patent ductus arteriosus
PE pulmonary embolism, edema
PEA pulseless electrical activity
PEEP positive end-expiratory pressure
PERRL pupils equal, round and reactive to light
PET positron emission tomography
PFIB perfluoroisobutene
pH potential of hydrogen
PICC peripherally inserted central catheter

PIH pregnancy-induced hypertension
PJC premature junctional complex
PMI point of maximal impulse
PMS premenstrual syndrome
PO by mouth, orally
PPD purified protein derivative (TB skin test)
PPE personal protective equipment
PPV positive pressure ventilation
PPF plasma protein fraction
PQRST see OPQRST
PRBCs packed red blood cells
PRI PR interval
PRN as needed
PSA prostate-specific antigen
PSI pounds per square inch
PSVT paroxysmal supraventricular tachycardia
Pt patient
PT prothrombin time, physical therapy
PTSD post-traumatic stress disorder
PTT partial thromboplastin time
PVC premature ventricular complex
PVD peripheral vascular disease
q, Q every
q.i.d. four times per day
q.o.d. every other day
R regular (insulin)

RA rheumatoid arthritis
RBBB right bundle branch block
RCA right coronary artery
RL Ringer's lactate
RLQ right lower quadrant
ROM range of motion, rupture of membranes
RR respiratory rate
RSI rapid sequence intubation
RSV respiratory syncytial virus
RT respiratory therapy, right
RTS revised trauma score
RUQ right upper quadrant
s̄ without
SAMPLE s/s, allergies, meds, pertinent history, last oral intake, events leading up
Sao$_2$ oxygen saturation
SBP systolic BP
SC, SQ subcutaneous
SCC squamous cell carcinoma
SI stroke index
SLP speech language pathology
SLUDGEM salivate, lacrimate, urinate, defecate, GI distress, emesis, miosis or muscle twitching
SOB shortness of breath
Spo$_2$ pulse oximeter
ss, s/s signs and symptoms
STD sexually transmitted disease
SV stroke volume
SVC superior vena cava
SVR systemic venous resistance
T temperature
TB tuberculosis
TBSA total burn surface area
TCA tricyclic antidepressant
TCP transcutaneous pacing
TF tube feeding
TIA transient ischemic attack
t.i.d. three times per day
TKO to keep open (30 mL/hr)
TPN total parenteral nutrition
TPR temperature, pulse, respirations
TVP transvenous pacing
u unit
UA urinalysis
UC ulcerative colitis
UO urine output
URI upper respiratory infection
UTI urinary tract infection
VAD vascular access device
VF ventricular fibrillation
VRE vancomycin-resistant Enterococcus
VRSA vancomycin-resistant *Staphylococcus aureus*
VT ventricular tachycardia
WBC white blood count
WC wheelchair
WMD weapons of mass destruction
WPW Wolfe-Parkinson-White

Selected References

American Academy of Pediatrics, American Heart Association: *Neonatal Resuscitation Textbook*, ed 5. 2006.

American Heart Association: *Pediatric Advanced Life Support Provider Manual*, Dallas, 2006.

American Heart Association: *Guidelines for CPR and ECC*, Dallas, 2005.

Bledsoe, BE, Porter, RS, and Cherry, RA: *Brady Paramedic Care, Principles and Practice, Medical Emergencies*, ed 2 (vol 3). Pearson Education Inc, Upper Saddle River, New Jersey, 2006.

Bledsoe, BE, Porter, RS, and Cherry, RA: *Brady Paramedic Care, Principles and Practice, Trauma Emergencies*, ed 2 (vol 4). Pearson Education Inc, Upper Saddle River, New Jersey, 2006.

Bledsoe, BE, Porter, RS, and Cherry, RA: *Brady Paramedic Care, Principles and Practice, Special Considerations Operations*, ed 2 (vol 5). Pearson Education Inc, Upper Saddle River, New Jersey, 2006.

Bledsoe, BE, and Clayden, DE: *Brady Prehospital Emergency Pharmacology*, ed 6. Pearson Education Inc, Upper Saddle River, New Jersey, 2005.

Burnstein, JL, and Singer, AJ: *Emergency Medicine Pearls*, ed 2. FA Davis, Philadelphia, 2001.

Cascio, T, and Lipman, BC: *ECG: Assessment and Interpretation*. FA Davis, Philadelphia, 1994.

Deglin, JH, and Vallerand, AH: *Davis's Drug Guide for Nurses*, ed 9. FA Davis, Philadelphia, 2003.

Dillon, PM: *Nursing Health Assessment: Clinical Pocket Guide*. FA Davis, Philadelphia, 2004.

Dubin, D: *Rapid Interpretation of EKGs*, ed 6. Cover, Tampa, Florida, 2000.

http://wonder.cdc.gov/wonder/prevguid/p0000419/p0000419.asp
http://www.aafp.org/afp/20040215/885.html
http://www.cdc.gov/ncidod/hip/isolat/isotab_1.htm
http://www.drugs.com/cdi/
http://www.emedicine.com/emerg/topic22.htm

http://www.emedicine.com/EMERG/topic25.htm
http://www.emedicine.com/emerg/topic554.htm
http://www.emedicine.com/emerg/topic603.htm
http://www.emedicine.com/emerg/topic795.htm
http://www.fpnotebook.com/ER/Procedure/OxygnDlvry.htm link>
http://www.medical-library.org/journals/e_publish/secure/login.html
http://www.ncemi.org/cgi-ncemi/edtable.pl?TheCommand=Load&NewFile=pediatric_equipment_by_age&BlankTop=1
http://www.nlm.nih.gov/medlineplus/ency/article/000009.htm
http://www.nlm.nih.gov/medlineplus/ency/article/000031.htm#First%20Aid
http://www.publicsafety.net/12lead_dx.htm#hints
http://stimson.org/cbw/?sn=CB2001121892%20
http://www.unm.edu/~lkravitz/EKG/ekg.html

Kranpitz, TR, Leeuwen, AM, and Schnell, Z: *Davis's Comprehensive Handbook of Laboratory and Diagnostic Tests with Nursing Implications*. FA Davis, Philadelphia, 2003.

McKinney, ES, et al: *Maternal-Child Nursing*. WB Saunders, Philadelphia, 2000.

McSwain Jr., NE, and Frame S (eds.): *PHTLS, Basic and Advanced Prehospital Life Support, ed 5*. Mosby, St. Louis, 2003.

Purnell, L, and Paulanka, B: *Guide to Culturally Competent Health Care*. F.A. Davis, Philadelphia, 2001.

Rosen, P, Barkin, RM, et al: *Rosen and Barkin's 5-Minute Emergency Medicine Consult, ed 2*. Lippincott Williams & Wilkins, Philadelphia, 2003.

Sanders, MJ: *Mosby's Paramedic Textbook, ed 3*. Elsevier Mosby, St. Louis, 2005.

Taber's Cyclopedic Medical Dictionary, ed 19. FA Davis, Philadelphia, 2001.

Townsend, MC: *Nursing Diagnoses in Psychiatric Nursing: Care Plans and Psychotropic Medications, ed 6*. FA Davis, Philadelphia, 2004.

Townsend, MC: *Psychiatric/Mental Health Nursing: Concepts of Care, ed 4*. FA Davis, Philadelphia, 2003.

EMS TOOLS

Illustration Credit List

Page ii from Multnomah County, Oregon, Emergency Medical Services, Patient Treatment Protocols, 2007; Pages 4, 5, and 11 from Donald Venes, Editor, Taber's Cyclopedic Medical Dictionary, 19e, Philadelphia: FA Davis Company, 2001; Pages 5, 18, 19, 22 from Williams LS, Hopper PD, Understanding Medical Surgical Nursing 2e, Philadelphia: FA Davis, 2003; Page 12 courtesy of LMA North America Inc.; Pages 13,14 from King Systems Corporation; Pages 42, 74 from Myers E, RN Notes, 2e, Philadelphia: FA Davis, 2006; Page 30 from Jones S, ECG Notes, Philadelphia: FA Davis, 2005; Page 47 from American Heart Association; Page 52 from Singer A, Burstein J, Schiavone F, Emergency Medicine Pearls, 2e; Page 92 from National Fire Protection Association, 2007; Page 222 from Hockenberry MJ, Wilson D, Winkelstein ML: Wong's Essentials of Pediatric Nursing, ed.7, St. Louis, 2005, p. 1259. Used with permission. Copyright Mosby.

Index

A

Abandonment, 224
Abbreviations, 228–233
Abuse, 80–81
Acute mountain sickness, 87
Airway
   combitube, 14–16
   equipment/devices for, 4–5
   endotracheal tube, (adult) 10–11, (pediatric) 100, 111
   king LT-D/LTS-D airway, 13–14
   laryngeal mask, 12–13
   management of, 5–6, 71
   obstruction of, 21
Allergic reaction, 42–43
Altered mental status, 43–45
Amputations, 80
Anaphylactic shock, 62–64
Anaphylaxis, 42–43
Anthrax, 93, 96
Antidotes, 54–55
Aortic aneurysm, 46
APGAR score, 109
Artificial pacemaker, 37
Asthma, 57, 59
Asystole, 22, 37, 113
Atrial fibrillation, 25, 36
Atrial flutter, 36
Atrioventricular block, 37–38
Automatic external defibrillators, 20, 25–26

B

Biological agents, 93, 96–97
Bites, 81–82
   black widow spider, 81
   brown recluse spider, 82
   scorpion, 82
   snake, 82
Botulism, 93, 96
Bradycardia, 23–24, 35, 112
Bronchitis, 57, 59
Bronchospasm, 57
Bundle branch block, 32, 34–35
Burns, 82–84

C

Capnography, 2–3
Carbon monoxide, 53–54, 95
Cardiogenic shock, 62–64
Cardiopulmonary resuscitation, 20–21
Cardioversion, 27–28, 100–101, 112–113
Caustics, 54, 96
Cervical spine immobilization, 71
Chemical agents, 93, 97–98
Chickenpox, 115
Chlorine, 95
Chlorine phosgene tear gas, 93, 98
Choking, 21–22
Cholecystitis, 46
Cholinergic antidote, 149
Cholinesterase antidote, 157
Chronic obstructive pulmonary disease, 57
Cold injury, 85–86
Colloids, 102

INDEX

Combative patients, 68–69
Congestive heart failure, 57, 59
Continuous positive airway
  pressure, 7–8
Crackles, 58
Cricoid pressure, 6, 8
Cricothyrotomy, needle, 16–17
Crime scenes, 223
Croup, 115
Cushing reflex, 51
Cyanide
  antidotes for, 55, 128,
    132–133, 143, 160
  characteristics of, 94–95, 98

D

Death, 221–222
Decerebrate posturing, 52
Decompression sickness, 87
Decorticate posturing, 52
Defibrillation, 20, 25–26, 100
Delivery
  breech presentation, 123
  complicated, 122–124
  emergency, 121–122
Dermatomes, 221
Diabetic emergencies, 48–50
Drowning, 86

E

Eclampsia, 118–120
Electrocardiography
  components of, 32
  hypothermia effects on, 40
  ischemia assessments, 32–33
  lead placements, 30
  medication effects on, 39
  parameters of, 31

sample rhythms, 35–38
Emphysema, 57, 59
End-tidal CO2 detectors, 10
English-to-Spanish translation,
  226–227
Epiglottitis, 115
Evidence preservation, 223
Evisceration, 79
Extrapyramidal symptoms, 55

F

Falls, 74
First-degree atrioventricular
  block, 37
Flail chest, 77
Fluid resuscitation, 83
Frostbite, 85–86

G

Gastric reflux, 47
Gastroenteritis, 117
Glasgow coma scale, 75

H

Hazardous materials, 92
HAZMAT incident, 91–92
Head-tilt, chin-lift, 5, 18–19
Head-to-toe assessment, 72–73
Heart failure, 57, 59
Heat exhaustion, 88–89
Heatstroke, 88–89
Hemorrhage, 71
Hemorrhagic fevers, 93, 96
High altitude cerebral
  edema, 88
High altitude pulmonary
  edema, 88
High-altitude illness, 87–88

238

Hydrocarbons, 95
Hypercalcemia, 39
Hyperemesis gravidarum, 117
Hyperglycemia, 48–50
Hyperglycemic hyperosmolar nonketotic syndrome, 48
Hyperkalemia, 39
Hypertensive emergency, 50–51
Hyperthermia, 88–89
Hyperventilation syndrome, 57
Hypocalcemia, 39
Hypoglycemia, 48–50
Hypokalemia, 39
Hypotension, 61–64
Hypothermia, 40, 89–90
Hypovolemic shock, 62–64

I

Insulin shock, 48–49
Intracranial pressure, 51–52
Intraosseous access, 107–108
Intubation, 8–10
Ischemia, 32–33
Ischemic CP fibrinolytic checklist, 47
Ischemic stroke, 66–67
IV fluid drip rate, 125

J

Jaw-thrust maneuver, 5, 18
Junctional rhythms, 38

L

Left bundle branch block, 32, 34–35

M

Mandatory reporting, 222
Measles, 115
Meconium-stained amniotic fluid, 122
Meningitis, 115–116
Metric equivalents, 224
Modified chest leads, 30
Motor vehicle accidents, 73
Myocardial infarction, 33

N

Narrow-complex tachycardia, 25
Nasal cannula, 4
Nasopharyngeal airway, 5
Near drowning, 86
Needle chest decompression, 78
Needle cricothyrotomy, 16–17
Neonates. *See also* Pediatrics
  drug reference for, 111–112
  equipment size and depth for, 111
  resuscitation of, 110
Nerve agents, 93, 97–98
Neurogenic shock, 62–64
Non-rebreather mask, 4

O

Organophosphates, 95
Oropharyngeal airway, 4
Overdose, 53–55
Oxygen tank capacities, 8

P

Pacing, transcutaneous, 28–29
Pain
  abdominal, 41–42
  chest, 46–47
  referred, 220
  scale (English/Spanish), 220

INDEX

INDEX

Parkland formula, 83
Pediatrics. *See also* Neonates
  advanced life support,
    112–113
  developmental milestones,
    114
  endotracheal tubes, 100, 111
  illnesses, 115–117
  intraosseous access, 107–108
  pulseless arrest, 113
  quick reference guide, 99–106
  trauma score, 108
Phone numbers, 225
Physician on scene, 222
Placenta abruptio, 119–120
Placenta previa, 119–120
Plague, 93, 97
Pleurisy, 46
Pneumonia, 46, 59
Pneumothorax, 9
Poisonings, 53–55
Preeclampsia, 118–120
Pregnancy, 73
  complications during, 117–124
  emergency delivery, 121–122
  normal changes during, 118
Premature atrial complexes, 35
Premature junctional
  complexes, 35
Premature ventricular
  complexes, 36
Prolapsed cord, 123
Pulmonary edema, 57, 88
Pulmonary embolism, 47
Pulse oximetry, 1–2
Pulseless arrest, 22–23
Pulseless electrical activity, 22,
  113
Pulseless ventricular tachycar-
  dia, 22–23
Pupil gauge, 74

Q
Q waves, 33

R
Rales, 58
Rape, 91
Rapid cooling, 89
Rapid sequence intubation, 8–9
Rapid thawing, 85–86
Refusal of service, 223
Respiratory distress, 56–59
Respiratory syncytial virus,
  115–116
Restraints, 68–69
Rhonchi, 58
Right bundle branch block,
  34–35
Rubella, 115
Rule of nines, 84
Run report, 218

S
Scuba diving, 87
Second-degree atrioventricular
  block, 37–38
Seizures, 60–61
Septic shock, 62–64
Sexual assault, 91
Shock, 61–64
Simple face mask, 4
Sinus bradycardia, 35
Sinus rhythm, 35
Sinus tachycardia, 35
Smallpox, 93, 97